A–Z

OF THE

SAS

SIDGWICK & JACKSON

A–Z
OF THE
SAS

Peter Darman

I would like to thank the following people for their help with this
book:
Bruce Rutland, for his unstinting efforts with the overall design,
and particularly the maps.
Ian Westell, for his contributions to the text.
Darren Ketteringham, for sewing up the production end.

First published in Great Britain 1992 by Sidgwick & Jackson

This paperback edition published 1993 by Sidgwick & Jackson
an imprint of Macmillan General Books
Cavaye Place London SW10 9PG
and Basingstoke

Associated companies throughout the world

ISBN 0 283 06166 9

Copyright © Brown Packaging Limited

The right of Peter Darman to be identified as the author
of this work has been asserted by him in accordance with
the Copyright, Designs and Patents Act 1988.

9 8 7 6 5 4 3 2

A CIP catalogue record for this book is available from
the British Library

Printed and bound in Great Britain by
BPCC Hazell Books Ltd
Member of BPCC Ltd

Editorial and Design: Brown Packaging

Quoted excerpts taken from:
One of the Originals by Johnny Cooper, published by Pan
Books (1991).
SAS: The Jungle Frontier by Peter Dickens, published by
Book Club Associates (1983).
SAS: Operation Oman by Colonel Tony Jeapes, published
by William Kimber & Co. Limited (1983).

Title spread: A patrol moves out at dusk.

CONTENTS

A

'ABEL', OPERATION Codename of an SAS operation undertaken between 27 August and 22 September 1944 in eastern France by 82 soldiers of 3 French Parachute Battalion (3 SAS) under the command of Captain Sicand. The operation included several successful blocking actions and hit-and-run raids carried out in conjunction with *Maquis* units and troops of the advancing French First Army and the US Seventh Army which were attempting to capture the Belfort Gap – a strategic pass between the Vosges and Jura mountains.
(SEE Maquis; *Northwest Europe*)

ABSEILING Method by which a soldier with a rope and harness can make a quick descent from a helicopter, down the side of a building or a cliff face. Employed by the SAS in the field and on counter-terrorist operations such as Princes Gate. Also called rappelling.
(SEE *Counter Revolutionary Warfare Equipment; Princes Gate*)

ACCURACY INTERNATIONAL PM 7.62mm bolt-action sniper rifle produced by the British firm Accuracy International and used by the British Army and the SAS. Designated L96A1, it is equipped with a bipod, a 10-round magazine and a Schmidt and Bender telescopic sight which guarantees a first round hit at 600m

Left: Receiving instruction in military abseiling techniques. Note the rappelling harnesses around the soldiers' waists.

range, though the weapon is accurate up to 1000m. The counter-terrorist version has a monopod (single support) in the butt, enabling the rifle to be laid on the target and rested independently so that the marksman can keep a close eye on his target without having to take the weight of the rifle for long, tiring periods.

The 'Covert PM' variant is a suppressed version with a range of up to 300m which can be stripped and packed into an average-sized suitcase.

Type: bolt-action sniper rifle
Designation: L96A1
Calibre: 7.62mm
Weight: 6.5kg
Length: 1124-1194mm
Effective range: 600m
Feed: 10-round box magazine
Muzzle velocity: 330 metres per second

ACTIVE SERVICE UNIT The name given to an operational cell of the Irish Republican Army, usually comprising 3-4 members, occasionally up to 10. Units operate on the basis of an independent cell structure controlled by one individual to reduce the risk of betrayal. Actions include assassination, bombings, mortar attacks and ambushes of security personnel.
(SEE *Balcombe Street Siege; Gibraltar; Irish Republican Army*)

ADEN The Special Air Service conducted two types of warfare in its arduous three-year campaign in Aden: against the tribesmen of the mountainous Radfan region of the interior,

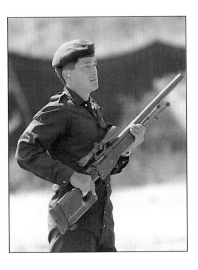

Above: The Accuracy International PM sniper rifle, as used by the SAS.

and an undercover counter-terrorist war against guerrillas operating in the port of Aden itself.

The port of Aden had been under British control since 1839 and, since 1937, had been ruled from Britain as a crown colony. In February 1959, six of the emirates, sultanates and various 'states' of the Western and Eastern Aden Protectorates came together to form the Federation of South Arabia (FSA) under the auspices of the British government. Another 10, together with the colony of Aden, had joined by the end of 1963. The various small states had agreed to federation on the understanding that the British would maintain a presence in the region after full independence, scheduled to be before 1968.

Above: A British Wessex helicopter flies over Aden in 1967. SAS counter-terrorist squads fought a deadly war against enemy guerrillas on the streets of the town.

In September 1962, the Soviet Union supported internal strife in neighbouring Yemen which led to the overthrow of the ruling Imam. The latter managed to escape and raised a royalist guerrilla force which waged war against the communists over the next eight years. A small mercenary force, covertly supported by the British and French governments and containing several former SAS soldiers, was subsequently organised and secretly based in the Aden Protectorate to aid the Imam.

The Yemen, which had some territorial claims on the FSA, began to support the two insurgent groups in the Protectorate, the National Liberation Front (NLF) and the Front for the Liberation of Occupied South Yemen (FLOSY). In December 1963, the federal authorities declared a state of emergency and called on the British government for military aid. In April the Federal Regular Army was withdrawn from the Radfan area and sent farther north to stop Yemeni-backed forces from infiltrating the Protectorate.

After the withdrawal the inhabitants of the Radfan, who were fiercely independent, were armed and trained by Egyptians and Yemenis to wage a guerrilla war against the British and

their supporters. In response, the British assembled Radforce – composed of 45 Commando, Royal Marines, B Company of 3 Para, two regiments of the Federal Regular Army, the 1st Battalion of the East Anglian Regiment and an SAS detachment from A Squadron – in April 1964. The force was supported by artillery units and transport and fighter aircraft from the RAF.

A Squadron established its base at Thumier, 100km north of Aden, just off the Dhala road near Habilayn airstrip. Tasked with regaining control of the Radfan, Radforce's assault was planned for 30 April. A Squadron's 3 Troop, under the command of Captain Robin Edwards, was ordered to seize a strategically important position, codenamed 'Cap Badge', in enemy territory prior to the main assault. This location would then be used as a para dropping zone (DZ).

Moving out on the night of 29 April, the 10 men of the patrol almost immediately came under fire as they made their way to 'Cap Badge'. Failing to reach their objective by daybreak, they laid up near a village some 5km from their destination. Their position was, however, compromised during the morning and they were forced to conduct a fighting retreat over the next 24 hours, during which Edwards was killed. The result was that the plans for the para drop were abandoned. Subsequent British military operations were less audacious and more carefully planned.

Later SAS missions, involving A, B and D Squadrons on rotation from operations in Borneo, took place in the hinterland and were mainly concerned with establishing covert observation posts to keep track of enemy movements. This role became particularly important as the British withdrawal date approached and enemy activity intensified. SAS patrols became increasingly concerned with preventing attacks on the main forward base at Thumier. In one of the last actions of the war, a patrol from 1 Troop, A Squadron, operating near the Yemeni border at Dhi Hirran, ordered an air strike against guerrillas trying to infiltrate the Federation.

In the port of Aden itself the SAS conducted counter-insurgency missions against the terrorists of the NLF. In the so-called 'Keeni Meeni' operations, troopers disguised as Arabs infiltrated the Crater and Sheikh Othman districts in twos and threes. Each SAS man was highly adept at rapidly drawing his Browning handgun from his *futah* (traditional flowing Arab robe) and firing it with deadly accuracy (an SAS close quarter battle range had been established in Aden). Operating from Ballycastle House, a block of flats in the Khormaksar military district, the 20-strong 'Keeni Meeni' unit's prime mission was the eradication of the Yemeni-trained assassins who were killing British Special Branch officers and their informers. Often the SAS soldiers would take with them a comrade dressed in Army uniform to act as bait for their trap.

The Regiment scored some notable successes in this urban guerrilla war. One one occasion two Arabs with guns drawn approached a vehicle containing two SAS troopers, only to be killed due to the speed that the latter drew and fired their handguns.

Unfortunately, there was no opportunity to develop a fully-fledged 'hearts and minds' campaign, as the British had already announced their intention of withdrawing from the colony. The only tangible value of the conflict in Aden to the SAS was the acquisition of basic experience in urban counter-terrorist warfare.

The British – and SAS – presence in Aden ended in November 1967. The new regime, the People's Democratic Republic of Yemen, was a Soviet-backed state which almost immediately tried to support the overthrow of the neighbouring regime of the Sultan of Oman.
(SEE *Ballycastle House; Edwards, Captain Robin; Front for the Liberation of Occupied South Yemen; 'Hearts and Minds'; 'Keeni Meeni'; National Liberation Front; North Yemen; Oman; Radfan; Thumier*)

ADOO Arabic word meaning 'enemy'. Used by the SAS in Oman to refer to the guerrillas of the People's Front for the Liberation of the Occupied Arabian Gulf (PFLOAG) and the Dhofar Liberation Front (DLF).
(SEE *Dhofar Liberation Front; Oman; People's Front for the Liberation of the Occupied Arabian Gulf*)

AGEDABIA Axis airfield on the North African coast near Benghazi in Libya's Cyrenaica province. Raided by an SAS team on the night of 21 December 1941. The party of five, commanded by Lieutenant W. Fraser, included Sergeants DuVivier and Tait and Privates Phillips and Byrne.

The five men were driven to within 16km of the target by Long Range Desert Group vehicles, and then made their way on foot. Arriving at the airfield in the early hours of the 21st, they laid up during the day and observed the target. That night they simply walked on to the airfield and planted their Lewes bombs on the aircraft. The raid was a great success, with 37 Italian CR42 fighter-bombers being destroyed. The SAS party itself suffered no casualties.
(SEE *Fraser, Major Bill; Lewes bomb; Long Range Desert Group; North Africa*)

AGHEILA Axis airfield on the Gulf of Sirte, North Africa. Raided by an SAS party led by Lieutenant 'Jock' Lewes during the night of 14 December 1941. However, as the airfield was only a staging post, there were no aircraft there when the raiders struck. Nevertheless, on the way back they did manage to blow up a number of Italian vehicles near a roadhouse at Mersa Brega.
(SEE *Lewes, Lieutenant John Steel 'Jock'; North Africa*)

AH HOI The leader of a group of Communist Terrorists in Malaya's Telok Anson swamp area. In February 1958, 37 men from D Squadron under Major Harry Thompson began a sweep of the swamp and after many days of difficult going surrounded his camp. Ah Hoi, nicknamed 'Baby Killer' for the murder of an informer's pregnant wife, surrendered to troops under the command of Captain Peter de la Billière and was then exiled to China.
(SEE *Communist Terrorist; de la Billière, General Sir Peter; Malaya; Malayan Races Liberation Army; Thompson, Major Harry*)

AH POY A Communist Terrorist district committee secretary killed

during Operation 'Ginger', a sweep carried out to the south of Ipoh in Malaya by members of A Squadron, 22 SAS, under Captain Johnny Cooper in 1954.
(SEE *Communist Terrorist; Cooper, Lieutenant-Colonel Johnny; Malaya; Malayan Races Liberation Army*)

AH-7 A version of Westland's high speed, highly manoeuvrable anti-tank helicopter capable of carrying up to nine passengers and two crew. Thanks to its performance, carrying capacity and armament, the Lynx has found favour with the SAS for the infiltration and exfiltration of personnel. The helicopter has seen extensive service with the Regiment, notably in Northern Ireland.

Type: anti-tank, liaison and transport helicopter
Crew: pilot, weapons officer and nine passengers
Range: 630km

Below: Fast and highly manoeuvrable, the AH-7 Lynx is ideal for the insertion of special forces into hostile territory.

Payload: 1766kg
Maximum speed: 211km/hr
Weapons: eight TOW anti-tank missiles; Hellfire anti-tank missiles; and 7.62mm machine gun mounts

AIMING POINT PROJECTORS
(SEE *Laser Aiming Systems*)

AIR TROOP One of the 16-man units, along with the Mountain, Boat and Mobility Troops, that make up an SAS squadron. The troop is further sub-divided into four fighting patrols. Members of the Air Troops, apart from their individual patrol skills, are highly trained in all aspects of parachuting.
(SEE *Boat Troop; Cross-training; Mobility Troop; Mountain Troop; Patrol Skills; Troop Skills*)

AKEHURST, BRIGADIER JOHN
Operational commander of the Sultan's Armed Forces in the latter stages of the conflict in Oman (1974-76). His successful strategy hinged on *firqat* groups, working with SAS support, establishing settlements in areas

where Dhofar Liberation Front guerrillas operated and then creating defensive lines to prohibit their movement into Oman from Yemen.
(SEE *Dhofar Liberation Front; Firqat; Oman; Sultan's Armed Forces*)

ALMONDS, LIEUTENANT 'GENTLEMAN' JIM
One of the original members of L Detachment who went on many early SAS missions in North Africa, including the attack on Nofilia airfield which ended in the death of Lieutenant 'Jock' Lewes. Almonds was captured during a disastrous raid on Benghazi in September 1942, but later escaped and went on to serve with the SAS in Europe.
(SEE *Benghazi; L Detachment; Lewes, Lieutenant John Steel 'Jock'; Nofilia; North Africa*)

'AMHERST', OPERATION Codename for the SAS effort to support the Canadian First Army as it advanced into Holland in early April 1945. The plan was for a large SAS party to parachute behind enemy lines and harry the German forces to prevent

them establishing a defensive line against the advancing Canadians. As the SAS troops would be lightly armed, it was anticipated that the Canadians would need to link up with them within 48 hours. In addition, the SAS was tasked with preserving a vital airfield at Steenwijk, preventing the destruction of 18 bridges and collecting intelligence.

The operation involved landing 3 and 4 French Parachute Battalions (3 and 4 SAS) – a total of 700 men and 18 jeeps – in the area of Groningen, Coevorden and Zwolle, northeast Holland. The drop took place on the night of 8 April. However, because of thick cloud the jeeps could not be delivered.

By and large the SAS units achieved most of their assigned tasks. For the loss of only 29 killed, 35 wounded and 29 missing, the SAS killed 270 enemy soldiers, wounded 220 and captured a further 187 during their various missions. Operation 'Amherst' ended on 16 April.

(SEE *Northwest Europe*)

AMMUNITION In the field SAS units employ standard British Army 5.56mm and 7.62mm ammunition. However, for hostage-rescue missions and other counter-terrorist operations, SAS units use a variety of specialist ammunition. In these situations the primary consideration is stopping power: the ability to neutralise an opponent with one bullet. In a hostage-rescue situation immediate neutralisation is imperative as a terrorist has to be stopped quickly to prevent him harming either the hostages or SAS team members.

The SAS, in common with other anti-terrorist forces around the world, employs 9mm calibre weapons in its operations. The disadvantage with the 9mm bullet is that, although it usually kills, it does not always stop, having a tendency to pass straight through the target's body and maybe hit a hostage. Therefore, research was undertaken to turn the 9mm bullet into a stopping

round. This has resulted in a number of different rounds being developed, although they all fit into two main categories: frangible rounds, which break up in the body, and accelerated energy transfer (AET) rounds, which flatten on striking a target and cause massive tissue damage.

Frangible rounds include the US Glaser Safety Slug. This consists of a small shotgun cartridge with a plastic cap fitted to the front. When it hits an uneven surface the cap fragments, causing the shot inside to spill out of the bullet. The speed of energy transfer results in massive systemic shock. The disadvantages of the round are its high cost and, more importantly, a hit on a non-combatant is invariably fatal. This means that the soldier has no opportunity to shoot through a hostage to hit a hostile.

The British 'Spartan' frangible round is a lead dust and polymer mix bullet which is designed to break up on impact. The 'Splat' round is a development of the 'Spartan', being a non-lead metal-and-polymer mix bullet designed to break up in the body but which can also penetrate soft-to-medium cover first without breaking up until it exits the far side.

There are three main types of AET profile round. First, 'Geco action', a hollow bullet with a plastic core. After firing the core falls away and, when the bullet hits the target, its construction causes it to tumble, resulting in high tissue damage and retention in the body. The second type, called 'equalloy', is made from an aluminium alloy and is thus extremely lightweight. It also remains in the body after impact. The third type of round is the French 'THV' bullet. The forward part of the bullet has a concave shape, resulting in massive tissue damage when it hits the body.

SAS counter-terrorist teams also employ a variety of shotgun ammunition in their operations, notably buckshot, armour-piercing, high explosive and Hatton rounds, the latter being designed to blow hinges off doors

without causing injury to the occupants of the room. The one major drawback with these specialist rounds is that counter-terrorist forces can only use manually operated shotguns as the shape of the cartridges and the low pressures produced are often insufficient to produce the gas blowback required to operate semi- or full-automatic models.

ANAK KAYAN Iban tribesman who did much to teach the Malayan Scouts the subtleties of tracking in the jungle.

(SEE *Malaya; Malayan Scouts*)

'APOSTLE', OPERATION Codename for the mission undertaken by HQ SAS Brigade, 1 and 2 SAS, all under the command of Brigadier Mike Calvert, to disarm the 300,000 German soldiers remaining in Norway at the end of World War II. An advance party arrived at Stavanger on 12 May 1945, and by the end of the month a total of 845 troops and 150 jeeps were in the country. The SAS Brigade was based at Bergen to administer the operation. The Germans gave no trouble, although there were clashes with Quislings (Norwegian collaborators) before the SAS returned to England at the end of August.

(SEE *Bergen; Calvert, Brigadier Mike*)

'ARCHWAY', OPERATION At the end of March 1945, two strong squadrons from 1 and 2 SAS, under the command of Majors Poat and Power respectively, were tasked with crossing the River Rhine to support the advance of the British 21st Army Group. Initially the SAS force, under the overall command of Lieutenant-Colonel Brian Franks and composed of 430 men, 75 jeeps and several trucks, was tasked with undertaking short-range reconnaissance for the 6th Airborne, 11th Armoured and 15th (Scottish) Divisions east of the Rhine around Wesel. They were then to carry out deeper penetration ahead of

Above: Arctic kit must be lightweight, durable and waterproof in addition to allowing freedom of movement.

the main Allied offensive into Germany.

The operation began on 25 March; by 3 May, having fought numerous battles against rearguard infantry and armoured forces, the SAS had reached Kiel. The high mobility of the SAS jeeps made a significant contribution to the rapid advance of the 21st Army Group.
(SEE *Franks, Lieutenant-Colonel Brian; Germany; Northwest Europe*)

ARCTIC KIT High winds and extreme cold are the two main dangers of

operating in Arctic regions, and so SAS members are provided with kit to prevent the onset of frostbite, trench foot and shock. Clothing is tough, light, windproof and waterproof and often made of natural materials such as cotton, wool and fur. A layered approach is usual, with windproof clothing worn over waterproof suits or thermal liners that maintain body heat. Individuals often purchase silk vests and 'long johns' to wear next to the skin. Two pairs of mittens are worn: the outer pair offering protection against wind and water covers the inner pair. Headgear is vital and SAS members favour the arctic cap with its fold-down ear flaps or the standard GS cap. Footwear is

influenced by the type of mission but many troopers prefer to wear the German ski-mountaineering boot. Other specialist kit includes the bergen rucksack, snow shoes and cross-country skis.

ARDENNES The SAS played only a minor part in the defeat of the German Ardennes Offensive which began on 16 December 1944. The only units involved were the Belgian battalion and one French battalion. They were mainly engaged in ground reconnaissance operations in the region to support Allied units.
(SEE *'Franklin', Operation; 'Regent', Operation*)

ARMALITE The early version of the M16 automatic rifle, designated the AR-15, designed by Eugene Stoner and produced by the Fairchild Aircraft Company in the late 1950s. The weapon was subsequently produced under licence by Colt and designated the M16. The Armalite, because of its compact size, was particularly suited to close-quarter jungle fighting, and was used in such a role by the SAS in Borneo. It is also a favoured terrorist weapon.
(SEE *M16*)

ARTISTS RIFLES The career of the World War II SAS ended with the regiments being disbanded in October 1945 but, following renewed War Office interest in the commando-style concept, the unit was re-activated as 21 SAS (Artists) in 1947. The Artists Rifles, formed in 1859 and with a distinguished fighting record in World War I, had acted as an Officer Training Unit in World War II and, following a short period of de-activation, became part of the Territorial Army and affiliated to the Rifle Brigade.
(SEE *Special Air Service*)

ASKAR An armed Arab tribesman. Approximately 30 *askars* from northern Oman fought alongside the SAS

Above: A detachment of Artists Rifles on parade outside the Royal Academy of Art, London, just after World War II. The unit was resurrected in 1947 as 21 SAS.

at the Battle of Mirbat in July 1972.
(SEE *Mirbat; Oman*)

ATHLIT After March 1943, Athlit, in Palestine, became the base of the newly-designated Special Boat Squadron. The SAS trained at the base for operations in the eastern Mediterranean and for the landings in Sicily, with particular emphasis being placed on mountain warfare.
(SEE *Special Boat Squadron*)

ATKINSON, TOMMY RAF instructor who was responsible for training SAS personnel in the various freefall parachuting techniques in the post-World War II era.

AUSTRALIAN SAS The Australian SAS began life as the 1st SAS Company in July 1957. The unit was awarded regimental status on 4 September 1964. At this date the regiment consisted of Headquarters and Base Squadron (Training Cadre), the 1st and 2nd 'Sabre' Squadrons and the 151st Signals Squadron.

In February 1965, both fighting squadrons were deployed to Borneo: the 1st was stationed in Brunei; the 2nd went to Sarawak. Australian SAS squadrons were also involved in the Vietnam War, where they served in rotation from 1966 to 1971.

Today, the Australian SAS has two main areas of responsibility. First, its operatives are trained in long-range reconnaissance – essential skills given the vastness of the Australian continent. Second, since 1979 it has become a crack counter-terrorist unit

trained in hostage-rescue techniques, as well as being responsible for the protection of oil and gas platforms in the Bass Strait. In addition, the regiment's hostage-rescue unit has undertaken training with other units, notably the British SAS.

Right: SAS training at Athlit in 1943.

B

'Badged' Term used to denote those potential recruits to the SAS who have successfully passed through the rigours of Selection and Continuation Training to be granted entry into the ranks of the Regiment. A 'badged' SAS soldier serves a probationary period of 12 months, which starts from the date on which he was first selected for training.
(SEE *Continuation Training; Selection Training*)

Bagnara Port in southern Italy which was seized by the Special Raiding Squadron (in fact 1 SAS, which had been renamed after the end of the African campaign), commanded by Lieutenant-Colonel Mayne, on 3 September 1943. The aim of the operation, codenamed 'Baytown', was the disruption of German lines of communication in southern Italy, which would make a determined defence against the Allied advance less likely (British and US forces had landed at Salerno and crossed the Straits of Messina from Sicily on 3 September).

However, the transport laid on by the Royal Navy left much to be desired: one of the two landing craft provided broke down and the other ran aground. Eventually, all the SAS troops and their equipment had to transfer to four much smaller landing

Left: The beige beret and winged dagger of a 'badged' SAS man. Right: Armed police at the Balcombe Street siege in December 1975.

craft. They were subsequently landed late on the wrong side of the bay. The mission was only a moderate success.

Light resistance was encountered and the town was quickly captured, but the SRS soon came under enemy mortar and machine-gun fire from the surrounding hills. Probing forward in small groups, the SRS skirmished around Bagnara for three days before making contact with Allied troops advancing from Reggio.

The operation cost the SRS five killed and 17 wounded, and afterwards the Squadron was withdrawn to Sicily for a rest.
(SEE *Italy; Mayne, Lieutenant-Colonel 'Paddy' Blair; Special Air Service; Special Raiding Squadron*)

Bagoush Axis airfield on the North African coast. The SAS conducted a

jeep raid against it on the night of 7 July 1942. The party included David Stirling and 'Paddy' Mayne, and the mission was the first in which enemy aircraft were attacked by jeeps.

Driving onto the runway, the three vehicles riddled each aircraft with machine-gun fire as they passed. Receiving no casualties themselves, the SAS destroyed 37 aircraft. An SAS raid was also mounted against the same airfield on the night of 26 July 1942 as a diversion for a much larger operation against Sidi Haneish airfield.
(SEE *Jeep; Mayne, Lieutenant-Colonel 'Paddy' Blair; North Africa; Sidi Haneish; Stirling, Lieutenant-Colonel David*)

Balcombe Street Siege On 6 December 1975, a four-man Irish Republican Army (IRA) Active

Right: British Army troops on patrol in South Armagh, 'Bandit Country', an area of high IRA activity.

Service Unit, which had just mounted an attack on a restaurant, took over a flat in Balcombe Street, London, and held a middle-aged couple hostage. Armed police quickly surrounded the flat. On the morning of the eighth day, by which time the siege had reached stalemate, media reports suggested that an SAS unit was in the vicinity. This information was heard by the terrorists on a radio set inside the flat and resulted in their immediate surrender to the authorities.
(SEE *Active Service Unit; Irish Republican Army*)

BALLYCASTLE HOUSE Location of the SAS HQ in the Khormaksar military complex near the port of Aden, and from where counter-terrorist 'Keeni Meeni' undercover operations were launched from 1966.
(SEE *Aden; 'Keeni Meeni'*)

BALUCHIS Inhabitants of Baluchistan (once part of Oman but now part of Iran and Pakistan) who were traditionally employed as soldiers in the army of the Sultanate of Muscat and Oman. In late 1958, when the SAS was first deployed to the country, the Sultan, Said bin Taimur, distrusting the local tribes, followed tradition and filled his 800-strong army with Baluchis (who were usually officered by British expatriates on contract). The Baluchis, although they made brave and hardy soldiers, did not speak Arabic, a fact which did not endear them to the indigenous population and created difficulties for the SAS 'hearts and minds' campaign in the country.
(SEE *'Hearts and Minds'; Oman; Said bin Taimur, Sultan*)

'BANDIT COUNTRY' British Army term for South Armagh, an area of Northern Ireland on the border with the Irish Republic that has seen con-

siderable IRA activity since the outbreak of the 'Troubles' in the Province in 1969.
(SEE *Irish Republican Army; Northern Ireland; South Armagh*)

'BAOBAB', OPERATION Codename for one of a series of raids conducted by 2 SAS in support of the Anzio landings (Operation 'Shingle' – 22 January 1944) designed to sever strategic railway lines which transported German supplies down through Italy. 'Baobab' was undertaken by a small party from 2 SAS and involved destroying a vital bridge between Pesaro and Fano on Italy's east coast. The men were landed on the coast on 30 January and successfully destroyed the bridge with explosive charges.
(SEE *Italy; 'Maple', Operation*)

BARCE Axis airfield in North Africa. Raided by the SAS on the night of 8 March 1942. The party, led by Major Bill Fraser, was transported to the target in vehicles of the Long Range

Desert Group. However, only one aircraft and a number of trucks were found at the site on arrival and, though these were destroyed by the SAS, it was a rather poor return for the effort involved.
(SEE *Fraser, Major Bill; Long Range Desert Group; North Africa*)

'BARKER', OPERATION One of a number of missions conducted throughout August and September 1944 to protect the open right flank of General Patton's US Third Army as it advanced through France to the River Rhine and the German frontier.
   On 13 August, 27 men from 3 French Parachute Battalion (3 SAS), commanded by Lieutenant Rouhan, jumped into the Saone-et-Loire area of the Massif Central. Their mission was to disrupt enemy movements and support the local *Maquis*. The operation was over by 19 September, by which time large-scale damage – 3000 casualties including 500 prisoners – had been inflicted on the Germans.
(SEE *Maquis; Northwest Europe*)

BARKWORTH, MAJOR ERIC
Intelligence officer of 2 SAS who, after World War II, headed the SAS War Crimes Investigation Team that looked into the murder of SAS personnel by German troops carrying out Hitler's infamous 'Commando Order' of October 1942. Several bodies were uncovered at Gaggenau near the Rotenfals concentration camp in Germany which proved to be the remains of captured SAS men involved in Operation 'Loyton'. Barkworth's work continued until 1949, by which time several of those responsible for the atrocities had been tried by military courts sitting at Wuppertal and hanged.
(SEE *Hitler's Commando Order; 'Loyton', Operation; Northwest Europe*)

'BASHA' Slang SAS term for a temporary shelter made from locally avail-

Below: 'Bashas' can be constructed from man-made or natural materials.

able materials such as large leaves and branches in jungle areas. Also used to refer to small canvas tents, barrack rooms, houses or beds.

'BAYTOWN', OPERATION Codename for the SAS mission to capture the Italian port of Bagnara in September 1943.
(SEE *Bagnara; Italy*)

BEACONSFIELD Location of the Royal Army Education Corps School of Languages. Individual SAS soldiers often attend crash courses in a particular language at the school prior to being sent to a country where the language is spoken. During the campaign in Oman (1970-76), for example, SAS soldiers undertook intensive, 10-week courses in colloquial Arabic before they were sent overseas.
(SEE *Patrol Skills; Troop Skills*)

'BEASTING' A practice, now abandoned, that saw SAS instructors

attempt to de-motivate recruits on Selection Training by suggesting they take a short break or give up altogether, particularly during the 'beat-up' marches that take place during Selection.
(SEE *'Beat-up' March; Selection Training*)

'BEATING THE CLOCK' SAS slang for staying alive. Those who die in action have their names inscribed on plaques originally fixed to the base of the Regimental Clock Tower at Stirling Lines, hence the expression. When the new barracks block, Stirling Lines, was completed the tower was left in place but the plaques were re-sited outside the Regimental Chapel.
(SEE *Stirling Lines*)

'BEAT-UP' MARCH Part of SAS Selection Training which sees recruits undertake a number of progressively harder marches over the Brecon Beacons. Initially undertaken in pairs

Right: A member of the Belgian 1st Para-Commandos in the Congo, 1964.

and then individually, the marches are designed to test both mental and physical strengths with recruits expected to navigated by map and compass between a number of rendezvous points. Those who fail are 'Returned to Unit' (RTU'd).
(SEE *RTU'd; Selection Training*)

BECKWITH, COLONEL CHARLES
US Special Forces veteran who saw action in Vietnam and with the SAS in Malaya in the early 1960s. In 1977 he was tasked with raising the United States' own counter-terrorist unit known as Delta Force. Delta Force's first batch of recruits underwent basic training at Hereford.
(SEE *Delta Force*)

'BEERCAN' Codename given to one of the SAS objectives during the assault on the Jebel Akhdar, Oman, in January 1959.
(SEE *Jebel Akhdar; Oman*)

'BEGONIA', OPERATION Following the surrender of Italy in September 1943, large numbers of British prisoners of war (POWs) escaped from their camps after their Italian guards had abandoned their posts. Operation 'Begonia' involved detachments from 2 SAS making contact with these men and guiding them to beaches along the Adriatic coast, from where they would be evacuated by sea.

Small parties were either landed from the sea between Ancona and Pescara or parachuted in farther inland. The drops were made on 2 October; the seaborne landings took place between 4 and 6 October.

The operation was not a great success. Contact was made with hundreds of POWs but only a handful were evacuated. Due to bad planning boats would arrive at a rendezvous to discover that there were no POWs to be picked up, and vice versa. Over 60 SAS men were employed in an opera-

tion which repatriated no more than 50 POWs.
(SEE *Italy*)

BEIHAN Site of a safe house in the interior of Aden provided by Sharif Hussein to shelter ex-SAS men involved in a covert operation against the Yemenis in 1962.
(SEE *North Yemen*)

'BELFAST CRADLE' SAS soldiers on operations traditionally do not use a sling to carry their rifle; rather, they hold the weapon crooked in their forearms. This 'Belfast Cradle' allows a quicker response to any surprise contacts with the enemy.

BELGIAN 1ST PARA-COMMANDO BATTALION
In memory of the regi-

ment's origins as part of the SAS Brigade in World War II, its 1st Battalion wears a maroon beret with SAS wings. The regiment's most memorable operation in recent years was the rescue of European nationals in Stanleyville, Congo, in 1964.
(SEE *Belgian Independent Parachute Company*)

BELGIAN INDEPENDENT PARACHUTE COMPANY
A World War II SAS unit, otherwise known as 5 SAS.
(SEE *Special Air Service*)

BENGHAZI Port on the North African coast which, during World War II, served as an Axis logistics centre. As such it became an SAS target, although the three attempts to hit objectives within the port resulted in disappointment. However, the missions were indicative of the daring which remains a notable feature of SAS operations.

In mid-March 1942, a party led by David Stirling managed to infiltrate the town and get to the harbour. However, the water was too rough to make use of the collapsible canoe that was to be used to reach the ships at anchor. In any case, it was soon discovered that the canoe had been damaged during the journey. The attack was therefore aborted.

In May 1942, a second attempt was made by Stirling to hit Axis shipping at Benghazi. On the 21st Stirling, accompanied by five others in the 'Blitz Buggy', headed towards the town. Bluffing their way through roadblocks, the party entered the town and again made for the harbour. The plan was to use two inflatable dinghies to place limpet mines on the ships. However, both dinghies were found to be damaged and the mission was again abandoned. The men stayed hidden in the town for two days while they fixed the truck, which had been damaged on the way to the port.

One particular incident of note is that on the way back from the harbour the party, complete with dinghies and limpet mines, had to

pass the guardhouse. One of the SAS soldiers, Captain Fitzroy Maclean, convinced the Italian sentries that they were German officers conducting sabotage training and demanded to know why hadn't they turned out the guard as they passed? Speechless, the Italians rapidly formed a line as Stirling and the rest passed. Bluff was often an integral part of SAS operations in North Africa.

The third attempt was made on 13 September 1942, but Stirling's column of jeeps and trucks faced an alerted garrison and did not get near the port. In the subsequent action the SAS lost four killed, 20 jeeps and 25 trucks destroyed, plus many wounded.
(SEE *'Blitz Buggy'; Maclean, Captain Fitzroy; North Africa; Stirling, Lieutenant-Colonel David*)

BENINA Major Axis airfield and repair workshop in North Africa during World War II. Raided by the SAS on no less than three occasions in 1942, though with mixed results. The first assault on the night of 8 March found no aircraft present. The second raid on 25 March, led by David Stirling, destroyed five aircraft. On the night of 13 June, led by Stirling again, the SAS party destroyed two aircraft and a number of workshops.
(SEE *North Africa; Stirling, Lieutenant-Colonel David*)

BENNETT, REGIMENTAL SERGEANT-MAJOR BOB One of the original members of L Detachment, Bennett joined the SAS after serving with the Brigade of Guards and No 8 Commando. He saw action with 1 SAS for most of the war, serving in North Africa, Italy, Northwest Europe and Norway. When the SAS was reformed, he served with B Squadron, Malayan Scouts, in Malaya and, before retiring in 1962, he was 21 SAS's regimental sergeant-major. His awards include the British Empire

Left: An SA-80 rifle with the current standard-issue British Army bergen.

Medal and the Military Medal.
(SEE *North Africa; Northwest Europe*)

'BENSON', OPERATION On 28 August 1944, six soldiers from the Belgium Independent Parachute Company (5 SAS), commanded by Lieutenant Kirschen, were parachuted into northeastern France at a point southeast of Amiens to collect intelligence concerning German troop strengths and movements. The men suffered numerous injuries on landing and so, after contacting the Resistance, were taken to a sympathetic doctor. The latter had, the day before, stolen a map from a German officer which contained detailed information about the positions of enemy divisions on the Somme. This valuable information was transmitted to headquarters, though not before the SAS party had conducted a firefight with a German patrol which had accidentally stumbled upon them. The operation ended on 1 September.
(SEE *Belgian Independent Parachute Company; Northwest Europe*)

'BERGBANG', OPERATION Took place between 2 and 12 September 1944. An unsuccessful mission conducted by 41 members of the Belgian SAS in the Liege-Aachen-Maastricht area to aid the local Resistance and sever German communications east of the River Meuse. The men were dropped too far from the operational area and bad weather dispersed the group over a wide area.
(SEE *Northwest Europe*)

BERGE, COMMANDANT GEORGE Free French officer who was an early recruit to the SAS in North Africa. On the night of 13/14 June 1942, Berge, in conjunction with Captain George Jellicoe of the Special Boat Section, three Free French operatives and a Greek officer, Lieutenant Costi, attacked the German airfield at Heraklion, Crete. The raid itself was a success as 21 aircraft were destroyed, but German patrols, possibly acting

Above: The Blackburn Beverley was an extremely sturdy transport aircraft.

on intelligence provided by an informer, surprised Berge and his three compatriots. One Frenchman was killed, with Berge and two others being captured. After interrogation, they were executed. Jellicoe and Costi made good their escape.
(SEE *Crete; Jellicoe, Earl George; Special Boat Section*)

BERGEN Town on the coast of Norway that became the operational base for SAS Brigade HQ and 1 and 2 SAS in late May 1945. The units were involved in the disarmament of German garrison troops, but their mission was hardly arduous and they returned to England in August.
(SEE *'Apostle', Operation*)

BERGEN Standard-issue British Army backpack which is used by the SAS.

BERKA Site of two Axis airfields on the outskirts of Benghazi: Berka Main and Berka Satellite. The latter was raided by the SAS on the night of 8 March 1942, with 15 aircraft being destroyed. A second SAS attack on both airfields was mounted on the night of 13 June. The assault on Berka Satellite, led by 'Paddy' Mayne, was unsuccessful, the party being stopped by enemy sentries and forced to retire. However, at Berka Main the SAS destroyed 11 aircraft.
(SEE *Benghazi; Mayne, Lieutenant-Colonel 'Paddy' Blair; North Africa*)

BEVERLEY A rugged and reliable transport aircraft, nicknamed the 'Flying Pig', built by the Blackburn Company, which saw service from 1955 to 1967. Used to support the SAS in Malaya, Oman and the Rad-fan. Capable of carrying large loads such as helicopters or vehicles and able to take off from small airfields and jungle strips, it was an invaluable asset in low-intensity operations. It had a top speed of 238km/hr, a range of 2100km and could carry 94 troops or 70 paratroopers.

BFT Battle Fitness Test. Early stage of the SAS Selection process which is based on the tests faced by all infantry and airborne soldiers in the British Army. Recruits, initially running as a group, have to cover two and a half kilometres in 13 minutes and then complete a solo run over the same distance in 11.5 minutes.
(SEE *Selection Training*)

'BIN' SAS slang for someone or something, e.g. a plan, being rejected. Particularly used to described those who fail the SAS selection process ('binned').
(SEE *RTU'd; Selection Training*)

'BINGO BOOK' Term for the journal containing the names of wanted terrorists, suspect addresses and missing vehicles which is carried by individual SAS soldiers while on active duty in Northern Ireland. The list is constantly amended and updated by British military intelligence.
(SEE *Northern Ireland*)

BIRDSTRIKE A dangerous and potentially lethal occurrence that can lead to the destruction of a helicopter or aircraft. Birds sucked into engines can cause rapid and irreversible power failure, as seems to have happened in one instance in the 1982 Falklands conflict. While cross-decking from HMS *Hermes* to HMS *Intrepid* on 19 May, a Sea King helicopter suffered a birdstrike, crashed into the sea and

sank. Twenty men died, the majority from D Squadron, 22 SAS.
(SEE *Falkland Islands*)

'BIVI-BAG' Slang for an item of standard British Army and SAS kit – a waterproof one-man sheet used as a temporary shelter.

'BLITZ BUGGY' Vehicle used by David Stirling during SAS operations in North Africa. Acquired in early 1942, the vehicle was a Ford V-8 staff car modified for SAS desert operations. The windows and roof were removed and a large spare fuel tank added. Two Vickers 'K' guns were mounted on the front and one on the rear. The vehicle was painted a drab olive grey colour to resemble a German staff car, and the new enemy air recognition panel was painted on the bonnet every month. The 'Blitz Buggy' was destroyed when returning from the successful raid against Bagoush airfield on 7 July 1942, when it was caught in the open by Italian aircraft and set alight by gunfire.
(SEE *Bagoush; Benghazi; Stirling, Lieutenant-Colonel David; Vickers 'K'*)

BLONDEEL, CAPTAIN Commander of the Belgian Independent Parachute Company attached to the SAS Brigade. Took part in Operations 'Noah' (August-September 1944), 'Regent' (December 1944-January 1945) and 'Larkswood' (April-May 1945) in Northwest Europe.
(SEE *Belgian Independent Parachute Company; 'Larkswood', Operation; 'Noah', Operation; Northwest Europe; 'Regent', Operation*)

BOAT TROOP One of the 16-man units, along with the Air, Mountain and Mobility Troops, that make up an SAS squadron. Members of the Boat Troops are specialists in all aspects of the operation of small boats and canoes, as well as combat swimming and diving.
(SEE *Air Troop; Mobility Troop; Mountain Troop; Patrol Skills*)

BODY ARMOUR SAS soldiers on counter-terrorist duties, either in Northern Ireland or for hostage-rescue work, wear a variety of body armour. Examples include jackets produced by the UK firms Bristol Engineering and Armourshield. The latter's GPV 25 vest is worn for hostage-rescue work and is capable of defeating attack from high velocity 9mm, .357 Magnum and 7.62mm bullets. Bristol's Type 18 armour jacket is specially designed not to interfere with the wearer's movements during operations. All models are designed to be lightweight, though guaranteeing maximum stopping power through the use of such materials as Kevlar.
(SEE *Counter Revolutionary Warfare Equipment*)

BODYGUARDING Following the end of the Aden campaign in 1967, the SAS offered the British government its best marksmen for bodyguard duties. They were subsequently engaged in training bodyguards for foreign diplomats whose safety was deemed to be in the interests of Britain. In some instances SAS soldiers themselves acted as bodyguards until indigenous personnel could be trained, as in the case of Sultan Qaboos of Oman during the period immediately following his palace coup against his father, Sultan Said bin Taimur, in 1970.

The construction of the 'Killing House' at Hereford in the early 1970s, a project specifically designed for counter-terrorist and hostage-rescue training, also resulted in a honing of the Regiment's bodyguard skills, as the qualities required in the 'House' are quick thinking and speedy reaction at close quarters.

The Regiment provides training for both foreign and domestic clients, a notable example of the latter being the Metropolitan Police's VIP protection squad. In addition, SAS soldiers continually act as bodyguards for the British Prime Minister, senior government ministers and members of the Royal Family on overseas visits, as well as for Foreign Office diplomats on high-risk foreign assignments.
(SEE *'Killing House'; Said bin Taimur, Sultan; Qaboos, Sultan*)

BONNINGTON, LIEUTENANT CHARLES Commander of one of the teams that took off from Bagoush airfield, North Africa, in five Bristol Bombay transports on the SAS's first, disastrous operation in November 1941. High winds and poor visibility forced the aircraft carrying Bonnington's command to make an emergency landing. Later, after taking off and heading back to Tobruk, they were hit by anti-aircraft fire and pursued by an enemy fighter. The two crew and one SAS man died when the Bombay crash-landed; the remainder, including Bonnington himself, were captured.
(SEE *Bagoush; 'Crusader', Operation*)

BORDER SCOUTS Name of the irregular forces raised and trained by the SAS during their campaign in Borneo (1963-66). They were created by Major-General W. Walker, Director of Operations Borneo, as part of an effort to establish a defensive intelligence network along the long, vulnerable border with the Kalimantan province of Indonesia.

Recruited from the indigenous tribes of the region, they were trained by SAS soldiers in a number of jungle camps. These camps were all identical: a simple longhouse to accommodate the Scouts, with a smaller one for their instructors. The SAS soldiers were responsible for all aspects of training, discipline and administration. The training programme was eventually handed over to the Gurkha Independent Parachute Company.

The Scouts, although armed and trained as paramilitaries, were not combat troops, a fact brought home in September 1963 when a Scout post at Long Jawi, 45km from the border, was all but wiped out by a large party of well-equipped Indonesians. After

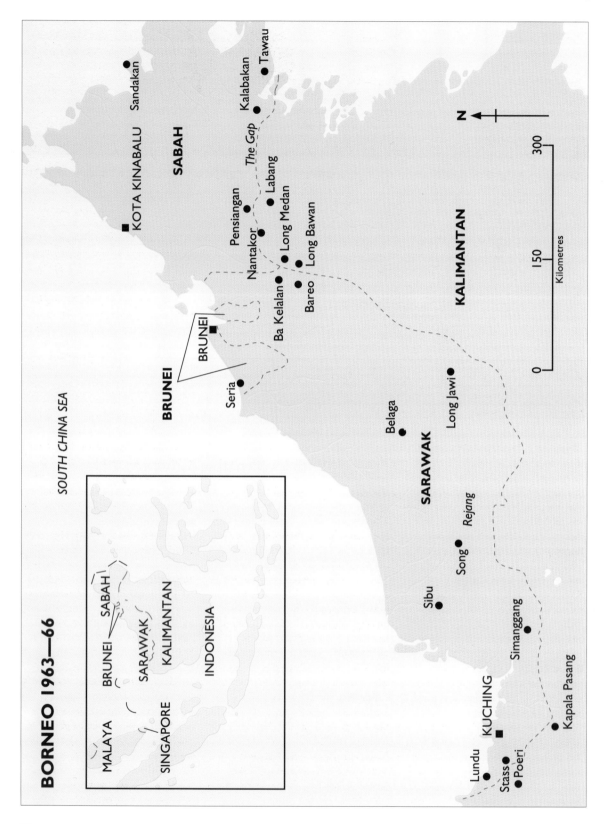

BORNEO 1963—66

MALAYA
SINGAPORE
BRUNEI SABAH
SARAWAK
KALIMANTAN
INDONESIA

SOUTH CHINA SEA

SABAH

Sandakan

Tawau
Kalabakan

The Gap

KOTA KINABALU

Labang
Pensiangan
Long Medan
Nantakor
Long Bawan

BRUNEI

BRUNEI
Ba Kelalan
Bareo

KALIMANTAN

Seria

N

300

150

0

Kilometres

Long Jawi

Belaga

SARAWAK

Song
Rejang

Sibu

Simanggang

KUCHING

Lundu
Stass
Poeri
Kapala Pasang

Above: An SAS patrol with riverboats on one of the countless waterways of Borneo. These craft were invaluable for transporting men quickly from one area to another.

this incident Walker changed their role to purely intelligence gathering. It was in the latter role that they proved their worth to the SAS, by being the Regiment's 'eyes and ears' along the border, and thus aided the British military effort. Often two or more Scouts were added to individual SAS patrols to facilitate communications with the indigenous inhabitants. (SEE *Borneo; Cross-Border Scouts*)

BORNEO The SAS conducted a highly successful campaign in the jungles and mountains of Borneo between 1963 and 1966.

Malaya, the former British colony, was lobbying hard for the formation of a new political entity in the region, comprising Sabah, Sarawak, Brunei, Malaya and Singapore, to be called the Federation of Malaysia. This idea

was supported by Britain but opposed by President Sukarno of Indonesia, who saw it as a threat to his ambitions to expand his country's frontiers. He therefore sought to do everything in his power to wreck the plan.

In December 1962, a rebellion led by anti-Malaysian elements broke out in the Sultanate of Brunei, but was quickly suppressed by British forces. In early 1963, Sukarno began to infiltrate insurgents from Kalimantan into Borneo. These were increased when Sabah and Sarawak (though not Brunei or Singapore) were officially incorporated into Malaysia in September 1963. The British, in response, organised a force of Malaysian, British and Commonwealth troops to contain the insurgents. The Special Air Service formed part of this effort.

The task facing Major-General W. Walker, the British commander in Borneo, was a formidable one. He had only five battalions to cover over 1500km of jungle-covered border. In addition, he had to contend with an internal threat in the shape of the Clandestine Communist Organisation (CCO), whose recruits came mainly from Chinese settlers in Sarawak.

A Squadron, 22 SAS, arrived in Borneo in early 1963, accompanied by the Regiment's commander, Lieutenant-Colonel John Woodhouse. At first Walker wanted the SAS to act as a mobile reserve, dropping by parachute onto the jungle canopy to recapture any village helicopter landing pads which had been taken by the Indonesians. Woodhouse, rightly believing that this tactic would result in high casualties and would be a waste of their talents, convinced Walker that SAS troops would be better suited to operating in small patrols along the border, where they could provide early warning of any communist or Indonesian military incursions. Walker agreed to Woodhouse's proposals.

The task facing the SAS was a daunting one. As well as consisting of jungle and swamp, and infested with snakes, lizards and wild pigs, the area was inhabited by primitive peoples – Land Dyaks, Muruts and Punans – whose pastimes included headhunting. In addition, the squadron was composed of only 70 troopers. However, the SAS proved itself up to the task in hand. By operating in two- or three-man patrols the squadron was able to field 21 patrols along the

entire length of the border. They usually operated in the jungle for long periods. One from D Squadron, for example, stayed in the jungle in the Long Jawi area for six months.

A 'hearts and minds' campaign formed a large part of SAS operations. The standard procedure was for the patrol to establish contact with the local inhabitants and gain their trust. This invariably took time, but the troopers' understanding of the natives, a skill learnt in Malaya, was their greatest asset in the 'hearts and minds' campaign. In addition, many individuals spoke Malay which greatly facilitated communications. The patrols often lived with the locals,

sharing their longhouses by the rivers and helping with the planting and harvesting of crops. The trust built up between these people and the SAS, however, was mainly due to the work of the patrol medic in curing the natives' ills. In return for this help, the SAS picked up valuable intelligence concerning enemy strengths and movements. The soldiers also encouraged them to carry on their cross-border trading, knowing that they would bring back news of Indonesian movements. In one instance in early 1963, for example, traders informed the SAS of enemy activity in the Kalimantan villages of Kapala Pasang and Gun, which indicated that they were forward staging posts for cross-border raids.

The SAS also trained some locals as paramilitaries known as Border Scouts, providing them with weapons and uniforms. However, the Scouts were best suited to intelligence gathering rather than deployment as conventional infantry. The Cross-Border Scouts, on the other hand, were natives who, from the summer of 1964, were trained by the SAS for raids into Kalimantan.

The patrols also undertook their own reconnaissance of the area, establishing likely ambush sites and potential helicopter landing zones. All intelligence collected was relayed back to SAS headquarters on high-frequency radios, where it could be acted upon immediately.

The Indonesian incursions began in April 1963, by which time A Squadron had fully established a 'hearts and minds' policy with the indigenous population. In May D Squadron relieved A, and began paying particular attention to likely infiltration points: the plains along parts of Sarawak's western frontier; tracks leading through Stass at Long Jawi; the valleys south of Pensiangan; and the estuaries of eastern Sabah and

Left: An SAS patrol in Borneo off-loads at the edge of the jungle.

Above: SAS soldiers prepare for a mission in the Sarawak region of Borneo. By the mid-1960s, the Regiment had dashed Indonesian hopes of occupying the area.

Kalabakan. The period up to the end of 1963 also saw D Squadron undertaking reconnaissance of the previously unexplored jungle area in southern Sabah known as 'The Gap'.

The winter of 1963-64 witnessed an increase in the number of Indonesian incursions into the regions of Sabah and Kalimantan. D Squadron mounted a number of long-range patrols and SAS personnel, because of their knowledge of the terrain and excellent relationship with the local inhabitants, began to assist regular infantrymen in intercepting infiltrators by guiding them to ambush sites. In June 1964, the British government authorised Walker to launch the first top secret 'Claret' raids across the border. The first, undertaken with the

aid of intelligence provided by the SAS, was against the Indonesian camp at Nantakor and was completely successful.

B Squadron was reformed in January 1964 (G Squadron would be formed in 1966 from Guardsmen who had been undertaking SAS-type patrols with the Guards Independent Parachute Company on the central Sarawak border) and it, together with A, conducted a number of 'Claret' missions. During the winter of 1964–65, patrols from B Squadron were concentrated in the Pueh range of hills of western Sarawak, a favourite route for CCO agents making their way to Lundu where a number of communist cells were located. D Squadron replaced A in early 1965

and also carried out cross-border recce missions. One such operation, in the Sentimo swamp, resulted in the sinking of an Indonesian river craft.

SAS operations in 1965 were aimed at preventing any Indonesian occupation of Sarawak or Sabah. The cross-border raids also continued, especially along the Koemba River near Poeri. In late May D Squadron was replaced by A, which was commanded by Major Peter de la Billière at the time. In August, working closely with the Gurkhas, he launched a series of cross-border raids which met with varying success. The search for an elusive foe often ended in frustration. In September 1965, for example, 12 four-man patrols from A conducted a three-week search for a CCO camp in the area between the headwaters of the Sempayang and Bemban Rivers, but nothing was found.

Above: Box-type ambush operations are characterised by long periods of boredom interspersed with short, violent bursts of action. Such missions demand nerves of steel.

SAS activity, which continued into 1966, did, however, convince the Indonesians that Britain would continue to support Malaysia. The Indonesian military leadership began to lose faith in their president and, in March, Sukarno was overthrown in a coup. Five months later Indonesia made peace with Malaysia.

The campaign in Borneo is an outstanding example of the tenacity, resourcefulness and skill of the individual SAS soldier, and illustrates that a small number of properly trained and motivated men can achieve results out of all proportion to their numbers. Walker himself stated: 'I regard 70 troopers of the SAS as being as valuable to me as 700 infantry in the role of "hearts and minds", border surveillance, early warning, stay behind, and eyes and ears with a sting'.

(SEE *Border Scouts; Brunei; Clandestine Communist Organisation; 'Claret' Operations; Cross-Border Scouts; de la Billière, General Sir Peter; 'Hearts and Minds'; Iban Tribesmen; Malaya; Walker, Major-General Walter; Woodhouse, Lieutenant-Colonel John*)

'BOSS' Term used by individual SAS troopers and noncommissioned officers when addressing their officers, the usual 'Sir' being reserved for officers of other regiments. This informality is a consequence of the close relationship between officers and men and the lack of time the SAS has for stiff military formalities and class distinctions. The high professionalism and self-imposed standards of discipline within the Regiment ensure that this informality does not turn into slackness.

BOUERAT Port on the North African coast. In January 1942 Benghazi fell to the British, an event which led David Stirling to believe that Bouerat, 480km to the west, would become the new supply centre for the *Afrika Korps*. He therefore decided to mount a raid against the port to blow up shipping in the harbour.

Stirling and 12 SAS men, accompanied by two Special Boat Section personnel and transported by the Long Range Desert Group, set off on 17 January. Their equipment included a collapsible canoe which they intended to use to plant bombs on the ships. However, the truck carrying the party ran into a gully during the journey and the canoe was damaged. Undeterred, they carried on and entered the port on the night of 23 January.

To their surprise they found there were no enemy sentries around the town and, unfortunately, no shipping in the harbour. However, undeterred, they split up into small groups and hunted for targets. They managed to blow up a number of warehouses, petrol tankers and the harbour radio station before retreating with no loss. (SEE *Benghazi; Long Range Desert Group; North Africa; Special Boat Section*)

BOURGOIN, COMMANDANT One-armed commander of 4 French Parachute Battalion (4 SAS). Took part in Operations 'Dingson' (June 1944) and 'Spenser' (August-September 1944) in World War II. (SEE *'Dingson', Operation; Northwest Europe; 'Spenser', Operation*)

BOX-TYPE AMBUSH A standard operating procedure used by SAS fighting patrols to deal with an enemy threat. SAS men – usually a four-man patrol though sometimes a larger number – establish positions on both flanks and in front of the enemy. When the enemy troops have entered the 'kill zone', the fourth SAS man moves into the rear to prevent any retreat. The ambush is then sprung. Larger box-type ambushes can be mounted with troop-sized units. (SEE *Loughall; Four-man Patrol; SOPs*)

BRADBURY LINES The former name of the SAS barracks at Hereford which has been the headquarters of 22 SAS since 1960. The buildings were in a somewhat poor state of repair and so a new barracks block was built, the

construction work being completed in 1984. It was re-named Stirling Lines in honour of the Regiment's founder, Lieutenant-Colonel David Stirling. (SEE *Special Air Service; Stirling, Lieutenant-Colonel David; Stirling Lines*)

BRADSHAW, CORPORAL ROBERT Member of B Squadron, 22 SAS, who took part in the action at Mirbat, Oman, on 19 July 1972. Bradshaw was responsible for coordinating the strafing and bombing runs by Omani Strikemaster jets that did much to blunt the attack by the *adoo*. The corporal was awarded a Military Medal for his part in the defence of town. (SEE Adoo*; Mirbat; Oman*)

BRECON BEACONS Mountain range in south Wales. Location for SAS selection and training courses. The barren, rugged terrain, which is often exposed to high winds, driving rain and sleet, is ideal territory for cross-country endurance marches and navigation exercises. (SEE *Selection Training*)

BREN GUN The SAS has used the Bren gun, which is still in British Army service, since its formation in World War II. Being reasonably lightweight, it was often carried by patrol lead scouts, especially in the jungle terrain of Malaya, because of its good blend of firepower and accuracy. It is no longer employed by the SAS, having been superseded by the

Colt Commando and M16.
  Type: light machine gun
  Designation: L4A4
  Calibre: 7.62mm
  Weight: 8.68kg
  Length: 1156mm
  Effective range: 600m
  Rate of fire: 520 rounds per minute (cyclic)
  Feed: 30-round box magazine
  Muzzle velocity: 838 metres per second
(SEE *Colt Commando; M16*)

'BRIGGS PLAN' Name given to the scheme devised by Lieutenant-General Sir Harold Briggs, Director of Operations, during the 'Emergency' in Malaya (1948-60). Briggs based his plan on the highly innovative ideas of Major J. M. Calvert (later commander of the Malayan Scouts), who in 1950 had written an in-depth report on how to defeat the enemy terrorists. The views laid out therein were to form the basis of the 'Briggs Plan'. This was designed to protect the many isolated Chinese communities and prevent the communists extracting money and supplies from them. Beginning in late 1950, thousands of Chinese occupying 410 settlements were relocated to defended villages (*kampongs*) or other safe areas where they could be protected. The 'Briggs Plan' also formed part of a later, largely successful, strategy to deny food to the terrorists. (SEE *Calvert, Brigadier Mike; Malaya; Malayan Scouts*)

THE 7.62MM BREN GUN

Above: The High Power is one of the most popular handguns in the world.

Calibre: 0.5in (12.7mm)
Weight: 39kg
Length: 1653mm
Effective range: 1800m
Rate of fire: 450-600 rounds per minute (cyclic)
Muzzle velocity: 810 metres per second
(SEE *Jeep*; *Vickers 'K'*)

BROWNING HIGH POWER The handgun currently in service with the SAS. Popular, robust and reliable – it works first time, every time – it is ideal for counter-terrrorist operations. It seems likely to be replaced in the near future by the Glock range of handguns.

Type: semi-automatic handgun
Designation: FN High Power Mk 3
Calibre: 9mm
Weight: 882gm
Length: 200mm
Effective range: 40m
Rate of fire: single shot
Feed: 13-round magazine
Muzzle velocity: 350 metres per second
(SEE *Glock Handguns*)

BRITISH ARMY TRAINING TEAM
Name given to the SAS detachments which arrived in Oman from July 1970 onwards to support the regime of Sultan Qaboos who had deposed his father, Sultan Said bin Taimur, in a palace coup in the same month. The detachments were called training teams so that officials could deny that any British combat troops were present in Oman. The first two teams were based at Taqa and Mirbat.
(SEE *Mirbat*; *Oman*; *Qaboos, Sultan*; *Said bin Taimur, Sultan*)

BROOKE, LIEUTENANT-COLONEL OLIVER Took command of 22 SAS

in 1953 while the Regiment was serving in Malaya. Although Brooke had little experience of special forces, he proved a capable leader and strict disciplinarian. Brooke helped devise an appropriate 7-14 day ration pack and placed great emphasis on 'hearts and minds' exercises. He also suffered a severe leg fracture after 'tree-jumping' into an operational area.
(SEE *'Hearts and Minds'*; *Malaya*; *'Tree-jumping'*)

BROWNING .5IN Heavy machine gun which was mounted on World War II SAS jeeps to supplement the firepower of the Vickers machine guns also carried on the vehicles.

Type: air-cooled machine gun
Designation: M2HB

BRUNEI A former British protectorate in Southeast Asia. In December 1962, the scene of a revolt engineered by a young Brunei sheikh, named Azahari, who desired to be prime minister of a country encompassing Brunei, Sarawak and Sabah, to be called North Kalimantan. The British rushed in troops from Singapore and the revolt was crushed in eight days. The conflict did not directly involve the Special Air Service, A Squadron arriving in Brunei in January 1963. However, approximately 1000 of the guerrillas fled into the jungle and joined forces with the Clandestine Communist Organisation (CCO), which the SAS would encounter in Borneo.
(SEE *Borneo*; *Clandestine Communist Organisation*; *'Haunted House'*)

Right: Members of the 'Bulbasket' party photographed in the Vienne area, 1944.

'BRUTUS', OPERATION On 2 September 1944, 19 men of the Belgian Independent Parachute Company (5 SAS) were dropped east of the River Meuse in the Belgian Ardennes to contact the Belgian Secret Army and another party of 5 SAS, commanded by Captain Blondeel, which had parachuted into the French Ardennes on 16 August 1944.

'Brutus' did manage to relay some intelligence back concerning German movements and also supplied large numbers of weapons to the Resistance. However, by mid-September the party had linked up with advancing Allied forces and then retired to Brussels.

(SEE *Blondeel, Captain; 'Noah', Operation; Northwest Europe*)

'BULBASKET', OPERATION One of the two SAS missions designed to interrupt German military movements in southern France and prevent reinforcements reaching the Normandy area following the D-Day landings on 6 June 1944.

The commander of the party, Captain Tonkin, had 43 men from B Squadron, 1 SAS, plus a Phantom patrol (F Squadron, GHQ Liaison Regiment (Phantom) was attached to the SAS Brigade as a signal section; its task was to relay intelligence from forward positions back by wireless to GHQ). In all, Tonkin commanded 55 men.

On 6 June, Tonkin and another officer were parachuted into the Vienne area to establish a suitable base and make contact with the Resistance. Five days later the main party was dropped in four groups, with orders to undertake sabotage acts before linking up with Tonkin. They achieved some success: the Poitiers-Tours railway line was severed in two places and a train on the Bordeaux-Saumur line was derailed. One group was dropped way off target, landing in the small town of Airvault where one trooper was captured and the rest had to flee for their lives.

In addition, Tonkin had discovered several trains with petrol wagons in the sidings at Chatellerault. He radioed for an RAF strike on them, which took place on 11 June. The 2nd SS Panzer Division *Das Reich* was at that time making its way north to Normandy and intended to refuel at Chatellerault. The air strikes which destroyed the fuel tankers delayed the advance of the German division.

The SAS and *Maquis* carried out a number of actions against railway lines in the area, although German troops concentrations made them hazardous. On 17 June, four jeeps and their drivers were parachuted to the 'Bulbasket' party to aid mobility. The operations to cut railway lines continued, although with only four jeeps there were severe limitations to what could be achieved. A new base was established in some woods near Verrieres on 25 June but security was lax and, on 3 July, the camp was attacked by enemy troops.

Although many SAS men and *Maquis* managed to escape, the Germans killed several men and captured 33, who were subsequently executed. Although Tonkin managed to rally 11 SAS men and five from Phantom, 'Bulbasket' had been rendered defunct. Therefore, SAS Brigade HQ extracted the survivors by aircraft on 7 and 10 August. They were replaced by soldiers from 3 SAS.

(SEE *'Houndsworth', Operation; Maquis; Northwest Europe; Phantom*)

'BULLSHIT' In SAS parlance 'bullshit' has two meanings: any action which serves no real purpose, such as cleaning kit way beyond the point of it being clean, tidy and functional; or talking a load of rubbish.

'BUMPED' SAS term used to describe when a friendly patrol is observed and/or attacked by the enemy.

'BUNYAN', OPERATION On 3 August 1944, Lieutenant Kirschen and 21 men of the Belgian Independent

Parachute Company (5 SAS) were dropped into the Chartres area west of Paris to harry the retreating Germans east and north of the River Loire. They inflicted a number of casualties on the enemy forces in addition to relaying intelligence back to headquarters concerning bombing targets. The operation was completed by 15 August.

(SEE *Belgian Independent Parachute Company; Northwest Europe*)

BURST MORSE RADIO Technique used by SAS teams in the field to avoid the enemy identifying their positions by homing in on their radio transmissions. Messages are encoded into Morse and then sent at high speeds, thereby making it difficult to get a fix on the patrol's exact location.

BUSHMAN IDW The Bushman Individual Defence Weapon is an example of the new generation of small arms that will be in service with special forces in the twenty-first century. It is a lightweight submachine gun driven by a lithium battery, which regulates the rate of fire at 450 rounds per minute, increasing to 1400 rounds per minute unregulated. The regulated rate of fire has been calculated as being the optimum rate to balance the forces in the weapon, enabling accurate one-handed fire (every shot is delivered from the same muzzle location, an attractive feature for counter-terrorist and hostage-rescue operations). Currently undergoing evaluation, there is a strong possibility that it will enter the SAS armoury.

Calibre: 9mm
Weight: 2.92kg (empty)
Length: 276mm
Effective range: 150m
Rate of fire: 450 rounds per minute (regulated); 1400 rounds per minute (unregulated)
Feed: 20-, 28-, or 32-round box magazine
Muzzle velocity: 352 metres per second

C

C-130 Long-range four-engined transport aircraft used to carry SAS personnel and their equipment. Operatives also use the Hercules for HAHO and HALO parachute jumps. A modified version, the MC-130, has been specifically designed for special forces use. Equipped with electronic jamming equipment, secure communications devices and precision navigation systems, it is usually deployed on low-level deep-penetration missions.

Refuelling probes and the Fulton STAR extraction system are also fitted to the aircraft.

  Type: long-range transport aircraft
  Crew: four/five
  Range: 4002km
  Payload: 19,686kg or 92 troops
  Maximum speed: 618km/hr
(SEE *HAHO; HALO*)

CADS The controlled aerial delivery system (CADS) has been designed by the UK firm Wallop Defence Systems to deliver payloads of weapons, ammunition and other supplies of up to 550kg in weight to ground locations accurately. The system consists of a ramair parachute, an airborne guidance unit (AGU) and a radio transmitter. The AGU, which is automatically activated on deployment, controls the parachute in response to signals from the transmitter on the ground. The latter can work in remote control mode for clandestine missions at night, or manually, where the payload-carrying parachute is visi-

Below: The C-130 Hercules long-range transport aircraft. Rugged, reliable and able to use short airstrips, the Hercules is ideal for supporting special forces operations.

Above: Brigadier Mike Calvert (left) commanded the SAS Brigade in World War II and raised and led the Malayan Scouts during the campaign in Malaya. Calvert's vision was instrumental in the re-birth of the Special Air Service in 1952.

ble. The unit has a maximum control range of 20km, and the load can be landed within 100m of its target.

'CALIBAN', OPERATION Codename for a mission undertaken by 26 troopers of the Belgian Independent Parachute Company (5 SAS), led by Lieutenant Limbosch, between 6 and 11 September 1944. They were dropped southeast of Bourg Leopold, northeast Belgium, to sever German communications west of the River Meuse. However, the men were widely dispersed, resulting in only limited activity. 'Caliban' fizzled out somewhat when the Belgians were reached by advancing British troops. (SEE *Belgian Independent Parachute Company; Northwest Europe*)

CALVERT, BRIGADIER MIKE A key figure in the post-World War II history of the SAS. Calvert, nicknamed

'Mad Mike', joined the Royal Engineers in 1933 and, after a spell in China as an observer during the latter part of the decade, held a post in Military Intelligence Research where he helped organise guerrilla units that were to be used if Britain was invaded. Other duties included training commandos from New Zealand and Australia, and guerrilla groups for China.

Calvert was next posted to Burma where he met the legendary Major-General Orde Wingate. Together they raised the Chindits, a force created to operate deep behind Japanese lines on sabotage and interdiction missions. In 1944 Calvert, now commanding the Chindits' 77th Indian Infantry Brigade, was awarded the DSO and bar, and the US Silver Star. Returning to Europe towards the end of the war, Calvert was given command of the SAS Brigade in March

1945, a position he would hold until the unit was disbanded in October.

In 1950 Calvert, a staff officer in Hong Kong, was asked by General Sir John Harding, Commander-in-Chief Far East Land Forces, to make an analysis of the Malayan Emergency and suggest means of defeating the Communist Terrorists (CTs). Several months later, after extensive and exhausting field research, Calvert presented his paper. He drew two main conclusions: first, Malaya's Chinese villagers should be moved into fortified settlements to keep them out of the clutches of the CTs; second, a special military force able to operate in the jungle for long periods should be raised and trained.

Both concepts were accepted and Calvert was ordered to raise his special military force which was to be named the Malayan Scouts. Recruits came from three main sources: from the thousands of military personnel dotted about the Far East, particularly ex-members of the SOE, Force 136 and Ferret Force; from a body of

Above: During Operation 'Canuck' the SAS placed Union Jack flags on commandeered vehicles to prevent them being strafed by Allied fighter aircraft.

Rhodesians that Calvert had helped select; and from a territorial unit that was organising a detachment for service in Korea, 21 SAS.

Calvert also devised the new unit's operational procedure. A detachment of up to 14 men would be despatched into the jungle and establish a defendable base, from where small patrols of three to four men would be sent out into the jungle to gather intelligence, spring ambushes and destroy enemy bases. A key part of Calvert's method was the waging of a 'hearts and minds' campaign designed to gain the confidence of the indigenous population who would in turn aid the Malayan Scouts' patrols. Calvert's

methods gradually began to pay dividends, although he was invalided home in 1952. Nevertheless, the success of his theories had done much to aid the return of the SAS to the regular Army's order of battle. In 1952, the Malayan Scouts became 22 SAS. (SEE *'Briggs Plan'; Communist Terrorist; Ferret Force; Force 136; 'Hearts and Minds'; Malaya; Malayan Scouts; SOE*)

'CANDYTUFT', OPERATION 'Saxifrage' and 'Candytuft' were two operations run in conjunction which were designed to cut the railway line that ran down the east Italian coast between Ancona and Pescara. The

small detachment from 2 SAS led by Major Roy Farran landed on the coast on the night of 27 October 1943. They spent the next six days behind enemy lines, operating in abysmal weather. They blew up the railway line in several places and mined the main coast road before being extracted by motor torpedo boat, minus two troopers who had been captured. (SEE *Farran, Major Roy; Italy; 'Saxifrage', Operation*)

'CANUCK', OPERATION Canadian Captain Buck McDonald led a party from 2 SAS into northern Italy in early 1945. His mission was to disrupt enemy communications between the Italian Riviera and northern Italy. McDonald and his team were able to equip and organise partisans who,

aided by a 75mm howitzer, were able to overcome the garrison of Alba, a small town near Turin.
(SEE *Italy*)

CASEVAC SAS abbreviation of casualty evacuation. Transportation of injured by helicopter to hospital.

'CHAIRMAN MAO SUIT' Standard British Army quilted, insulated suit designed for troops operating in extremely cold conditions. Used by SAS troopers in the Falklands War.

CHALLENOR, SERGEANT 'TANKY' Member of 2 SAS involved in Operation 'Speedwell' in 1943. He and a lieutenant were able to destroy two trains and a tunnel on the Bologna-Genoa line and a further train on the Pontremoli-La Spezia line. In an epic of endurance, it took Challenor several months to reach Allied lines, fighting off bouts of malaria and making two successful escape attempts after being captured. He later saw action in 1944-45, particularly in Operation 'Wallace'.
(SEE *Italy*; *'Speedwell', Operation*; *'Wallace', Operation*)

CHAPMAN, LANCE-CORPORAL ROGER One of the SAS men responsible for the defence of the Omani town of Mirbat on 19 June 1972. Chapman won a Military Medal for his part in the action.
(SEE *Mirbat; Oman*)

'CHAUCER', OPERATION Conducted by 22 troopers of the Belgian Independent Parachute Company (5 SAS) between 28 July and 15 August 1944. Two parties were dropped by parachute (the first, led by Lieutenant Ghys, on 28 July; the second, led by Captain Hazel, on 9 August) into the area northwest of Le Mans, northwest France, to harry the retreating Germans. However, they were dropped too late and had to operate on foot. As a result, they only met the tail of the retreating enemy.

(SEE *Belgian Independent Parachute Company; Northwest Europe*)

'CHESTNUT', OPERATION Designed to support the Allied invasion of Sicily, Operation 'Husky' (9 July 1943), the mission was a lesson in how good planning and logistical support are essential for successful military operations.

The plan called for two small parties from 2 SAS to be inserted into northern Sicily to disrupt enemy communications. 'Pink' party, led by Captain Pinckney, was ordered to sever roads and telephone lines on the northeast coast of the island, as well as destroy the Catania-Messina railway line. 'Brig' party, commanded by Captain Bridgeman-Evans, was detailed to attack hostile convoys and the enemy HQ near Enna.

The two parties were dropped on the night of 12 July, both encountering serious difficulties almost immediately. Most of the equipment and radios of 'Pink' party were damaged on landing, and the men were widely scattered. 'Brig' was dropped too near the urban areas with the result that the enemy were alerted (Bridgeman-Evans was captured but later escaped). A reinforcement drop was scheduled for the night of 13 July, but, because the aircraft failed to contact either party (a result of the damaged radios), no men were dropped. No further forces were committed to the operation.

Though most of the SAS men on the ground managed to get back to Allied lines, they had achieved very little. The inadequate preparations for the mission had made success unlikely: most of the troops had no experience of landing as a fighting force (after they had landed it took Pinckney a long time to assemble his men); there had been no rehearsal; and, most importantly, the plan was changed a number of times (originally, for example, the parties were to be landed by submarine).
(SEE *Sicily*)

CH-47 Twin-blade transport helicopter commonly known as the Chinook. The SAS use a modified version of the standard military model. Extras can include an inflight refuelling probe, radar for low-level flying and special glass-fibre blades that can withstand gunfire.

Type: transport/assault helicopter
Crew: three
Range: 1370km
Payload: 12,700kg or 44 troops
Maximum speed: 291km/h

Below: Special forces CH-47 Chinook helicopters, including this particular model, were used to insert SAS teams into Kuwait and Iraq during the 1991 Gulf War.

Above: While being totally alien to other units of the British Army, the 'Chinese Parliament' is a common event within the SAS. Just prior to an operation, every member of the unit has an opportunity to voice his opinion and make suggestions.

'CHINESE PARLIAMENT' An informal meeting often held by the commanding officer of an SAS patrol, troop or squadron before an assault or operation to discuss the plan of action. Although the commander will have his own plan, anyone is free to suggest ideas, which are discarded or adopted according to the situation. Most likely the commander's plan will be retained, but occasionally an excellent idea will come 'out of the blue'.

The 'Chinese Parliament' recognises that individual troopers (who were often noncommissioned officers before they joined the Regiment) can possess considerable experience, despite their lowly SAS rank. It is also part of one of the founding principles of the Regiment that the SAS tolerates no sense of class.

CHINOOK
(SEE *CH-47*)

CIVIL ACTION TEAM Established in Oman after July 1970, the SAS CAT was an important part of the 'hearts and minds' campaign in the country. Each team consisted of four troopers and always included a medic and at least one Arabic speaker. The teams immediately established a clinic wherever they were based (the first two CATs were located at Taqa and Mirbat) to administer treatment to the locals and their livestock. In this way the Dhofaris came to trust the SAS soldiers, a fact which in turn aided the Sultan's cause. Each CAT reported on the supplies of food and water in the area in which it operated, and this information was used by the

Omani government's Civil Aid Department to distribute food relief. CATs did not train *firqat* units. In Mirbat, for example, they carried on with their social work while another SAS troop conducted military training. The CAT programme was a very successful part of the SAS campaign in Oman and made a significant contribution to the victory of Sultan Qaboos. All CATs were withdrawn from Oman in 1976.
(SEE *British Army Training Team; Firqat; 'Hearts and Minds'; Mirbat; Oman; Qaboos, Sultan*)

CLANDESTINE COMMUNIST ORGANISATION Chinese terrorist group based largely in the Sarawak region of Borneo, where it had large and active cells in many of the towns. President Sukarno of Indonesia supplied the CCO with arms, and allowed the communists to train in Kalimantan prior to their incursions

Above: The charred remains of the terrorist car which was fired upon by members of the security forces in Coagh, Northern Ireland, in June 1991. Note the bullet holes highlighted with chalk. Three known terrorists died in the incident.

into Borneo. However, border surveillance and patrols mounted by the SAS placed a major constraint upon CCO freedom of action.
(SEE *Borneo; Brunei*)

'CLARET' OPERATIONS Top secret cross-border missions undertaken during the Borneo conflict in the 1960s. Because of frequent Indonesian incursions into Sarawak, it was decided to mount cross-border raids (eventually to a depth of 10km) to pre-empt the build-up of enemy forces in Kalimantan by attacking their forward bases.

The first 'Claret' mission, in June 1964, based on intelligence provided by the SAS, was a successful attack on the Indonesian camp at Nantakor. SAS four-man patrols also carried out cross-border raids (the Regiment had conducted cross-border reconnaissance missions from December 1963), the men being lightly armed and carrying a minimum of supplies in their bergens. Calling themselves the 'Tip

Toe Boys' because they hit and then vanished quickly, the SAS ambushed enemy units moving down tracks and rivers and set booby traps. If a man was killed he was immediately stripped of any identification and buried. Wounded often had to march or crawl back across the border, as there was little opportunity for helicopter evacuation. 'Claret' missions, which also involved infantry and Gurkha units, ceased in March 1966, when there was an army coup in Indonesia against President Sukarno. The incursions succeeded in their purpose of making Indonesian raids into Borneo too costly. In addition, the SAS trained a team of 40 specially selected Border Scouts for cross-border 'Claret' missions, called the Cross-Border Scouts.
(SEE *Bergen; Border Scouts; Borneo; Cross-Border Scouts*)

CLAYMORE MINE American directional anti-personnel mine especially

useful for laying along jungle tracks. Used by the SAS in Borneo, the Claymore comprises a rectangular iron box with spikes fitted to the base for stability. It contains 700 ball bearings set in an explosive bed and is detonated by remote control or trip wire. On detonation, the balls are blasted out in a 60 degree arc which is lethal to a range of 45m.

CLOSE QUARTER BATTLE HOUSE
(SEE *'Killing House'*)

COAGH SHOOTING On 3 June 1991, three IRA men were killed in the main street of Coagh, County Tyrone, Northern Ireland, when their Vauxhall Cavalier car was fired upon by members of the security forces. The soldiers responsible, part of a 'specialist covert army operation' (believed to be SAS), fired around 200 shots into the car. The vehicle exploded in flames and smashed into a wall; its occupants – Peter Ryan, Lawrence McNally and Tony Dorris – were all known terrorists. However, the fact that there were no attempts to stop the car, specifically the failure

Above: The Colt Commando is an extremely reliable and compact weapon. It has been used by the SAS in Borneo and, more recently, in Northern Ireland.

to issue a verbal warning to halt, or arrest those inside again raised the spectre of a shoot-to-kill policy operating in the Province.
(SEE *Northern Ireland*)

COCKERILL, HARRY Served with the SAS in World War II and provided a study (January 1965) that was made available to the SAS on the Radfan tribes that the unit would face in Aden.
(SEE *Aden; Radfan*)

COIN Counter-insurgency. Any action taken by a government and its armed forces to prevent or neutralise the activities of insurgent, guerrilla or rebel groups. As shown by the SAS in Malaya, Oman and Borneo, a viable 'hearts and minds' campaign is an essential ingredient of a successful COIN campaign.
(SEE *Borneo; 'Hearts and Minds'; Malaya; Oman*)

'COLD COMFORT', OPERATION
On 17 February 1945, a 13-strong party from 3 Squadron, 2 SAS, was dropped by parachute north of Verona, northern Italy, with orders to block the railway line leading to the

Brenner Pass. Success would result in the Germans being unable to send troops south through the Alps. However, the party was scattered on landing and, because of adverse weather conditions, resupply was all but impossible. In addition, the local inhabitants, being of Germanic origin, proved to be hostile. The group's commander, Captain Littlejohn, and Corporal Crowley were captured and subsequently executed under Hitler's Commando Order. The party was evacuated by the end of March having failed in its mission.
(SEE *Hitler's Commando Order; Italy*)

COLLINS, LIEUTENANT IAN G.
SAS liaison officer with Airborne Corps HQ, based at Moor Park outside London, with responsibility for planning, training and various other staff duties. Among the roles he suggested for the SAS at the close of the war in Europe were the disarmament of German troops in Norway, the hunting down of war criminals in Germany and deployment to the Far East.
(SEE *'Apostle', Operation*)

COLUMBIA Beginning in the late 1980s, members of 22 SAS have travelled to Columbia to train police commandos in long-range patrol techniques. This is to allow them to infiltrate areas where drugs are being produced, to destroy the factories and kill or capture the criminals. This is part of a on-going US/British effort to combat so-called 'narco-terrorism' in South America.

COLT COMMANDO A compact version of the M16 rifle designed for combat at close quarters, the Commando is a favoured weapon of the British Special Air Service. In service since the early 1960s, its small size makes it particularly useful for counter-terrorist operations in Northern Ireland.
Type: automatic rifle
Designation: Model 733

Above: Over the intensive 14 weeks of Continuation Training students learn all the skills needed for them to become effective members of a four-man patrol. For those men who pass, it is the start of service with the world's most famous elite unit.

Calibre: 5.56mm
Weight: 3.23kg
Length: 760mm (butt extended);
680mm (butt telescoped)
Effective range: 400m
Rate of fire: 700-1000 rounds per
minute (cyclic)
Feed: 20- or 30-round box magazine
Muzzle velocity: 829 metres per
second

COMBAT AND SURVIVAL TRAINING
(SEE *Continuation Training*)

COMMUNICATIONS Because intelligence gathering plays such a vital role in SAS operations, the Regiment needs access to reliable, rugged communications equipment. Such systems used by the SAS include the

Clansmen High-Frequency set, the MIL/UST-1 satellite communications system and the state-of-the-art PRC 319. In addition, for counter-terrorist/hostage-rescue work the Regiment uses compact communications kit which allows individuals to keep in contact while freeing hostages or engaging terrorists. An example of the latter is the range of covert communications accessories built by the UK firm Davies Industrial Communications, which includes a wide range of miniature microphones and receivers which can be fastened to clothing, hung around the neck or fitted to the inside of respirators.
(SEE *Counter Revolutionary Warfare Equipment; Counter Revolutionary Warfar Wing; PRC 319*)

COMMUNIST TERRORIST The term used to describe the guerrillas of the Malayan Races Liberation Army who fought the SAS in Malaya.
(SEE *Malaya; Malayan Races Liberation Army*)

CONTINUATION TRAINING The 14-week course following Selection Training in which the prospective troopers learn basic SAS skills to enable them to become effective members of a four-man patrol. They are taught standard operating procedures (SOPs) for the SAS four-man unit; for example, how to move through hostile territory; the arcs of fire of each patrol member; and how to conduct contact drills.

Each student receives instruction in signalling, a vitally important skill for long-range patrols operating in hostile territory. All SAS troopers must achieve British Army Regimental

Above: Respirators, flame-proof suits, submachine guns and integral communications systems are all essential items for the Counter Revolutionary Warfare soldier.

Signaller standard which includes being able to transmit and receive Morse Code at a minimum of eight words a minute. In addition, tuition is given in SAS field medicine techniques, which combine sophisticated drugs with primitive medical knowledge, and basic demolition skills.

After being taught these fundamentals the students then go on to Combat and Survival training, where they learn all aspects of living in hostile environments: building shelters, finding food and water, laying traps and lighting fires. The Combat and Survival phase ends in an Escape and Evasion exercise in which the prospective SAS trooper must avoid capture by the 'enemy' (usually a local infantry battalion). However, at the end of the exercise all that are still free are obliged to surrender themselves. They are then taken to an interrogation centre, where they

undergo a 24-hour Resistance-To-Interrogation exercise. They are subjected to various forms of mental stress, all designed to make them reveal information to their interrogators. Many men crack at this stage, which results in them being rejected by the Regiment.

Those that get through have then finished Continuation. However, they still have to go on to successfully complete Jungle Training and a static-line parachute course before they are accepted into the SAS.
(SEE *Escape and Evasion; Four-man Patrol; Jungle Training; Patrol Skills; Selection Training; SOPs; Special Air Service; Static-line Parachuting Course; Patrol Skills*)

'COONEY', OPERATION On 7 June 1944, 54 men of 4 French Parachute Battalion (4 SAS) were dropped 'blind' between St Malo and Vannes with orders to cut railway lines throughout Brittany. The force, divided into 18 three-man teams, managed to cut a number of railway lines before dispersing and joining the SAS base established by the 'Dingson' party.
(SEE *'Dingson', Operation; Northwest Europe*)

COOPER, LIEUTENANT-COLONEL JOHNNY One of the original members of L Detachment in World War II, Cooper joined the unit via a spell with the Scots Guards (in which David Stirling was a junior officer) and 8 Guards Commando. Arriving in North Africa in February 1941, Cooper spent time with Layforce before volunteering to serve in Stirling's new command. Cooper was trained as a navigator and went on many of the SAS's desert missions, usually as a member of Stirling's own party. In 1943, Cooper was sent to an Officer Cadet Training School and at the end of that year flew back to Britain, where he was closely involved in the creation and training of the SAS Brigade in preparation for the liberation of Europe.

Following D-Day Cooper, now a troop commander in A Squadron, 1 SAS, took part in Operation 'Houndsworth' and in March 1945 crossed the Rhine at Wesel at the start of a campaign that would take him to Kiel. Shortly after the end of the war, Cooper accompanied most of the brigade to Norway to assist in the repatriation of German troops.

After a brief spell with the 6th Battalion, Green Howards, Cooper was demobilised in January 1947, though he joined the Territorial Army as a lieutenant a year later. At the beginning of 1951, he rejoined the regular Army and was posted to Malaya to serve with 22 SAS. During his time in Malaya, Cooper held many positions within the regiment – commander of C, B and A Squadrons, officer in charge of transport, operations officer, and recruiting officer – and rose to the rank of major. Cooper saw much active service during the 'Emergency' and had one particularly bad accident while 'tree-jumping' into the jungle. In January 1959, Cooper and his A Squadron were suddenly withdrawn from Malaya and transferred to Oman.

Whilst in Oman, Cooper took part in one of the Regiment's most famous and successful operations: the storming of the rebel-held Jebel Akhdar. Mopping up operations followed before Cooper returned to the UK in December 1959. At the beginning of the following year, Cooper left 22 SAS to take up the post of company commander of the Omani Northern Frontier Regiment and then as second-in-command of the Muscat Regiment. However, Cooper was soon to be again involved with the SAS.

In 1963, Cooper was asked to lead a clandestine mission into Yemen, the scene of a recent left-wing coup, to discover the precise nature of Egyptian involvement in the country's affairs, to discover the Egyptians' order of battle in the country, to aid forces loyal to the deposed ruler and

to provide medical assistance to the local tribes. Cooper had three spells in the Yemen before completing his mission in the early part of 1966.
(SEE *'Houndsworth' Operation; Jebel Akhdar; L Detachment; Malaya; Oman; Stirling, Lieutenant-Colonel David; 'Tree-jumping'*)

'CORPORATE', OPERATION

Codename for the British effort to retake the Falkland Islands in 1982.
(SEE *Falkland Islands*)

COUNTER REVOLUTIONARY
WARFARE
In general terms, CRW is akin to counter-insurgency (COIN) warfare in meaning. However, as applied to the SAS it has a more specific definition. The Regiment's training makes it particularly well suited to CRW, and small-sized SAS teams are expected to conduct the following missions in times of war: infiltrate the area of operations by sea, air or land; gather intelligence concerning the location and movement of guerrilla forces; ambush and harass insurgents; undertake assassination and demolition operations in insurgent-held areas; border surveillance; establish a 'hearts and minds' policy to win over the local inhabitants; and train and liaise with friendly guerrilla forces operating against the enemy. The SAS currently conducts intelligence gathering and ambush operations against the Irish Republican Army (IRA) in Northern Ireland, and its campaign there would, in many respects, be classed as CRW in nature. However, one important point must be made: the Regiment does not liaise or conduct operations with Loyalist terrorist organisations in the Province.

The SAS also includes bodyguarding and hostage-rescue as part of its CRW duties.
(SEE *COIN; Counter Revolutionary*

Warfare Wing; 'Hearts and Minds'; Irish Republican Army; Northern Ireland)

COUNTER REVOLUTIONARY
WARFARE EQUIPMENT
The clothes worn and equipment carried by SAS soldiers during hostage-rescue missions is thoroughly evaluated, tested and updated by the Regiment's Operations Research Wing at Hereford before it is used in action. The equipment currently used by the Regiment includes:

Clothing – Nomex fire-retardant suit
National Plastics AC100 composite helmet
GPV 25 body armour
Davies Communications CT 100 unit (worn inside the respirator)
Flame-retardant gloves
Abseiling harness
Ankle-high, rubber-soled boots

Weapons – Heckler & Koch MP5 submachine guns
Stun and CS grenades
Remington 870 pump-action shotgun
Browning High Power handgun

Other equipment – sledgehammer to break down doors and windows
Bag strapped to bottom of leg which holds the rope a trooper uses when abseiling down the side of a building (this prevents alerting anyone below of the forthcoming descent)
Pouch for three MP5 magazines
Two 13-round magazines for the High Power handgun are usually strapped to the left thigh before an assault
One High Power magazine is, additionally, strapped to the right wrist to facilitate a rapid magazine change
(SEE *Body Armour; Browning High Power; Heckler & Koch MP5 Submachine Gun; Remington 870; Stun Grenade*)

Right: The SAS puts great emphasis on cross-training. This ensures that all of its four-man patrols contain soldiers who are multi-skilled individuals capable of undertaking a wide variety of missions in any terrain.

COUNTER REVOLUTIONARY WARFARE WING

Following the massacre of Israeli athletes by the Palestinian 'Black September' group at the 1972 Munich Olympics, it was recognised that Britain needed a dedicated hostage-rescue unit to combat the threat of international terrorism. Established at Hereford in 1973, the Wing now has a permanent staff of 20 and trains every member of the Regiment's squadrons in all aspects of counter-terrorist skills. A main part of the training involves acquiring proficiency in close quarter battle (CQB) techniques, which includes a six-week marksmanship course. At first, a standard British Army CQB range, consisting of remotely-controlled targets which sprung up to test a soldier's reflexes, was used. However, while this was excellent for preparing individuals for fighting in built-up areas (FIBUA), it did not adequately prepare SAS troopers for hostage-rescue work. Therefore the 'Killing House' was built at Hereford to teach rapid entry and target indentification techniques and hostage-rescue skills.
(SEE *'Double Tap'; 'Killing House'*)

COVENTRY, MAJOR DUDLEY

Commanded the Parachute Regiment Squadron that joined the SAS in Malaya in 1955 and later commanded C Squadron of the Rhodesian SAS in the early 1960s.
(SEE *Rhodesian SAS*)

CRETE

Three Special Boat Section (SBS) parties – part of the SBS was at this time an element of the SAS – landed on Crete on the night of 7 June 1942 to destroy German aircraft at Kastelli, Timbaki and Maleme airfields. Only the assault on Kastelli was successful, a total of seven aircraft being destroyed.

Another operation took place one week later, when a party of SAS men, composed of Commandant Berge, Captain Jellicoe and three Free French noncommissioned officers, was

landed by submarine to attack the German airfield at Heraklion. This was one of the SAS raids undertaken on 13/14 June to support two convoys which were endeavouring to reach beleaguered Malta. The other airfields being attacked on the same night were at Derna, Benina, Berka, Barce and Martuba.

Berge and his party managed to destroy 21 aircraft on the night of 14 June, though only Jellicoe and one other got off Crete, the others being killed or captured. Despite SAS efforts, 15 of the 17 ships in the convoy were sunk by German aircraft, though the other two did reach Malta.
(SEE *Barce; Benina; Berge, Commandant George; Berka; Derna; Free French SAS; Jellicoe, Earl George; Martuba; North Africa; Special Boat Section*)

CROSS-BORDER SCOUTS

A force raised, trained and led by the SAS in Borneo during the war against Indonesian troops and communist guerrillas. The unit consisted of 40 specially selected Iban Dyaks trained for cross-border operations into Indonesian Kalimantan. It was believed by the British, correctly, that the Ibans would be adept at moving unseen through the jungle and, should a mission go wrong, they stood a better chance of getting out alive. Training began in the summer of 1964 under the supervision of Major John Edwardes of A Squadron, 22 SAS. The Scouts' first mission was in August, and thereafter they were active along the border, especially in western Sarawak and around Bemban.
(SEE *Border Scouts; Borneo; 'Claret' Operations; Edwardes, Major John*)

CROSS-TRAINING

Continual training and rotation through different troops ensures that every SAS soldier is a specialist in at least one patrol skill and, often, more than one troop skill. This results in four-man patrols containing an abundance of skills and experience.

(SEE *Air Troop; Boat Troop; Four-man Patrol; Mobility Troop; Mountain Troop; Patrol Skills; Troop Skills*)

'CRUSADER', OPERATION

British operation in North Africa which began on 17 November 1941. Devised by General Claude Auchinleck, Commander-in-Chief Middle East, it was designed to throw General Rommel, commander of the *Afrika Korps*, out of Cyrenaica. 'Crusader' was the occasion for the first raids by the newly formed L Detachment, SAS, which was to attack airfields at Tmimi and Gazala.

L Detachment, divided into five aircraft loads commanded by David Stirling, 'Paddy' Mayne, Eoin McGonical, 'Jock' Lewes and Lieutenant Bonnington respectively, was to be dropped by parachute on the night of 16/17 November. However, the drop was a disaster as the men were widely scattered, some being injured on landing. As a result, the operation had to be abandoned, individuals making their way to the rendezvous with the Long Range Desert Group (LRDG) as best they could. Only 22 of the 64 men dropped were picked up.

This first operation prompted a radical rethink concerning transportation to the target for future SAS missions. Stirling resolved never again to use parachute drops, but instead use vehicles, initially those of the LRDG.
(SEE *Bonnington, Lieutenant Charles; L Detachment; Lewes, Lieutenant John Steel 'Jock'; Mayne, Lieutenant-Colonel 'Paddy' Blair; North Africa; Stirling, Lieutenant-Colonel David*)

CUMPER, CAPTAIN WILLIAM 'BILL'

Explosives and canoe specialist who trained many recruits to the SAS in North Africa in 1941-42. Accompanied David Stirling during the raid on Benghazi (September 1942) and took part in the attack on the Greek island of Simi in July 1944.
(SEE *Benghazi; North Africa; Stirling, Lieutenant-Colonel David*)

D–E

Above: The RAF used Douglas Dakotas to support many SAS operations during World War II, most notably in northwest Europe in 1944-45.

DAKOTA The Douglas Dakota was one of the most famous transport aircraft of World War II. The basic United States Air Force (USAF) models were the C-47 Skytrain, used for transporting freight, and the C-35 Skytrooper, a version specifically designed for passengers. In addition, each aircraft was equipped with a glider towing cleat. To describe the Dakota as a work horse is something

of an understatement. It was, quite simply, one of the most important aircraft employed by Britain and America during the war. Notable examples of its widespread use include the Allied airborne landings around Arnhem and during Operation 'Overlord', the invasion of Normandy, both in 1944.

The Dakota was used extensively by the SAS to drop men and supplies

behind enemy lines in France and the Low Countries in 1944-45. After the war the Dakota continued in service around the world in the air forces and commercial airlines of many countries.

Type: twin-engined transport
Crew: three
Range: 2414km
Payload: 11,430kg; 20 paratroopers or 46 troops
Maximum speed: 322km/hr

DAVIS, SERGEANT BARRY
(SEE *Mogadishu*)

43

Above: Tony Deane-Drummond, at the time a lieutenant-colonel, photographed on the Jebel Akhdar in February 1959.

DEANE-DRUMMOND, MAJOR-GENERAL TONY Took charge of 22 SAS in 1958. Saw extensive action in Italy and northern Europe during World War II. While leading the SAS he planned the capture of the Jebel Akhdar in Oman in 1959. For his part in the action, Deane-Drummond was awarded a DSO.
(SEE *Jebel Akhdar; Oman*)

'DEFOE', OPERATION Between 19 July and 23 August 1944, Captain McGibbon-Lewis and 21 men of 2 SAS conducted an ineffectual reconnaissance of the Argentan area of Normandy. The failure of the mission was in the main due to the dithering British Second Army HQ which, when the party reported to it, was at a complete loss to know what to do with them. In addition, the party was inadequately supplied with radios and transport.
(SEE *Northwest Europe*)

Right: General Sir Peter de la Billière, one of the most successful soldiers ever to have worn the famous beige beret. Joining the Regiment as a captain during the Malayan campaign, he went on to command the entire SAS Group.

DE LA BILLIÈRE, GENERAL SIR PETER
A soldier who had a meteoric rise within the SAS, born of hard work, courage and the ability to get the job done. Space does not permit more than a brief synopsis of his career, though this short entry can never do justice to his contribution to the Regiment or the British Army as a whole.

Originally commissioned into the Durham Light Infantry, de la Billière joined the SAS as a captain in Malaya in 1955. In February 1958, he parachuted into the Telok Anson Swamp as a troop commander with D Squadron. Staying over 20 days in the swamp, he made a major contribution towards the capture of the notorious terrorist Ah Hoi. Between December 1958 and January 1959, he served with the SAS in Oman and took part in the assault on the Jebel Akhdar, his conduct in action winning him the Military Cross. In the winter of 1963-64, de la Billière served on attachment to the Federal Regular Army in Aden and, later in 1964, he was to serve as a major commanding A Squadron in the Radfan. He also established a Close Quarter Battle course for those troopers engaged in 'Keeni Meeni' operations in the colony.

He was next deployed to Borneo. In 1965 he undertook a thorough reorganisation of the SAS, improving such things as the transportation of supplies to patrols operating in the

Above: Sea Stallion helicopters on board the Nimitz *prior to Operation 'Eagle Claw', Delta Force's abortive attempt to free American hostages in Iran in 1980.*

jungle. He coordinated a three-week sweep by A Squadron of the area between the headwaters of the Bemban and Sempayang Rivers, and worked closely with the Gurkhas in a series of cross-border 'Claret' raids. True to SAS tradition, he conducted a series of lone reconnaissance expeditions in the jungle. In 1966 he was awarded a second Military Medal. Between 1972 and 1974, de la Billière was commander of 22 SAS and, four years and a Distinguished Service Order later, was appointed Director of the SAS and Commander of the SAS Group. He was responsible for turning the Regiment into a crack counter-terrorist unit, and played a critical command role in the Iranian Embassy siege in 1980, continually briefing Prime Minister Margaret Thatcher throughout the operation.

During the Falklands War in 1982,

by that time a brigadier, de la Billière ensured that the Regiment was included in the Task Force, convinced that the SAS was ideally suited for the campaign. Events were to prove him right.

The culmination of his career was to be as commander of the British forces sent to the Arabian Gulf in 1990 as part of the United Nations contingent against Iraq. Lieutenant-General de la Billière (who by this time had 15 years experience of the Arabian Gulf and spoke fluent Arabic) quickly established a close working relationship with Norman Schwarzkopf, the American general who commanded the Allied ground forces. The stunning success of the ground offensive in February 1991 was largely due to the success of the partnership and, as a reward, de la Billère was made a full general later in the year.

(SEE *Aden; Ah Hoi; Borneo; 'Claret' Operations; Gulf War; Jebel Akhdar; 'Keeni Meeni'; Malaya; Oman; Princes Gate; Radfan*)

DELTA FORCE Elite US counter-terrorist unit established in 1977, following the German anti-terrorist squad GSG 9's successful rescue operation at Mogadishu. The force is closely modelled on the SAS. Indeed Delta's founder, Colonel Charles Beckwith, served with the Regiment in the 1960s. Organised into two operational squadrons, the selection and training courses for Delta resemble those of the SAS. For example, Delta has its own version of the 'Killing House' called the 'House of Horrors'.

Trained to deal with terrorist incidents outside the USA, Delta's most famous mission to date was the abortive attempt to rescue the US Embassy hostages held in Iran in 1980 (Operation 'Eagle Claw'). Delta also

took part in the 1983 intervention in Grenada, the 1989 invasion of Panama and the 1991 Gulf War. The unit conducts frequent exchange training with other counter-terrorist forces: the SAS, GSG 9 and France's GIGN.
(SEE *Beckwith, Colonel Charles; GIGN; GSG 9; 'House of Horrors'; Mogadishu*)

DELVES, MAJOR CEDRIC Charismatic commander of D Squadron, 22 SAS, during the operations to recapture the Falkland Islands in 1982. Delves was awarded a DSO for his actions in the conflict, which included accepting the Argentinian surrender on South Georgia (22 April); leading the daring raid on Pebble Island (14/15 May); coordinating a diversionary attack against Darwin (21 May); and over-seeing SAS missions in the vicinity of Stanley, East Falkland, before the Argentinian surrender.
(SEE *Falkland Islands; Fortuna Glacier; Pebble Island; South Georgia*)

DEMPSEY, GENERAL MILES Very successful World War II British general who expressed great admiration for the SAS, having worked with it in Sicily and Italy. In a farewell speech, he outlined six reasons for the unit's success: good training, fair discipline, physical fitness, the men's confidence in their abilities, carefully planning, and the right spirit.

DEPONT TRAIN INCIDENT On 23 May 1977, South Moluccan terrorists hijacked a Dutch train travelling between Assen and Groningen, taking 49 people hostage. The train was suc-cessfully stormed three weeks later by members of the Royal Dutch Marines Close Combat Unit. SAS advisors were on the scene throughout the siege and offered the Marines stun grenades for their assault. In the event, the terrorists were distracted by fighters flying low over the train.

DERNA Location of an Axis airfield complex in North Africa. One of a

Above: The Depont train incident, 1977. A picture of the railway carriage contain-ing the terrorists and their hostages which was stormed by Dutch Marines.

number that were raided by the SAS on the night of 13 June 1942. The party for Derna consisted of Captain Buck, Lieutenant Jordan, Free French volunteers and a number of Special Interrogation Group personnel (Jewish immigrants to Palestine who spoke fluent German and dressed in German uniforms), as well as one ex-*Afrika Korps* man who had been recruited by Buck. Transportation consisted of four German trucks driven by the Jewish volunteers. However, the party was betrayed by the ex-*Afrika Korps* soldier before it reached the airfields and as a result only Buck, Jordan and two others made it back to the Long Range Desert Group rendezvous.
(SEE *Barce; Benina; Berka; Crete; Long Range Desert Group; Martuba; North Africa*)

'DERRY', OPERATION A very suc-cessful mission conducted by 89 men of 3 French Parachute Battalion (3 SAS) between 5 and 18 August 1944. The party, commanded by Commandant Conan, was parachuted into the area around Finisterre, Brittany, to hinder German move-ment towards Brest and to prevent

the destruction of the viaducts at Morlaix and Plougastel. Both objec-tives were achieved, with substantial damage and casualties being inflicted on the enemy.
(SEE *Northwest Europe*)

'DEVON', OPERATION Successful attack by the Special Raiding Squadron on the Italian town of Termoli in October 1943.
(SEE *Italy; Special Raiding Squadron; Termoli*)

DHOFAR Western province of Oman, approximately the size of Wales. Most of its inhabitants live on the Jebel Dhofar, which runs parallel to the sea. The *jebelis* are a proud, rugged people who have a different culture and social background to the Arabs and Baluchis who live in the north of the country. During the 1950s their lives were made worse by the repressive regime of the ruler of Oman, Sultan Said bin Taimur, who believed he could keep the forces of change at bay through isolation and autocracy. The alienation and resentment of the *jebelis* finally boiled over into open conflict in 1962, which resulted in the Sultan imposing even more repressive measures on Dhofar. This prompted the formation of the Dhofar Liberation Front.

The SAS's role in Dhofar (1970–76) included a 'hearts and minds' campaign designed to win back the Dhofaris to the Sultan's cause (Said bin Taimur had been overthrown by his son in July 1970). The Regiment realised this was the key to winning the war rather than military might. (SEE *Dhofar Liberation Front;* Firqat; *'Hearts and Minds'; Oman; Qaboos, Sultan; Said bin Taimur, Sultan*)

DHOFAR LIBERATION FRONT

Separatist party in Oman formed after 1962 in response to Sultan Said bin Taimur's repressive measures in Dhofar province. Essentially traditionalist in nature, emphasising the Moslem religion and the tribal structure, the DLF's aims were the modernization of the province and 'Dhofar for the Dhofaris'. Its fighters, some of whom had had military experience with other Arab armies, for example Saudi Arabia, were mostly poorly armed and equipped. In neighbouring Yemen another party, the People's Front for the Liberation of the Occupied Arabian Gulf (PFLOAG), made overtures to the DLF and suggested amalgamation.

PFLOAG was communist, had an abundance of money and weapons supplied by China and the Soviet Union, and was well organised and highly motivated. The DLF was at first lukewarm, but was eventually swayed by PFLOAG's money and modern weapons. The result was that the communists quickly dominated the DLF, establishing cells throughout the province and undermining the tribal structure through fear and coercion. By 1970 they had taken control of the whole of the Jebel Dhofar. However, their ruthlessness and arrogant attitude alienated many within the DLF. As a result the Dhofaris began to fight back, a move which prompted PFLOAG to order the disarmament of the DLF. This in turn

led to several gun battles between supporters of each party.

The split between the communist and the Moslem rebels aided the SAS, as many Dhofari guerrillas, disillusioned with events on the jebel, surrendered to the government (Sultan Qaboos had declared a general amnesty after taking power in 1970). Many of these men subsequently joined the *firqat* (units of ex-guerrillas trained and commanded by the SAS). (SEE *Dhofar; 'Hearts and Minds';* Firqat; *Oman; People's Front for the Liberation of the Occupied Arabian Gulf; Qaboos, Sultan; Said bin Taimur, Sultan*)

'DICKENS', OPERATION

Between 16 July and 7 October 1944, 65 men of 3 French Parachute Battalion (3 SAS) operated in the Nantes/Saumur area of western France. They were parachuted in to disrupt rail communications, to gather intelligence concerning enemy movements, and to organise the local Resistance. The mission was entirely successful, achieving the complete breakdown of the railway network in the area, and cost the Germans 500 troops killed and 200 vehicles destroyed. (SEE *Northwest Europe*)

'DINGSON', OPERATION

On 6 June 1944, 160 men and four jeeps of 4 French Parachute Battalion (4 SAS) landed by parachute in the Vannes area of Brittany. They established the 'Dingson' base and began organising the local Resistance and interrupting the movements of enemy forces. By 18 June the leader of the SAS party, Commandant Bourgoin, had equipped three battalions of Resistance and a company of gendarmes. However, these men had almost no military training and were lightly armed and, when the Germans attacked the base on the same day, they were easily scattered.

Around 40 SAS men made good their escape and established a new base near Pontivy, codenamed 'Grog'.

(SEE *Bourgoin, Commandant;* Maquis; *Northwest Europe*)

'DOOMSDAY', OPERATION

Mission by a large part of the SAS Brigade to disarm German troops stationed in Norway at the end of World War II. Also called Operation 'Apostle'. (SEE *'Apostle', Operation*)

'DOUBLE TAP'

Two shots fired in quick succession from a handgun. SAS close quarter battle (CQB) training for counter-terrorist/hostage-rescue operations previously stressed 'double taps' as suitable for neutralising a terrorist. However, in recognition of the fact that terrorists often carry sophisticated remote detonation devices and that two shots are often insufficient to stop a determined person, the Regiment now teaches sustained and accurate firepower to its recruits. For example, a fully trained trooper can discharge a magazine of 13 rounds from a High Power handgun in under three seconds. This firepower keeps a terrorist's hands away from any remote detonation buttons or weapons he or she may be carrying. Troopers are always taught to aim their shots at the trunk of the body, as it presents a larger target. (SEE *Browning High Power; 'Killing House'*)

'DRIFTWOOD', OPERATION

Unsuccessful part of Operation 'Maple' which involved attacks on railways in northern and central Italy in early 1944. Two four-man teams from 2 SAS were detailed to attack the Urbino-Fabriano and Ancona-Rimini lines. The exact fate of the raiders remains unclear. (SEE *Italy; 'Maple', Operation*)

DRUCE, CAPTAIN HENRY

Joined 2 SAS late in World War II and led a reconnaissance party into eastern France in August 1944 to prepare the way for Operation 'Loyton'. Following the arrival of the main force on 1 September, he took part in

numerous raids before breaking through enemy lines with valuable captured documents. Druce later took part in Operation 'Keystone'.
(SEE *'Keystone', Operation; 'Loyton', Operation; Northwest Europe*)

DUKE OF YORK'S BARRACKS, LONDON Location of SAS Group Headquarters. The highly secretive SAS Group Intelligence is also situated at the barracks. The Special Air Service comes under the overall control of the UK Special Forces Group which comprises a brigadier, a colonel as second-in-command, plus an 18-strong support staff. This body, which directs the SBS, is also housed at the Duke of York's barracks.
(SEE *Special Air Service; Special Boat Squadron*)

'DUNHILL', OPERATION On 3 August 1944, 59 men of 2 SAS, divided into five parties, were dropped into eastern Brittany, northwest France, to observe enemy movements in the Rennes/Laval area. However, the US breakout from Normandy meant that four of the parties were overrun within 24 hours of landing. The main result of the operation, which was completed by 24 August, was the rescue of 200 downed Allied airmen.
(SEE *Northwest Europe*)

DUNLOY SHOOTING On 10 July 1978, 16-year-old John Boyle, a Catholic from the village of Dunloy, County Antrim, Northern Ireland, discovered an Irish Republican Army (IRA) arms cache in the graveyard of the local church. The Boyle family immediately informed the Royal Ulster Constabulary (RUC), which passed on the information to the British Army. The latter called in the SAS which, under cover of darkness, moved a four-man team into the graveyard to keep the cache under surveillance.
However, the security forces had made two grave errors. First, by the

time the incident had been relayed to the SAS, the 'young man' who had found the weapons was inexplicably described as being a 'child'. Second, the RUC failed to warn the Boyle family to stay away from the graveyard until late on the morning of 11 July. By that time it was too late, John Boyle, out of curiosity, had returned to the graveyard.
The two SAS men in the nearby 'hide' saw John Boyle pull out a rifle from under the gravestone (the other two soldiers were hidden in a ruined farmhouse near the entrance to the graveyard). Knowing from his appearance that he was not the Boyle 'child', they deduced that he was an IRA terrorist. This appeared to be confirmed when Boyle apparently pointed the rifle in the direction of the SAS soldiers. Believing he was about to shoot, they immediately fired their weapons, killing Boyle instantly. The two soldiers, Corporal Bohan and Trooper Temperley, were charged with murder but were subsequently acquitted. The Dunloy shooting was held up by the IRA as proof of an SAS shoot-to-kill policy operating in the Province and, at the time, was extremely damaging to the Regiment's image. What the tragedy did bring home, however, was the need for the accurate transmission of intelligence between the various arms of the security forces in Northern Ireland.
(SEE *Irish Republican Army; Northern Ireland*)

E

E4A Surveillance unit of the Royal Ulster Constabulary in Northern Ireland. Its members are trained in surveillance and intelligence gathering techniques by the SAS at Hereford.
(SEE *Northern Ireland*)

EDWARDES, MAJOR JOHN Renowned and resourceful commander of A

Above: Sergeant Tasker, a member of Captain Edward's ill-fated patrol.

Squadron, 22 SAS, in 1963, during the conflict in Borneo. From the summer of 1964 until 1966 he led the locally raised Cross-Border Scouts with great success.
(SEE *Borneo; Cross-Border Scouts*)

EDWARDS, CAPTAIN ROBIN Leader of an ill-fated nine-man patrol from 3 Troop, A Squadron, 22 SAS, in the Radfan region of Aden. Setting out on 29 April 1964, the patrol was tasked with establishing a dropping zone for 3 Para. However, the SAS team was spotted by local tribesmen in the vicinity of Shab Tem village who opened fire on Edwards and his men. As the firefight intensified the SAS began to withdraw, but Edwards and Trooper Nick Warburton were killed and two others wounded. The survivors fought their way out against the odds. The bodies of Edwards and Warburton were later decapitated by the tribesmen and their heads put on display in the Yemeni city of Taiz.
(SEE *Aden; North Yemen; Radfan*)

EL DABA Axis airfield in North Africa during World War II. One of several targets raided by the Special Air Service on the night of 7 July 1942. The SAS party, led by Captain Jellicoe and Lieutenant Zirnheld and mounted on jeeps, failed to breach the airfield's defences, managing only to destroy a number of trucks. The airfield was raided again on the night of 11 July by Jellicoe, though by this time the defences had been strengthened and the attack had to be aborted. (SEE *Bagoush; Fuka; Jellicoe, Earl George; North Africa; Sidi Barrani; Zirnheld, Lieutenant Andre*)

EL FASCIA In December 1942, the newly formed B Squadron, 1 SAS, commanded by Major Vivian Street, was ordered to establish a base at El Fascia, 160km west of Tamit and behind enemy lines. The squadron's task was to raid as far as Tripoli, as part of the overall SAS effort to harry the Germans who were retreating after their defeat at El Alamein.

The operations in the El Fascia area were part of a wider SAS strategy devised by Lieutenant-Colonel David Striling, who believed that if his men made it dangerous for the enemy to move at night, then they would be forced to move during the day, thus becoming targets for the RAF.

While B Squadron was operating in the El Fascia area, A Squadron under Major 'Paddy' Mayne was ordered to hit the coast road between Agheila and Bouerat (a task the unit undertook with great relish and even greater success before being overrun by the advancing British Eighth Army).

B Squadron itself was divided into eight patrols, each having three jeeps. The base was established by 13 December, and a series of raids were mounted along the Tripoli-Bouerat road. However, these raids resulted in large numbers of enemy troops being diverted against the SAS, and the latter suffered high casualties as a consequence. The base was surrounded on the night of 23 December. Most of the remaining men surrendered, including Street, with only a few escaping to link up with A Squadron.

The story of Street is an interesting one. After he was captured he was put on an Italian submarine for transportation to the Italian mainland. However, en route the vessel was depth-charged and Street and six others managed to escape and were picked up by a Royal Naval vessel. He was then taken to Kabrit, the SAS's base, where he commanded 1 SAS (February to March 1943) before being replaced by a Lieutenant-Colonel Cator (SEE *Kabrit; Mayne, Lieutenant-Colonel 'Paddy' Blair; North Africa; Stirling, Lieutenant-Colonel David*)

ESCAPE BELT An item of clothing worn by all SAS soldiers on operations. It contains enough food and equipment for a trooper to survive for two days if he is forced to abandon his bergen. (SEE *Bergen; Escape and Evasion*)

ESCAPE AND EVASION The culmination of the Combat and Survival phase of Continuation Training. All

Below: Jeep-mounted SAS personnel scan the horizon for retreating German and Italian forces, North Africa, late 1942.

Above: Escape and Evasion makes heavy demands upon an individual's mental and physical reserves, and is made worse by the sense of isolation.

students must pass Escape and Evasion to gain entry to 22 SAS. The purpose is for individuals to evade capture by the 'enemy' (usually a local infantry battalion) by employing all the skills learnt during Combat and Survival: concealment, selecting routes, laying false trails, the best time for movement, and how to live off the land. All regular SAS soldiers usually wear an Escape Belt, consisting of high-calorie rations, hexamine fuel blocks, fishing line and hooks, a small knife, waterproofed matches, a button-compass and small-scale map. This will sustain a trooper for two days if he has been forced to abandon his bergen. However, Escape Belts are not worn on Escape and Evasion – the men are on their own.

Evasion techniques, like most military principles, are relatively simple. For example, when endeavouring to move through enemy territory unseen it is impressed upon recruits that any resting time before travelling is used to build up strength and evaluate the

forthcoming journey. This includes formulating alternative plans and courses of action to cope with as many eventualities as possible, or at least as many as can be thought of.

An individual is most vulnerable during periods of movement, and experience has taught that this is the time when many soldiers are captured. This is because they followed the easiest and shortest, and therefore most predictable, route, or failed to employ precautionary techniques such as camouflage and concealment.

SAS recruits are taught to avoid major roads and populated areas; to make full use of camouflage and concealment, particularly the cover of darkness, wooded areas, trees, bushes and other terrain features; and to conduct all movement at night. These rules are relatively simple, but learning them in a classroom and employing them on operations, when an individual may be cold, hungry and tired, are two different things. It is impressed upon SAS soldiers –

indeed it is one of the qualities looked for in prospective recruits – that when they are alone and in a potentially life-threatening situation, they must retain the capability for clear thought, as this will give them the greatest chance of getting out alive. Indeed, one of the things that sets SAS soldiers apart from other special forces troops is their ability to think straight in all situations.

At the end of the exercise those that have evaded capture are obliged to surrender themselves, after which they undergo a Resistance-To-Interrogation exercise. This lasts for 24 hours and subjects each student to intense psychological strain. As SAS soldiers often operate behind enemy lines, each man must be as prepared as possible for capture and subsequent interrogation. If he divulges any information other than name, rank, number and date of birth, he immediately fails Continuation.

As each student endures a vicious barrage of verbal threats, sensory deprivation and gentle coercion, he will remember his training: do not sign anything; always appear more tired than you actually are (no interrogator wants an unconscious prisoner, they will therefore terminate the questioning to allow him to recover); do not answer 'yes' or 'no' to questions, these words can be tape-recorded and added to a different question so, for example, to answer 'yes' to a supposedly innocent question such as 'are you alright?', can be turned into an admittance of responsibility for committing an atrocity; and do not waste precious energy in trying to break free when captured, it will invariably be wasted and, more importantly, it will not be available when needed during the interrogation.

After successfully completing Escape and Evasion, the students then go on to undertake Jungle Training in the Far East.
(SEE *Bergen; Continuation Training; Escape Belt; Jungle Training; Selection Training*)

F

Above: On patrol near Fitzroy, East Falkland. The SAS collected valuable intelligence concerning the movements and dispositions of enemy forces on the islands.

'FABIAN', OPERATION Originally codenamed 'Regan', 'Fabian' was a six-month mission conducted by five men of the Belgian Independent Parachute Company (5 SAS) who, between 16 September 1944 and 14 March 1945, operated around Arnhem, Holland. Their mission was to collect intelligence concerning enemy dispositions in northwest Holland and the location of V2 sites. However, although they did gather some useful information, the Belgians became heavily involved with the Dutch Resistance in helping Allied paratroopers escape in the aftermath of the landings around Arnhem in September 1944.
(SEE *Belgian Independent Parachute Company; Northwest Europe*)

FALKLAND ISLANDS Situated in the South Atlantic, some 13,000km from Great Britain, this island group consists of two main islands, West and East Falkland, and over 100 smaller ones. The climate is cool, damp and windy, and the terrain is mostly treeless moorland and rocky hills. Under British sovereignty since 1833, they were invaded by Argentina (which had a long-standing claim over the islands), led by a military junta headed by General Galtieri, on 2 April 1982. The British government, under the leadership of Margaret Thatcher, resolved to retake the islands by force if necessary. A Task Force was quickly assembled and sent south, Operation 'Corporate' was underway.

The SAS was to play a vital role during the subsequent military operations in May and June, which resulted in Argentinian forces on the

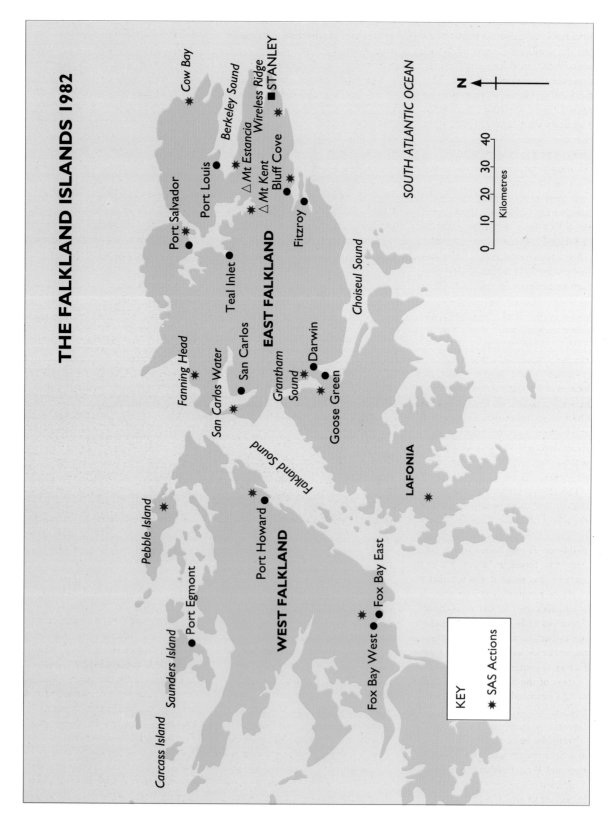

THE FALKLAND ISLANDS 1982

Cow Bay

Berkeley Sound

STANLEY

Wireless Ridge

Mt Estancia

Port Louis

Mt Kent

Bluff Cove

Port Salvador

Fitzroy

EAST FALKLAND

Teal Inlet

SOUTH ATLANTIC OCEAN

Choiseul Sound

Grantham Sound

Fanning Head

San Carlos Water

San Carlos

Darwin

Goose Green

Falkland Sound

LAFONIA

Pebble Island

Port Howard

WEST FALKLAND

Saunders Island

Port Egmont

Fox Bay East

Carcass Island

Fox Bay West

KEY
✳ SAS Actions

40
30
20
10
0

Kilometres

N

islands being defeated. The Regiment undertook a number of missions during the conflict including infiltration, surveillance, intelligence gathering, diversionary actions and raids. The SAS did not have the monopoly on special forces operations during the Falklands War, however. The Royal Marines' Special Boat Squadron (SBS) was also heavily involved, often cooperating closely with its SAS counterpart.

As soon as the Argentinians had invaded the islands, the Director of the SAS Group, Brigadier Peter de la Billière, and the commander of 22 SAS, Lieutenant-Colonel Mike Rose, lobbied hard for a Special Air Service presence in the Task Force. In the event, over half the Regiment would be involved in the campaign. Some troopers sailed south with the Task Force in the carrier HMS *Hermes*. Others were flown direct to Ascension Island, a vital staging post located approximately halfway between Britain and the Falklands. On 5 April, 66 men of D Squadron and support personnel flew to Ascension; the next day G Squadron and Regimental HQ were on their way there.

The British government decided that its first move would be against the island of South Georgia, which lay some 1200km east of the Falklands. It had been overrun by Argentine forces in March, but as its garrison was small it was felt that it could be recaptured at little cost. It would also send a clear message to Argentina of Britain's determination not to back down. An SAS party under the command of Major Cedric Delves, together with men of No 2 Section of the SBS and M Company of 42 Commando, Royal Marines, had successfully retaken South Georgia by 26 April.

From the beginning of May, SAS and SBS parties were put ashore on East and West Falkland to undertake a number of missions, the most important of which was to determine

which sites would be most suitable for a large-scale landing. The teams were inserted by Sea King helicopters from HMS *Hermes*, mostly at various locations between Stanley and the mouth of Falkland Sound on East Falkland. SAS activity was concentrated around Bluff Cove, the capital, Stanley, Berkeley Sound, Cow Bay, Port Salvador, San Carlos Water, Goose Green and Lafonia. On West Falkland around Port Howard, Fox Bay and on Pebble Island. The patrols reported back to the Task Force on the day-to-day movements and dispositions of the nearly 11,000 Argentinian soldiers on

Above: A patrol deplanes from a Scout helicopter near Goose Green during the Falklands War. Helicopters were widely used by the SAS during the campaign.

the islands, plus the 42 enemy helicopters and aircraft which would pose a threat to British land forces after they had been put ashore.

The SAS established many observation posts (OPs), or 'hides', on East and West Falkland throughout the conflict which reported back vital, timely intelligence to the command cell established in Admiral Woodward's flagship, HMS *Hermes*. This intelligence gathering continued for three weeks. Typical of the sort of work carried out by the SAS was the reconnaissance undertaken by G

Squadron's Captain Aldwin Wight on East Falkland. His four-man patrol had been landed on the island at the beginning of May to report on enemy movements around Stanley. They established a camouflaged OP on Beaver Ridge overlooking Stanley, and reported on enemy movements using a 'burst' radio (which encodes the message into morse and then transmits it in fractions of a second). Wight's patrol reported that the Argentinians had a night dispersal area for helicopters situated between Mount Kent and Mount Estancia. This intelligence was relayed to the fleet which despatched two Harrier

aircraft to attack the site. The result was that three enemy helicopters were destroyed. Wight and his men endured the confines of the OP for 26 days, being relieved on 25 May.

The SAS displayed their typical daring during the campaign. One OP, for example, was established in a wooden hulk in Darwin harbour. However, it was not all plain sailing. The Argentinians discovered an SAS 'hide' near Port Howard, West Falkland, on 10 June. They quickly surrounded it, though the occupants, Captain Hamilton, D Squadron, and

Above: The memorial to personnel lost in the Falkalnds War of 1982.

his signaller, decided to shoot their way out. Hamilton was killed as he covered the escape of his comrade, who was unfortunately captured shortly after. For his bravery, Hamilton was awarded a posthumous Military Cross.

Before the main landings, SAS teams were allegedly inserted onto the Argentinian mainland, although there are two versions of the precise nature of the operation. In early May a Sea King helicopter crash-landed near the Chilean port of Punta Arenas, some 650km west of the Falklands. It has been suggested that the aircraft landed an SAS party which operated near forward Argentine mainland air bases and reported back to the Task Force on the activity of enemy aircraft. Of particular interest were the Super Etendards at Rio Grande airfield which were capable of carrying the French Exocet anti-ship missile. This version maintains that several of the

SAS men were killed and captured, but that their mission was essentially successful. The prisoners were apparently secretly exchanged for Lieutenant Commander Astiz, captured on South Georgia, who was wanted by several countries for human rights abuses during Argentina's 'dirty war'.

The second version is slightly different. It maintains that at the beginning of May a Sea King took off from HMS *Invincible* and, three hours later, landed 40km from Rio Gallegos airfield. On board was a reconnaissance party tasked with gathering intelligence for a proposed attack on the airfield on 4 May by 70 troopers under the command of Lieutenant-Colonel Crooke, second-in-command of 22 SAS. The latter, loaded into two Hercules transports, were due to take off from Ascension Island, land at Rio Gallegos and destroy any aircraft there with grenade launchers and hand-held

anti-armour weapons. However, the Argentinians discovered the presence of the Sea King and the mission had to be aborted. Whatever the truth may be, it seems highly probable that the crashed Sea King was something to do with a secret SAS mission on the Argentine mainland.

Six days before the main landings, men of D Squadron undertook a spectacular raid on the enemy air base on Pebble Island, destroying 11 aircraft. The Regiment suffered a tragic loss on 19 May, however, when a Sea King helicopter carrying a large party of SAS soldiers, took off from *Hermes* to transfer the men to HMS *Intrepid*. When circling while waiting to land, the aircraft inexplicably crashed into the sea. Whether the accident was caused by a birdstrike or overloading and a tired crew will never be known, but 18 men of D Squadron died as a result.

On the night of 20 May, 40 men of D Squadron, led by Major Delves, mounted a diversionary raid in the

Darwin/Goose Green area to support the main landings which were to take place the next day at San Carlos. Landing north of Darwin by helicopter, and supported by gunfire from HMS *Ardent* in Grantham Sound, the men engaged the enemy garrison at Darwin. Determined to prevent the garrison from hindering the landings farther north, the SAS laid down such a ferocious barrage of fire that the Argentinians reported to Stanley that they were being attacked by a battalion.

Simultaneously, a group of SBS men, supported by an SAS mortar team, attacked and seized Fanning Head where an enemy OP was located. On their way back from Darwin, the SAS brought down a Pucara aircraft with a Stinger missile, a successful end to what had been a textbook diversion.

The British plan was to establish a strong beachhead at San Carlos and then launch an attack across East Falkland to take Stanley. The weeks after the landing saw the SAS and SBS supporting conventional forces by conducting deep-penetration patrols to locate enemy forward positions and drive in their outposts. On the night of 30 May, the SAS assisted 42 Commando in taking Mount Kent; five patrols were landed on West Falkland on 5 June; and on the night of 13 June a combined SAS, SBS and Royal Marines party headed by Major Delves raided Stanley harbour as a diversion for 2 Para's attack on Wireless Ridge. However, the party was discovered and, after being fired upon, dispersed to the hills, where its members were later picked up by helicopter. This was a somewhat ignominious end to the campaign which concluded on 14 June with the Argentinian surrender. However, the Regiment had played a vital role in the weeks before the main landings by inserting teams which, in extremely high-risk locations, were able to relay valuable information back to the Task Force.

The roll of honour for the campaign includes one Distinguished Service Order, two Military Crosses and one Military Medal.
(SEE *Birdstrike; de la Billière, General Sir Peter; Delves, Major Cedric; Fortuna Glacier; Pebble Island; South Georgia*)

'FAN DANCE' Name given to the 60km solo, timed navigation march which is the culmination of the series of day and night marches that make up Test Week of Selection Training. Named after Pen-y-fan, the highest peak in the Brecon Beacons, an area subject to rapid weather changes. The volunteer has to complete the route, which encompasses some of the highest peaks in the Brecons, in 20 hours to pass Selection. The march is also called 'Long Drag'.
(SEE *Brecon Beacons; Selection Training*)

FARRAN, MAJOR ROY Joined 2 SAS in the latter stages of the war in North Africa and later led Operation 'Narcissus', a daring attack on Axis positions in Sicily prior to Operation 'Husky', the main Allied landings. With B Squadron, he played a part in the action at Termoli in 1943, before withdrawing with his regiment to Britain to prepare for missions in France. Following D-Day Farran led his men on the highly successful Operation 'Wallace', and in December 1944 was sent to Italy as commander of 3 Squadron to launch another first-rate mission, Operation 'Tombola'.
(SEE *Italy; 'Narcissus', Operation; Sicily; Termoli; 'Tombola', Operation; 'Wallace', Operation*)

FENWICK, MAJOR IAN Commander of D Squadron, 1 SAS, who took part in Operation 'Gain' in France (June-August 1944). Fenwick was killed in action in the village of Chambon on 6 August.
(SEE *'Gain', Operation; Northwest Europe*)

FERNSPAEHTRUPPEN Germany's specialist long-range patrol units which, in time of war, would conduct SAS-style operations. Both units undergo training at the International Long Range Reconnaissance Patrol School at Weingarten in Bavaria.
(SEE *International Long Range Patrol School*)

'FERRET FORCE' Paramilitary unit set up during the Malayan Emergency (1948-60). Its purpose was to strike at the communists in their jungle bases as opposed to fighting a defensive war. It was formed in July 1948 by an ex-Chindit officer, R.G.K. Thompson of the government Planning Staff, and three former officers of Force 136. The force comprised volunteers from British, Gurkha and Malay battalions, the Malayan Police, as well as Iban trackers brought in from Borneo. 'Ferret' scouts led fighting patrols of regular infantry units into the jungle to hunt for communist bases. In its first operation, they led a battle group of British infantry and Gurkhas which resulted in the discovery of 12 guerrilla camps.

'Ferret Force' lasted for only a few months, most of its leaders having to return to other military duties or civilian life. Nevertheless, the idea of offensive jungle operations persisted, eventually leading to the reforming of 22 SAS for just such a role.
(SEE *Force 136; Iban Tribesmen; Malaya; Malayan Scouts*)

FIELD POLICE FORCE Part of the Federation of Malaya Police Force during the Malayan Emergency (1948-60). The Field Police Force deployed some 22 Jungle Companies of around 180 men each to fight the communists. The SAS worked with the Field Police Force during the implementation of the 'Briggs Plan', which involved the moving of large numbers of villagers into fortified settlements.
(SEE *'Briggs Plan'; Malaya*)

'FIRKINS' SAS nickname for the *firqat*.
(SEE *Firqat*)

FIRQAT Dhofari irregular units trained by the SAS during the war in Oman (1970-76). The acrimonious split between the Moslem and communist factions in the anti-government movement, plus the general amnesty granted by Sultan Qaboos, resulted in many of the former surrendering to the government.

In January 1971, Major Tony Jeapes, 22 SAS, arrived at Salalah, Dhofar province. He was soon visited by Salim Mubarak, a former senior figure in the Dhofar Liberation Front, who, together with two dozen men, had fought his way out of a communist encirclement on the Jebel Dhofar. He now advocated forming an anti-rebel group, a *firqat* (company), drawn from several tribes and to be called the *Firqat Salahadin*. Jeapes took up the idea and the SAS began training the men at Mirbat. Other tribal leaders began to offer men and the SAS was soon training other *firqats*.

The initial number of men in each company was between 30 and 40, but the units quickly grew as success encouraged recruitment. Their first action was at Sudh, 30km east of Mirbat, which was successfully taken by the *Salahadin* on 24 February 1972. The *Firqat Salahadin* had 68 men by late April, and the combined *firqat* strength was 450. Other *firqats* included *Firqat A'asifat, Firqat Al Nasr, Firqat Tariq Bin Zeead* and *Firqat Southern Mahra*. At the end of the war they had a combined strength of 2000 men.

The *firqat* were not conventional infantry, but rather operated as reconnaissance troops, a forward screen, and as general intelligence gathering forces (which often meant picking up gossip from the next village). The end of the war saw the break-up of the *firqats*, as each split into its tribal and family groupings.

(SEE *Dhofar Liberation Front; Jeapes Brigadier Tony; Mirbat; Oman; Qaboos, Sultan;* Salahadin, Firqat)

'FIVE FRONTS' CAMPAIGN Strategy devised by Lieutenant-Colonel Johnny Watts, Commanding Officer of 22 SAS, for conduct of the Oman campaign (1970-76). The SAS would wage the war on five 'fronts':

1) Establishing an intelligence cell
2) Establishing an information cell to ensure the population was properly informed about the government's civil aid programme, and also to counter the propaganda of the enemy's Radio Aden
3) A medical officer backed up by SAS medics
4) A veterinary officer
5) Raising Dhofari troops to fight for the Sultan

The plan was devised as a catalyst whereby the SAS would train the Omanis in the above five tasks, eventually leaving them to do everything themselves. Watts realised that the success of the plan depended on the Omani government wanting to improve the lot of its people. Fortunately, Sultan Qaboos was eager to enlist SAS help and so the 'Five Fronts' campaign was implemented.
(SEE *British Army Training Team; Oman; Qaboos, Sultan; Watts, Lieutenant-Colonel Johnny*)

5 SAS
(SEE *Special Air Service*)

FIVE-MAN PATROL In his original memorandum concerning the use of small parties to attack targets behind enemy lines, David Stirling argued that the five-man patrol was the ideal unit, as it combined the minimum firepower requirements with the maximum possibilities of surprise. It was subsequently discovered that the number could be reduced to four men. Today, the four-man patrol is the smallest SAS operational unit,

although the Australian SAS still uses five-man patrols.
(SEE *Australian SAS; Four-man Patrol; Patrol Skills; Stirling, Lieutenant-Colonel David*)

'FLASH BANG' SAS slang for a stun grenade.
(SEE *Stun Grenade*)

'FLAVIUS', OPERATION Codename for the SAS operation against the Irish Republican Army (IRA) terrorists in Gibraltar in March 1988.
(SEE *Gibraltar; Irish Republican Army*)

FOLBOT Two-man collapsible canoe used by the SAS, Commandos and Special Boat Squadron in World War II. A Folbot accompanied David Stirling during his raid on Benghazi in March 1942. The canoe had a wooden frame inside a rubberized canvas cover, was 1.52m long and equipped with a rudder.
(SEE *Benghazi; Special Boat Squadron; Stirling, Lieutenant-Colonel David*)

FORCE 136 Clandestine resistance force set up by the British Special Operations Executive (SOE) during World War II to attack enemy targets in Japanese-occupied Malaya. The unit, led by British military personnel, trained and armed members of the local Chinese community to conduct a hit-and-run campaign against the Japanese, using the jungle for bases.

After the war the communists who had been recruited into Force 136 turned their guns on the British administration in Malaya. Their leader, Chin Peng, was an ex-member and had been awarded an OBE for his efforts against the Japanese. Ironically, many non-Chinese members of Force 136 were to join 'Ferret Force' and, later, the Malayan Scouts.
(SEE *'Ferret Force'; Malaya; Malayan Scouts; SOE*)

FORT BROOKE One of the jungle bases built by the SAS during its Malayan campaign, Fort Brooke was constructed at the end of 1953 in the Cameron Highlands. The forts were invariably situated deep in the jungle on cleared sites, and were usually reached by helicopter or aircraft. From these outposts long-range patrols were launched against the Communist Terrorists.
(SEE *Communist Terrorist; Malaya*)

4 SAS
(SEE *Special Air Service*)

14TH INTELLIGENCE UNIT
Covert British Army intelligence gathering organisation. Formed in the early 1970s to work in Northern Ireland, its recruits, who come from the Army on secondment, are trained by the SAS in the rudimentary elements of clandestine warfare: surveillance, agent running and communications. It was set up in recognition of the fact that the Army could only gain the upper hand in Ulster if it had access to a continual flow of accurate, timely intelligence. In addition, relations between the Army and the Royal Ulster Constabulary have often been strained, resulting in the latter frequently withholding information. The Army therefore wished to have access to its own independent flow of information.
(SEE *Northern Ireland*)

FORTUNA GLACIER Located on the island of South Georgia. During the 1982 Falklands War it was the scene of a near-disastrous SAS operation. Mountain Troop, D Squadron, 22 SAS, was landed on the glacier to establish observation posts (OPs) around Leith, prior to the recapture of the island by British forces. Simultaneously, the Special Boat

Right: A wrecked Wessex helicopter on Fortuna Glacier, South Georgia, in April 1982.

Squadron was tasked with establishing OPs around Grytviken.

The commander of the SAS during the South Georgia operation, Major Cedric Delves, originally wanted his men to be landed on the southwest side of the island and then trek 32km to reach Leith. This plan was dropped as being too unrealistic due to South Georgia's harsh terrain and severe weather conditions. However, he would not allow his men to land on the northeast coast, fearing they would be spotted by the Argentinian forces. Fortuna Glacier was therefore a compromise.

The 16-strong troop, commanded by Captain John Hamilton, was landed on the glacier at midday on 21 April by Wessex helicopters from HMS *Antrim* and HMS *Tidespring*. The plan was to divide into four patrols: one to observe Leith, one Stromness, one Husvik and one to survey Fortuna Bay for possible landing sites. Each man carried 35kg of equipment and there were, in addition, the 300kg *pulks* to be pulled across the snow. The going was slow; by the time darkness began to fall they had travelled just 800m. A blizzard then blew up which swept away one of the two tents. Faced with a real danger of hypothermia and frostbite, Hamilton was forced to request evacuation.

The next morning three helicopters, led by a radar-equipped Wessex flown by Lieutenant-Commander Stanley, flew up the glacier in a blizzard. Failing to find the men on the ground, they were forced to fly back to the ships to refuel. The SAS party was located at the second attempt, and the troopers were promptly loaded into the aircraft. However, the weather closed in and two of the helicopters crashed while attempting to take off. Stanley in the remaining Wessex returned to *Antrim*, refuelled, and went back carrying a medical party, blankets and supplies. A break in the weather allowed Stanley to pick up the SAS soldiers and the other two helicopter crews. The heavily loaded aircraft was then expertly flown back to *Antrim*. Stanley quite rightly won a Distinguished Service Order for his bravery, but the loss of the two Wessex helicopters was a grave blow to the South Georgia operation.
(SEE *Delves, Major Cedric; Falkland Islands; Hamilton, Captain John; Pulk; South Georgia; Stanley, Lieutenant-Commander Ian*)

FOUR-MAN PATROL Originally conceived by David Stirling, and later refined by Brigadier Mike Calvert and Lieutenant-Colonel John Woodhouse in Malaya, the four-man

Above: Though a four-man patrol is not a large unit, modern automatic weapons allow it to lay down heavy firepower at a moment's notice.

patrol is the smallest SAS operational unit and the cornerstone of the Regiment's art of war. Four men are recognised as being the ideal tactical number to maximise the chances of surprise, while at the same time having sufficient firepower and mobility. Each SAS troop is made up of four fighting patrols, of four men each. In addition, cross-training ensures each patrol member is a specialist in at least one SAS patrol skill.

(SEE *Cross-training; Five-man Patrol; Patrol Skills; Special Air Service; Stirling, Lieutenant-Colonel David; Troop Skills*)

FRAME CHARGE Rapid entry device used primarily by counter-terrorist units during hostage-rescue operations. The explosive, in strip form, can blow precision holes through doors, brickwork and steel, and can be used to blow in windows. Frame charges were used by the SAS at the Iranian Embassy in 1980.

(SEE *Princes Gate*)

FRANCHI SPAS 12 The Special Purpose Automatic Shotgun (SPAS) can fire up to four shots a second. Also capable of semi-automatic and pump-action fire, the gun uses a wide range of ammunition including buckshot, solid slug and CS rounds. It is ideally suited to counter-terrorist and hostage-rescue operations as a special scattering device designed for indoor shooting can be fitted to the muzzle to produce an instantaneous spread of pellets.

Type: 12-gauge automatic shotgun
Weight: 4kg
Length: 930mm (stock extended), 710mm (stock folded)
Effective range: 50m
Feed: seven-round internal magazine plus one in the chamber

FRANCHI SPAS 15 The Special Purpose Automatic Shotgun (SPAS) is a follow-on to the SPAS 12, having a box magazine instead of a tubular one. The gun is also capable of semi-automatic and pump-action fire.

Type: 12-gauge automatic shotgun
Weight: 3.9kg (without magazine)
Length: 915mm (stock extended), 700mm (stock folded)
Effective range: 50m
Feed: six-round box magazine

'FRANKLIN', OPERATION Between 24 December 1944 and 25 January 1945, 186 men of 4 French Parachute Battalion (4 SAS) operated around St. Hubert and Houffalize, the Belgian Ardennes, to support the left flank of the US VIII Corps during the German Ardennes Offensive. The party, mounted on 31 jeeps, was commanded by Captain Puech-Samson. The major part of the operation consisted of reconnaissance and fighting alongside regular troops.

(SEE *Northwest Europe*)

FRANKS, LIEUTENANT-COLONEL BRIAN A key figure in the early days of the SAS, Franks joined the unit after spells with Phantom and the Commandos. He saw service in Italy with the Special Raiding Squadron as the unit's second-in-command and then became comman-

Above: A photograph taken in the North African desert in 1942 which amply conveys the swagger and panache of the Free French volunteers who joined the SAS.

der of 2 SAS during the liberation of Europe following D-Day, after its original commander, Lieutenant-Colonel Wiliam Stirling, had resigned. He played a prominent role in Operations 'Loyton' and 'Archway' before the defeat of Germany.

At the end of the war, he helped in the re-establishment of the SAS and became the first commander of 21 SAS in 1947. Franks was also tasked with hunting down German war criminals responsible for the murder of captured SAS personnel.
(SEE *'Archway'; Operation; Artists Rifles; Barkworth, Major Eric; 'Loyton', Operation; Phantom; Special Raiding Squadron; Stirling, Lieutenant-Colonel William*)

FRASER, MAJOR BILL One of the original members of L Detachment who took part in many of the raids in North Africa. He won a Military Cross for his part in the mission against Agedabia airfield in December 1941, and won renown for an epic 320km slog through the desert after a raid against Marble Arch airfield. From April 1943 he commanded One Troop of the Special Raiding Squadron (SRS) and, when the SRS reverted to 1 SAS, he led A Squadron. In Europe he played an active role in Operations 'Houndsworth' and 'Archway', being wounded during the latter.
(SEE *Agedabia; 'Archway', Operation; 'Houndsworth', Operation; L Detachment; Marble Arch; Special Raiding Squadron*)

FREE FRENCH SAS French volunteers were associated with the SAS from December 1941, when Commandant George Berge and a group of parachute-trained volunteers joined the unit in North Africa. The Free French contingent soon grew in number and became operational in March 1942. Though they were part of the SAS and wore the same uniforms and insignia, they were in reality a separate unit because of language difficulties. Nevertheless, they took an active part in the war against the enemy, and by the end of the campaign in North Africa they made up a full squadron of 1 SAS.

In mid-March 1943, the squadron was handed over to the Free French

Army, but the men were later to form the nucleus of the two Free French parachute battalions that joined the SAS Brigade prior to D-Day and became 3 and 4 SAS respectively.
(SEE *Berge, Commandant George; Special Air Service*)

FRELIMO Abbreviation of *Frente de Libertação de Moçambique*, a Marxist liberation movement in Mozambique which waged a guerrilla war against the Portuguese rulers of the country between 1964 and 1974, and became the dominant political power in Mozambique after independence in 1975. The Rhodesian SAS conducted joint operations with Portuguese forces against Frelimo in Mozam-

Below: A group of British infantry soldiers in 'full battle order'.

bique. After 1975 the SAS continued its operations against the guerrilla bases inside Mozambique, from where raids were often launched into Rhodesia. These continued until the war in Rhodesia stopped in 1979.
(SEE *Rhodesian SAS*)

FRONT FOR THE LIBERATION OF OCCUPIED SOUTH YEMEN Arab nationalist group involved in a violent campaign against the British in Aden. The movement was backed by President Nasser of Egypt who, having seen his support for adjoining Yemen result in the Yemen Arab Republic being proclaimed in September 1962, hoped that he could establish another Arab nationalist state by aiding FLOSY. To this end Nasser provided training, camps and weapons for FLOSY's guerrillas. However, the other nationalist group

in Aden, the National Liberation Front, was antagonistic towards FLOSY, resulting in many armed clashes over who would rule the country after the British departed.
(SEE *Aden; National Liberation Front*)

FUKA Site of two Axis airfields in North Africa. Fuka Main and its satellite were subjected to SAS jeep raids on the night of 7 July 1942. The airfields were heavily guarded, however, with the result that only eight aircraft were destroyed at Fuka Main and six at the satellite field.

Fuka Main was raided again on the night of 12 July, the SAS managing to destroy 22 aircraft.
(SEE *Bagoush; El Daba; North Africa; Sidi Barrani*)

'FULL BATTLE ORDER' SAS term for fully armed.

G

GABES GAP Situated in Tunisia between the Great Sea Erg and Gabes on the coast. In January 1943, the Eighth Army under Montgomery was advancing towards Tunis and driving Rommel's forces into an ever-shrinking pocket. To support this offensive the SAS was tasked with numerous reconnaissance and raiding missions behind enemy lines. David Stirling and a party mounted on five jeeps were heading through the Gap to attack Sousse, a port used by the Germans to bring in supplies. However, on 22 January they were surrounded by a group of Germans and Stirling was captured.
(SEE *North Africa; Stirling, Lieutenant-Colonel David*)

'GAFF', OPERATION On 25 July 1944, Captain William Lee and six men of 2 SAS were parachuted into the area of Rambouillet, southwest of Paris. Their orders were to kill or capture Field Marshal Erwin Rommel at his headquarters at La Roche Guyon on the Seine. After lying up for two days, they learned that Rommel had been wounded by aircraft fire on the 28th. The SAS party then decided to mount a series of foot patrols in the Seine area, which resulted in a number of trains being derailed and trucks destroyed. On 12 August, they attacked a German headquarters in the town of Mantes and killed 12 enemy soldiers. The SAS team linked up with US forces a few days later.
(SEE *Northwest Europe*)

'GAIN', OPERATION D Squadron, 1 SAS, under the command of Major Ian Fenwick, was tasked with severing railways and enemy lines of communications southwest of Paris immediately after the D-Day landings. An advance party was parachuted into the forest of Fontainebleau to establish contact with the *Maquis*, and to find a suitable location for an SAS base. Men and jeeps were subsequently parachuted into the area throughout the rest of June and early July.

The first operations were carried out on foot, including two successful attacks on the Orleans-Pithiviers line. Subsequent attacks were undertaken with jeeps, although missions were hindered by informers in the ranks of the Resistance. This resulted in bases being changed periodically for fear of betrayal. Several SAS parties also ran into enemy ambushes. On 6 August, the squadron's camp was attacked by the Germans and scattered. Fenwick himself was killed when his jeep became involved in a firefight with German troops in the village of Chambon.

The rest of the squadron continued operating until the middle of August, when it was united with advancing US troops. 'Gain' had been extremely successful. The SAS teams inflicted substantial casualties and damage on the enemy. However, the many informers in the Resistance, and the fact that the Germans executed a number of SAS men they had captured, were timely reminders of the dangers inherent in operating behind enemy lines.
(SEE *Fenwick, Major Ian;* Maquis; *Northwest Europe*)

'GALIA', OPERATION Mission conducted by 34 men of 3 Squadron, 2 SAS, commanded by Captain Walker-Brown. On 27 December 1944, they were parachuted into the area between Genoa and La Spenzia in northern Italy to support the forthcoming offensive by the US Fifth Army. This involved disrupting enemy communications and liaising with local partisans. Operating under near-arctic conditions, the SAS party managed to inflict 150 casualties and destroy 25 vehicles, as well as sending back intelligence concerning prime bombing targets. At one point the Germans carried out a sweep of the area with 6000 troops to find the SAS soldiers, who had employed surprise and spread rumours to convince the enemy they were larger in numbers than they actually were. The withdrawal of the party was completed by mid-February 1945. Walker-Brown was awarded the Distinguished Service Order for his leadership during 'Galia'.
(SEE *Italy*)

GAMBIA Scene of a highly successful SAS covert operation carried out in 1981. In late July of that year, 500 Cuban- and Libyan-backed rebels had mounted a coup while the country's President Jawara was attending the wedding of Prince Charles and

Above: President Jawara of Gambia, who was restored to power by the SAS.

Lady Diana Spencer in London. As well as seizing the capital Banjul, they had also taken hostage 28 senior officials, as well as one of Jawara's wives and her four children.

Formerly a British colony, Gambia had retained close ties with the UK after it gained independence in 1965. It was a peaceful country whose armed forces totalled less than 1000 men. Britain, after consulting with America and France (which had excellent relations with Senegal, Gambia's neighbour), decided to send a small SAS team to Gambia.

At Hereford the second-in-command of 22 SAS, Major Ian Crooke, decided he and two others would go to Banjul immediately. They first flew to Paris dressed in civilian clothes – carrying grenades, weapons and a satellite communications system in their bags – and then to Banjul on an Air France flight, using diplomatic contacts to get round security checks.

The French, meanwhile, consulting with Jawara and London, had despatched some French-trained paratroops from Senegal. These troops had secured the airport by the time the SAS arrived, but the rebels still had control of the capital. Jawara had given Crooke permission to rescue the hostages and defeat the coup.

Crooke and his men made their way to the British Embassy, where he discovered that Jawara's wife and children had been moved to the capital's Medical Research Centre. The SAS men headed for the Centre and quickly overpowered the sentries at the gates. The guards inside the hospital were effectively disarmed by a British doctor, who persuaded them to lay down their weapons as they were causing distress to the patients. The SAS then freed the wife and her children and took them back to the British Embassy.

Crooke and his colleagues then rallied a small group of Senegalese troops, who had been repulsed by the rebels, and proceeded to assault their positions. After four days the coup had collapsed and Jawara was once more ruler of the country.

GARTHWAITE, CAPTAIN SIMON

SAS officer who worked closely with the *firqat* in Oman. He was killed in April 1974 while trying to rescue a *firqat* soldier who was pinned down by enemy fire.
(SEE Firqat)

GEBIRGS UND WINTERKAMPF SCHULE

(SEE *Mountain and Winter Warfare School*)

GEMINI LANDING CRAFT

Inflatable boats used by the SAS and Special Boat Squadron that are ideally suited for waterborne insertion of special forces. Powered by either 18 or 40 horsepower outboard motors, Geminis come in three sizes: a 12-man version (5.2m long), a 10-man version (4.5m long), and an eight-man model (4m long).

GERMANY

Crossing into Germany in the early months of 1945, the SAS carried out a number of reconnaissance missions. Two squadrons drawn from 1 and 2 SAS took part in a recce mission east of the River Rhine at Wesel (Operation 'Archway'). During Operation 'Larkswood', the Belgian SAS gathered intelligence for the advance of the Canadian 4th Armoured Division as it moved into northwest Germany. 1 SAS worked in conjunction with the Canadians and Belgians during the assault on Wilhelmshaven (Operation 'Howard'). All SAS units were back in Britain by the end of May 1945. In general, SAS operations in Germany were ill-conceived. By working in the reconnaissance role and closely tied to regular formations, the SAS columns were subjected to several ambushes and losses were disproportionately high. The general hostility of the population also served to aggravate the problem. Ideally, the jeep-mounted patrols should have been used on deep-penetration hit-and-run raids.
(SEE *'Archway', Operation; 'Howard', Operation; 'Larkswood', Operation*)

GHALIB, BIN ALI

Imam (religious leader) of the tribes in the interior of Oman who, with his brother Talib, fomented rebellion against the country's ruler, Said bin Taimur, in 1957. The Jebel Akhdar, the seat of their power, became the setting for an outstanding SAS operation.
(SEE *Jebel Akhdar; Oman; Said bin Taimur, Sultan*)

GIBRALTAR

Scene of a controversial counter-terrorist operation carried out by the SAS on 6 March 1988, when an Irish Republican Army (IRA) unit, comprising Daniel McCann, Sean Savage and Mairead Farrell, were engaged and killed. Following the SAS killing of eight IRA terrorists at Loughall in May 1987, the British security and intelligence services went on high alert for any retaliation. But where? The IRA selected Gibraltar as being a 'soft' target, but one strongly identified with British 'imperialism'. In November 1987, Savage and McCann, known IRA members, were in southern Spain under false names. London had been notified of their

GERMANY AND HOLLAND 1945

NORTH SEA

BALTIC SEA

Kiel ●

Lübeck ●

Bremerhaven
Wilhelmshaven ●   ●   Hamburg ●
Oldenburg   Lüneburg ●
Groningen ●   ●
LARKSWOOD   Weser
Assen ●
AMHERST
HOWARD
Zwolle ●   Hanover ●
HOLLAND   KEYSTONE   Osnabrück ●   ● Minden
Enschede ●
Arnhem   ARCHWAY
●
Münster ●
Rhine ● Wesel
GERMANY

Elbe

N

KEY

AMHERST: SAS Operations

BELGIUM

0   50   100

Kilometres

LUXEMBOURG

presence by the terrorist experts in Madrid's *Servicios de Informacion* office. To the British government this could only mean that they were either going to kill someone out of the nearly quarter of a million British residents on the Costa del Sol or, more likely, attack a British Army target in Gibraltar (there were 1500 service personnel on the Rock).

The next few months witnessed an intense amount of surveillance and cooperation between British and Spanish police, counter-terrorist and intelligence agencies. The changing of the guard outside the Governor of Gibraltar's residence was considered the terrorists' most likely target (the IRA admitted on 7 March 1988 that the target was indeed the changing of

the guard and band parade ceremony of the 1st Battalion, the Royal Anglian Regiment, due to take place on 8 March). In December, therefore, the ceremony was postponed, ostensibly for refurbishing work on the guardhouse, though in fact to give the intelligence services more time to prepare for the arrival of the terrorists.

Above: A column of armoured SAS jeeps in Germany, early 1945.

In late February 1988, MI5 recorded several journeys made to the Rock by an Irish woman travelling under the false name of Mary Parkin, who was seen observing the guard ceremony (this unidentified person was undoubtedly carrying out reconnaissance for the main party). On 1 March, she was back again, and this time followed the route taken by the bandsmen. The next day, the Joint Intelligence Committee in London decided a bombing was imminent. It therefore notified the Joint Operations Centre (which included an SAS liaison officer) which decided to despatch an SAS Special Projects Team to Gibraltar.

On 3 March, 16 troopers from Hereford flew to the Rock. When they arrived they were fully briefed about the terrorists, their identities and the type of mission they were on. It was stressed to the soldiers

that it was highly likely they would carry out a 'button job', i.e. detonate a bomb with a radio-control device. Although the operation to apprehend the terrorists, codenamed 'Flavius', was carefully coordinated between the local Special Branch and police, MI5 and the SAS, the information given to the latter was incorrect on three critical points. First, that the three terrorists were armed; second, that the car they would drive into Gibraltar would contain a bomb and would not be a 'blocker' (an empty vehicle used to occupy a space which would subsequently be filled by the car containing a bomb); and, finally, that the bomb would be set off by remote control (in fact the IRA team had decided to use a time bomb).

The SAS were given orders to arrest the terrorists, but they could use their weapons 'if those using them had reasonable grounds for believing that an act was being committed or about to be committed which would endanger life or lives

and if there was no other way of preventing that other than with firearms' (these are the words used at the inquest in September 1988).

On 4 March, Savage and McCann flew into Malaga airport, where they were met by Farrell. Their subsequent movements are not known as the Spanish police temporarily lost them. However, they were located before they entered Gibraltar on 6 March. The IRA team had in fact hired two cars, one to take them to the Rock and the other to transport the bomb (this vehicle was subsequently found in Marbella, with 60kg of Semtex explosives and detonators, by Spanish police).

On 6 March, the SAS had four men on the streets in plain clothes, backed up by armed Gibraltar policemen and MI5 surveillance officers. The troopers were armed with High Power handguns and spare magazines. In addition, each man was equipped with a radio-microphone concealed in his collar to provide continuous communications with the operations room.

At around 1430 hours, the terrorists were identified as having entered Gibraltar, Savage in a Renault 5 car, McCann and Farrell walking across the border. All three then headed towards the town centre, Savage parking the car in the main square. At 1450 hours, all three terrorists walked into the square and strolled along a line of parked cars, pausing in front of their Renault. A few minutes later they walked out of the square and headed for the Alameda Gardens, a short distance away. At 1525 hours, they returned to the square to once again look at the Renault, then turned and headed north to the border. An SAS bomb disposal expert from the operations centre ran over to the parked Renault and reported that the car could contain a bomb, although he wasn't able to make a detailed examination.

At 1540 hours, the police commissioner, Joseph Canepa, signed over the power of arrest to the military, effectively giving the SAS control of the situation. On the ground the soldiers continued to trail the terrorists. Shortly afterwards the IRA team split, with Farrell and McCann carrying on towards the border and Savage heading back towards the square. At around 1600 hours, a police car which was trailing the terrorists was recalled to police HQ so a vehicle would be available to take the IRA team to gaol after their arrest. The car swung around and turned on its siren, which was immediately heard by the IRA team.

The next few seconds were confused, but a picture of events can be pieced together from the subsequent evidence given by the four SAS soldiers at the inquest. Soldier 'A' made eye contact with McCann, who 'moved, in what I deemed an aggressive action, across the front of his body. I thought "Mad" McCann was definitely going for the button.' 'A' then fired his handgun once at

McCann, hitting him in the back. He saw Farrell 'going for her bag' and shot her once. He then shot McCann three more times. 'B', seeing Farrell draw a large shoulder bag across her body, drew his High Power and shot her twice – 'in my mind she made all the actions to carry out the detonation of a radio-controlled device' – before firing five shots at McCann.

When Savage split from the other two, soldiers 'C' and 'D' followed him. When he heard the shots he spun round, at the same time 'C' shouted 'stop'. Seeing Savage put his right hand down to his jacket pocket, both 'C' and 'D' opened fire, and kept on firing until he was 'no longer a threat to initiate that device' (they too believed he was carrying a detonator); he was hit by between 16 and 18 bullets.

The death of the three terrorists resulted in questions being asked about the amount of control exercised over the SAS, whether they had a licence to kill, and had the British government, specifically Prime Minister Margaret Thatcher, ordered them to kill the terrorists, not capture them? The debate raged throughout the following months and was not extinguished by the inquest's verdict in September that the three had been lawfully killed. Though the

operation did result in the neutralisation of an IRA unit, the publicity surrounding the affair was deemed negative from the Regiment's point of view as it prefers to work covertly, well away from the attention of the media.

(SEE *Browning High Power; Irish Republican Army; Loughall; Northern Ireland*)

GIGN *Groupement d'Intervention de la Gendarmerie Nationale*. Elite French counter-terrorist unit established in November 1973. GIGN's members frequently undertake exchange training with the SAS to practise counter-terrorist and hostage-rescue tactics.

'GIMPY' SAS nickname for the GPMG.
(SEE *GPMG*)

GLOCK HANDGUNS The Austrian manufacturer Glock GmbH produces an innovative range of 9mm calibre handguns for military, paramilitary and police use. The body of the weapons are made from high-resistance polymer material, making them extremely lightweight. In addition, the Glock 18 has a fire selector assembly and can accommodate a large magazine (33 rounds), which

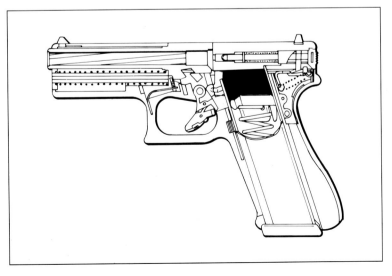

Above: The GPMG, one of the most reliable machine guns in the world, has accompanied the SAS on many of its missions. Its replacement is the LSW.

turns it into a small machine pistol capable of automatic fire.

The Glock 18 thus gives special forces, SWAT teams and military and police personnel the option of firing automatic bursts from a lightweight handgun. The Glock range of handguns seems set to enter the SAS armoury as a replacement for the Browning High Power.

Glock 17

Weight: 890g (with full magazine)

Length: 188mm
Feed: 17-round magazine
Muzzle velocity: 360 metres per second

Glock 18

Weight: 636g (with empty magazine)
Rate of fire: 1300 rounds per minute (cyclic)
Feed: 17, 19 or 33-round magazine
Muzzle velocity: 360 metres per second

Glock 19

Weight: 836g (with full magazine)
Length: 177mm
Feed: 15-round box magazine
Muzzle velocity: 360 metres per second

'GOBBO', OPERATION Originally codenamed 'Portia', 'Gobbo' was conducted between 27 September 1944 and 17 March 1945 in northern Holland. Lieutenant Debefre and six men of the Belgian Independent Parachute Company (5 SAS) were parachute into the area around Drente to gather information con-

the Indonesians, which the *golok* resembles.

GOOSE GREEN
(SEE *Falkland Islands*)

GPMG The British Army's general purpose machine gun (GPMG) has, since the late 1950s, been employed by the SAS in their operations around the world, often to give small-sized patrols additional firepower. Fitted with a bipod, the weapon is light enough to be fired from the hip with the aid of a sling. When mounted on a tripod, the GPMG can be used in the sustained-fire role. In a four-man SAS patrol, the weapon's ammunition is usually distributed throughout the team as on extended operations it is common for 1000 rounds or more of GPMG rounds to be carried.

> Type: machine gun
> Designation: L7A2
> Calibre: 7.62mm
> Weight: 10.9kg
> Length: 1232mm
> Effective range: 1800m
> Rate of fire: 750-1000 rounds per minute (cyclic)
> Feed: belt
> Muzzle velocity: 838 metres per second

'GRANBY', OPERATION Codename for the British military deployment to the Gulf following Iraq's invasion of Kuwait. Movements commenced on 9 August 1990, when RAF Tornado aircraft landed at Dhahran air base in eastern Saudi Arabia to assist the Allied air-defence screen. SAS and Special Boat Squadron contingents were flown out to the Gulf later that month.
(SEE *Gulf War*)

GRENADES SAS teams on active service tend to rely on the firepower they can put down with their personal weapons during any contact with the enemy. Nevertheless, all troopers are fully trained in the use

of British and foreign grenades, from the state-of-the-art models in service in the West to the stick variety in service with the Chinese and the aged Soviet models which date back to World War II.

The fragmentation grenade currently used by the British Army is the L2A2; other models available include the E105, which can be fitted with a trip wire mechanism for perimeter defence; the Mk 4 smoke grenade designed for rapid concealment of troops, buildings and vehicles; and the E108 incendiary grenade, used for sabotage and general destruction. In addition, there are various smoke grenades that discharge coloured smoke, ideal for evacuation of special forces teams from jungle and other locations of poor visibility.

Special forces adopt a number of rules concerning the use and carrying of grenades while on operations. Each member of the unit, for example, always carries a mixture of grenades, such as fragmentation, white phosphorus, CS and smoke. Fragmentation grenades are excellent for inflicting casualties, whereas CS grenades can be used to stop or slow down pursuing enemy troops. CS

Below: The SAS are trained to use all grenades, including these from Iraq.

cerning enemy movements and to discover whether it was feasible to establish an SAS base in the area. They quickly established an intelligence network and, operating in civilian clothes, began providing excellent intelligence about German movements. The plans for the base, however, had to be abandoned as the area had no cover.
(SEE *Belgian Independent Parachute Company; Northwest Europe*)

GOLOK Jungle knife used by the SAS. The name derives from the fighting machete originally used by

grenades can also throw dogs off a scent trail in wet weather, as the smoke hangs low to the ground.

L2A2
Type: anti-personnel grenade
Weight: 395g
Delay time: 0.5 seconds to 4.4 seconds
Lethal radius: 10m

Haley and Weller E105
Type: fragmentation grenade
Weight: 580g
Number of fragments: 2000
Delay time: 4 seconds to 4.5 seconds

Haley and Weller E108
Type: incendiary grenade
Weight: 530g
Burn time: 60 seconds

Schermuly Mk 4
Type: screening smoke grenade
Weight: 650g
Burning times: 60 to 120 seconds

There are, in addition, several grenade launchers and rifle grenades which are ideally suited to special forces missions. These weapons are significant force multipliers for small-sized SAS teams. The M203 grenade launcher, for example, was used by the Regiment during the Falklands War. Grenade launchers such as the M203 are traditionally mounted beneath the barrel of a rifle, though they can also be used on their own. The Hilton Gun Co. of the UK has developed an add-on grenade launcher which can be fitted to the SA-80 and is currently undergoing tests. If accepted for use, it will be used in future SAS operations.

There are also numerous rifle grenades available for special forces use. These are placed on the muzzle of a rifle and launched by discharging a round into the base of the grenade. Rifle grenades are designed for various tasks: anti-armour, riot control and long-range fragmentation.

Hilton HG 40
Type: grenade launcher
Calibre: 40mm
Weight: 1.50kg
Length: 388mm
Effective range: 375m
Muzzle velocity: 75 metres per second

FN-Bullet-Through
Type: anti-personnel and anti-vehicle rifle grenade
Calibre: 39mm
Weight: 320g
Length: 189mm (retracted); 290mm (extended)
Effective range: 300m (5.56mm rifle); 400m (7.62mm rifle)

MECAR ARP-RFL-40BTU M260
Type: anti-armour rifle grenade
Calibre: 40mm
Weight: 390g
Length: 330mm
Maximum range: 300-400m

MECAR HE-RFL-35BTU M262
Type: blast and fragmentation rifle grenade
Calibre: 35mm
Weight: 400g
Length: 288mm
Maximum range: 300-400m
Number of fragments: 300 plus

Below: The great advantage of rifle grenades is that they can be fired from the muzzle of a conventional infantry rifle, thus being ideal for special forces units.

Above: GSG 9 members undergoing helicopter assault training. This unit is one of the most highly trained and motivated counter-terrorist organisations in the world.

'GREEN SLIME' SAS name for members of the Intelligence Corps which derives from the colour of the latter's berets.

GREVILLE-BELL, LIEUTENANT ANTHONY Served with the SAS in World War II. After the war, he raised M Squadron, 21 SAS, for service in the Korean War (1950-53). The squadron was diverted to Malaya where it formed the basis of 22 SAS, along with the Malayan Scouts.
(SEE *Korean War; Malaya; Malayan Scouts*)

'GROG', OPERATION Codename for mission originally called 'Dingson'.
(SEE *'Dingson', Operation*)

GRYTVIKEN
(SEE *South Georgia*)

GSG 9 *Grenzschutzgruppe* 9. German counter-terrorist unit. Formed on 26 September 1972, following the murder of 11 Israeli athletes at the Munich Olympic Games at the hands of Palestinian terrorists. In common with other Western counter-terrorist units, GSG 9 conducts frequent exchange training with similar foreign organisations, such as the SAS.

GSG 9's first commander, Ulrich Wegener, a member of the German border police and an expert on terrorism, quickly established links with the SAS, leading to the latter aiding GSG 9 in the rescue at Mogadishu airport in 1977. Wegener in turn helped the SAS plan the assault on the Iranian Embassy in 1980. These close links have benefited both sides. For example, the SAS adopted the Heckler & Koch MP5 range of sub-machine guns for counter-terrorist operations after seeing them in action at Mogadishu.
(SEE *Heckler & Koch MP5 Submachine Gun; Princes Gate; Mogadishu*)

GULF WAR The war between the forces representing the United Nations and Iraq (17 January-27 February 1991) provided an excellent example of the high standards of training and professionalism of Britain's Special Air Service. The Regiment, together with a substantial number of US special forces, as well as members of the Special Boat Squadron, made a significant contribution to the eventual Allied victory.

Iraq invaded Kuwait on 2 August 1990, quickly overrunning the tiny oil-rich state. Later that month, soldiers of 22 SAS were reportedly flown out to Saudi Arabia as part of Operation 'Desert Shield'. They were carrying large quantities of hand-held

Above: US and British special forces were vital in helping to disable Iraq's air-defence network, such as this radar complex, at the start of 'Desert Storm'.

laser designators which would be crucial during the air campaign of the war. Eventually over half of 22 SAS went to the Gulf, in addition to selected personnel from 21 and 23 SAS, the Territorial Army units. All British and American special forces were controlled by the Allied Special Operations Command of Central Command (SOCCENT). The fact that the British commander in the Gulf, Lieutenant-General Peter de la Billière, had served with the SAS meant special forces units were given full confidence in their abilites, and were not viewed with suspicion and hostility, as is often the case with military high commands.

Allied special forces were inserted into Kuwait and Iraq almost immediately after the Iraqis had occupied the country, though it is unknown whether they were allowed to enter Iraq itself before the coalition's November 1990 decision to prepare for offensive action. Three methods of insertion were used: by RAF Special Duties Flights or USAF Special Operations Squadrons; by vehicle, the SAS using 'Pink

The SAS, like its US counterparts, carried out a variety of missions during the war including training escaped Kuwaiti soldiers at the Regiment's base in Oman to act as guides for special forces missions inside Kuwait; capturing numerous pieces of Iraqi kit for threat-assessment purposes; and acting as a link between the Allied forces being built up in Saudi Arabia and the Kuwaiti resistance. However, their most important mission was the collection of intelligence concerning Iraqi command centres, bunkers, nuclear, biological, chemical (NBC) weapons, as well as the general movement of men, aircraft, armour and food supplies. The SAS quickly established many concealed observation posts, from which information was transmitted back to Saudi Arabia by means of SATCOM equipment. Individual SAS soldiers reportedly moved around behind enemy lines disguised as Arabs and speaking Arabic, all the time collecting intelligence concerning the location of high-priority targets. It has been suggested that teams even infiltrated Baghdad itself.

SAS deep reconnaissance missions played an integral part in the first stage of the air campaign. The first wave of air strikes were directed against the Iraqi Air Force, surface-to-air missile (SAM) and anti-aircraft artillery sites, NBC and conventional armaments factories, communications, oil refineries, transportation systems, radar sites and command-and-control centres. The laser-guided bombs carried by Allied aircraft, such as the GBU-15 and GBU-10 Paveway II, require the target to be 'warmed' or 'painted' throughout their flight, the weapon homing in on the spot of intense light. The target can be illuminated in three ways: by a designator on the aircraft itself; from an accompanying aircraft; or by a designator on the ground. Of the three, the ground option is the most desirable because the bomb can be

directed with pinpoint accuracy to go through a door or a window. SAS teams carrying large camera-like designators mounted on tripods illuminated many important targets for Allied aircraft during the first days of 'Desert Storm'. They also planted small, disposable transmitters around Iraqi military sites which jammed communications just prior to a land or air assault.

However, there were intelligence mistakes made during 'Desert Storm', the most notable being the bombing of the Baghdad baby milk factory and the Amiriya bunker. The Allies stated just after the attack on these two locations – and no other official US or British version has since been proffered – that the factory was a biological weapons plant and the bunker was a command-and-control centre. The bunker's bombing resulted in the estimated deaths of 300 civilians and was widely condemned at the time by the international community. However, these two incidents must be set next to the wealth of valuable information which was collected by British and US special forces in Kuwait and Iraq during the war.

On 18 January, the first Scud surface-to-surface (SSM) missiles were launched against Israel in an attempt to bring the Jewish state into the war. The SAS was immediately ordered into western Iraq and tasked with hunting down the mobile launchers and destroying them. (Iraq had correctly perceived that Israel's entry into the war would have destroyed the unity which existed in the coalition against it – almost the only correct assessment Iraq made during the war). Fortunately, because of Allied air supremacy, teams mounted on 'Pink Panthers', Light Strike Vehicles and other dune buggy-type vehicles were able to roam around the desert almost at will. Satellite photography would identify a Scud launcher, the information being quickly relayed to an

Panther' Land Rovers and Light Strike Vehicles (unconfirmed reports have stated that the latter encountered mechanical difficulties during the conflict, resulting in a heavy reliance on the more reliable 'Pink Panthers'); or by making high altitude, low opening (HALO) or high altitude, high opening (HAHO) parachute descents with their SATCOM and SATNAV equipment in their backpacks.

Above: Destroyed Iraqi hardened aircraft shelters in Kuwait. Units such as the SAS assisted the Allied air campaign by pinpointing targets such as these for friendly aircraft, in addition to conducting their own sabotage missions.

AWACs aircraft in the skies above the war zone; this would then be communicated to a waiting SAS unit via their SATCOM equipment. It was a deadly cat-and-mouse game which, on the whole, was won by the Allies. In one incident, for example, three Scuds and their launchers were reportedly destroyed in an SAS ambush.

Other direct action missions conducted by the Regiment included seizing high-ranking Iraq officers for interrogation, destroying bridges and contaminating enemy aircraft fuel

Left: An American Black Hawk helicopter transporting an SAS Light Strike Vehicle during the Gulf War. Cooperation between US and British special forces was a feature of this war.

(alledgedly one of the reasons the Iraqi Air Force made such a poor showing in the war). In all, 52 medals and other honours were awarded to individuals of the British special forces for their actions during the Gulf War. There was, of course, a price to pay for this daring. Four members of the Regiment, plus a sapper attached to the SAS, were killed in the war, three of whom allegedly died from heat exhaustion and lack of food and water in the desert near the Syrian border (other sources reported that SAS personnel were subjected to the extreme cold of the desert night and that their diesel fuel froze, which resulted in several deaths due to hypothermia). In addition, captured Allied airmen have stated that five SAS prisoners had

their finger nails pulled out while being tortured by the Iraqis.

The Gulf War stands as a superb example of the high standards of SAS training and equipment, and how that training has prepared it for the modern battlefield. The success of extremely expensive high-tech weapons during the conflict, while not insubstantial, must not be allowed to mask the qualities which units such as the SAS, as well as the Allied forces in general, brought to the war – excellent morale, good leadership, strict discipline, comprehensive training and good equipment – and that ultimately these qualities are, and throughout history have always been, the deciding factors in who is the winner and who is the loser.

(SEE *de la Billière, General Sir Peter; HAHO; HALO; Land Rover; Light Strike Vehicle; 'Pink Panther'; Special Air Service; US Special Forces*)

H–I

'HAFT', OPERATION Seven men from 1 SAS were dropped near Le Mans, northwest France, on 8 July 1944. Their mission was to collect intelligence on German troop movements and dispositions, report potential targets for Allied aircraft, and establish contact with the *Maquis*. The operation continued until 11 August, by which time some very useful intelligence had been gathered.
(SEE Maquis; *Northwest Europe*)

'HAGGARD', OPERATION Conducted by 52 men of B Squadron, 1 SAS, under the command of Major Lepine, who were later reinforced by a jeep troop from 3 French Parachute Battalion (3 SAS). The objective was to establish a base south of the River Loire between Nevers and Gien and harass the retreating Germans and sever their lines of communications.

The operation was originally planned for late July 1944, but SOE objected as its forces were in the area. The advance party was, therefore, dropped on 10 August but, as the Americans were advancing so quickly, it was decided to drop the main party near Villequis to cover the two major roads leading east from Bourges. Despite some aggressive patrolling the SAS found few worthwhile targets. The operation was completed by 23

Left: A member of the Parachute Regiment equipped for a HALO jump. Apart from the SAS, soldiers of Pathfinder Platoon are also trained in HALO techniques.

September, when the party was ordered north to link up with the 'Kipling' base.
(SEE *'Kipling', Operation; Northwest Europe; SOE*)

HAHO High Altitude, High Opening. A parachute technique employed by the SAS for insertion into hostile territory. The trooper, wearing an oxygen mask, exits the aircraft at an altitude of 10,000m, freefalls for 8-10 seconds, then deploys his 'chute at around 8500m. He then makes a gentle flight to the ground – which can take between 70 and 80 minutes – by which time he will have travelled a distance of up to 30km.

The advantage of HAHO parachuting is that SAS teams can leave an aircraft well outside hostile areas and then land silently inside enemy territory, without the noise of their aircraft alerting the opposition. Individual soldiers can control their direction of drift and land into the wind; they can also control their rate of descent and stall their 'chutes on landing for increased safety. HAHO was reportedly used by the SAS in the 1991 Gulf War.
(SEE *Gulf War; Parachutes*)

HALO High Altitude, Low Opening. Parachute technique employed by the SAS. Similar to HAHO, during which the soldier exits the aircraft at an altitude of 10,000m, except that the 'chute is deployed at around 760m. HALO

allows SAS teams to land together, an important factor considering most operational HALO descents are conducted at night.

As with HAHO, the parachutist's personal equipment includes oxygen breathing kit, main controllable ramair parachute, reserve 'chute, helmet with headset, altimeter, plus equipment for his mission on the ground. The SAS reportedly used HALO descents during the 1991 Gulf War.
(SEE *Gulf War; HAHO; Parachutes*)

HAMILTON, CAPTAIN JOHN Commanding officer of Mountain Troop, D Squadron, 22 SAS, during the Falklands War. Hamilton played a prominent part in the recapture of South Georgia and took part in several SAS operations in the Falklands. The captain led a diversionary raid on Darwin just prior to the main amphibious landings at San Carlos, was involved in numerous skirmishes with Argentinian patrols and led the highly successful raid on Pebble Island airfield. Hamilton was killed on 10 June 1982, when he and another SAS man were discovered by a much larger Argentinian force based at Port Howard on West Falkland. The captain was awarded a Military Cross.
(SEE *Falkland Islands; South Georgia*)

'HARDY', OPERATION Fifty-five men and 12 jeeps from 2 SAS, commanded by Captain Grant Hibbert, were parachuted into eastern France between 27 July and 1 September 1944. Hibbert was ordered to establish

Above: The head-on contact drill in action. This tactic demands superb reflexes and the ability to fire a weapon instinctively and accurately.

a base on the Plateau de Langres, northwest of Dijon, and collect information concerning German activities. This was carried out and the party also conducted offensive actions against the enemy. Hibbert was joined in late August by Major Roy Farran's 'Wallace' party.
(SEE *Farran, Major Roy; Northwest Europe; 'Wallace', Operation*)

HARRISON, CAPTAIN DERRICK
Harrison volunteered for the British Army in 1940 and, after serving with the Cheshire Regiment in England and North Africa, was accepted into the Special Raiding Squadron. He fought with the squadron in Sicily and Italy and then took part in Special Air Service missions in France (Operations 'Kipling' and 'Hounds-

worth'). As the war drew to a close, Harrison, who had been awarded a Military Cross for his part in 'Kipling', took part in the SAS reconnaissance actions in support of the Canadian Army in northwest Germany.
(SEE *Germany; 'Houndsworth', Operation; 'Kipling', Operation; Northwest Europe; Special Raiding Squadron*)

'HARROD', OPERATION Conducted between 13 August and 24 September 1944 by 85 men of 3 French Parachute Battalion (3 SAS) under the command of Commandant Conan. This was part of the SAS support for the right flank of General Patton's US Third Army as it headed east to the German frontier. The party was parachuted into the area around Saone et Loire, central France, to disrupt enemy movements and bolster the local *Maquis*. 'Harrod' resulted in the destruction of bridges, roads and railway lines, though the cost to the party was 6 killed and 11 wounded.
(SEE *Maquis; Northwest Europe*)

HART, MAJOR L.E.O.T. Hart was the SAS Brigade major in charge of administration during 1944-45, and was the second-in-command of 21 SAS in 1947.
(SEE *Special Air Service*)

'HAUNTED HOUSE' Name of the SAS HQ during the Borneo campaign (1963-66). Given to the Regiment as a present by the Sultan of Brunei, it was located behind his palace in the capital. The building had an operations room, communications centre and living quarters. The locals believed it was haunted by the ghost of a young girl who had been brutally murdered some years before (the building had been used by the Japanese equivalent of the Gestapo during World War II). This had the advantage of keeping locals away, thus aiding secrecy.
(SEE *Borneo; Brunei*)

Above: 'Hearts and minds' in operation. An SAS trooper with locals in Borneo.

'HAWTHORN', OPERATION This raid on Sardinia, carried out on 7 July 1943, was in fact a Special Boat Section mission. It is frequently listed as being an SAS operation, probably because the commanding officer, John Verney, later joined the Special Air Service.
(SEE *Italy; Special Boat Section*)

HEAD-ON CONTACT DRILL An SAS standard operating procedure (SOP) devised for a four-man patrol while on the move. When contact is made with the enemy, each member moves reactively into a position that allows him to fire at the opposition without hitting a comrade. For example, if the patrol is moving in file, the three men behind the lead scout will break left and right and bring their weapons to bear on the enemy. This drill is espe-cially effective for jungle patrolling, when visibility is poor.
(SEE *Four-man Patrol; SOPs*)

'HEAD SHED' SAS slang for senior officers.

'HEARTS AND MINDS' A concept devised by the Military High Commissioner in Malaya, General Sir Gerald Templar, to defeat the com-munist insurgents. Subsequently became an integral part of SAS counter-insurgency warfare methods.

'Hearts and minds', as practised by the Regiment in Malaya, Borneo and Oman, concentrates on gaining the trust of the local inhabitants by learn-ing their language, customs and shar-ing their lifestyle, and thus winning them over. In Borneo, for example, SAS troopers lived with the natives in the jungle for often months at a time, assisting them in their everyday needs and providing medical care. In this way the locals would accept the SAS and be their 'eyes and ears', often providing valuable intelligence on enemy movements and dispositions. In addition, it was hoped that the locals, because of the aid provided by the SAS, would support the British, or whoever they fought for.

The policy often required extra training. Medics, for example, had to learn midwifery and dentistry, and troopers had to learn the local lan-guage. Above all, 'hearts and minds' required large quantities of tact, cour-tesy and patience. But the benefits, as Malaya, Borneo and Oman illustrate, were well worth it.
(SEE *Borneo; Malaya; Oman*)

HECKLER & KOCH MP5 SUB-MACHINE GUN Because of their excellent handling qualities, engineer-ing and reliability, the MP5 range of submachine guns are employed by the SAS in counter-terrorist and hostage-

Above: The Heckler & Koch MP5 submachine gun has been in service with the SAS since the late 1970s. It is one of the most finally engineered weapons in the world, which makes it very reliable and thus ideal for counter-terrorist missions.

rescue operations, a notable example being at the Iranian Embassy in 1980. Heckler & Kochs are also carried by members of the Regiment in Northern Ireland, where they are ideal for combating Irish Republican Army terrorists armed with Kalashnikov AK-47 machine guns.

Heckler & Koch MP5A2 and A3

The A2 version has a fixed butt stop whereas the A3 has a single metal strut stock which can be slid forward to reduce the overall length of the weapon.

Type: submachine gun
Calibre: 9mm
Weight: 2.55kg (empty)
Length: 680mm (fixed butt); 660mm (butt extended); 490mm (butt retracted)

Effective range: 200m
Rate of fire: 800 rounds per minute (cyclic)
Feed: 15- or 30-round box magazine
Muzzle velocity: 400 metres per second

Heckler & Koch MP5SD

The silenced version of the MP5. The silencer fitted to the barrel also acts as an expansion chamber for the propulsive gases, which reduces the gas pressure and so slows down the acceleration of the bullet. The bullet itself leaves the muzzle at subsonic velocity, thus preventing a sonic shock wave in flight. There are six versions of the MP5SD: the MP5SD1 has a receiver end cap and no butt stock; the SD2 has a fixed butt stock; and the SD3 a retractable butt stock. The

MP5SD4 resembles the SD1 but has a three-round burst facility in addition to single and automatic fire; the SD5 is the SD2 with a three-round burst facility; and the SD6 is the SD3 with a three-round burst facility.

Type: submachine gun
Calibre: 9mm
Weight, empty: 2.9kg (SD1); 3.2kg (SD2); 3.5kg (SD3)
Length: 550mm (SD1); 780mm (SD2); 610 or 780mm (SD3)
Effective range: 200m
Rate of fire: 800 rounds per minute (cyclic)
Feed: 15- or 30-round curved box magazine
Muzzle velocity: 285 metres per second

Heckler & Koch MP5K The short-
ened version of the MP5 was specifically designed for use by special police and counter-terrorist units. The MP5KA1 has a smooth upper surface

with a small end rearsight to enable withdrawal from clothing or a holster without the weapon catching. The A4 has a three-round burst facility as well as single and automatic fire; the A5 resembles the A1 but has, in addition, a three-round burst facility.

Type: submachine gun
Calibre: 9mm
Weight: 2kg
Length: 325mm
Effective range: 200m
Rate of fire: 900 rounds per minute (cyclic)
Feed: 15- or 30-round box magazine
Muzzle velocity: 375 metres per second

(SEE *Irish Republican Army; Northern Ireland; Princes Gate*)

HECKLER & KOCH 53 Basically an MP5 chambered for the 5.56mm cartridge, the HK 53 can be used either as a submachine gun or as an assault rifle. With a telescoping butt stock fitted the weapon is only 563mm long with the butt retracted. This, together with the fact that the 5.56mm bullet has a lethality and stopping power disproportionate to its size, has resulted in the HK 53 being employed by the Regiment for counter-terrorist work in Northern Ireland.

Type: submachine gun
Designation: HK 53
Calibre: 5.56mm
Weight: 3.68kg
Length: 563mm (butt retracted); 755mm (butt extended)
Effective range: 400m
Rate of fire: 700 rounds per minute (cyclic)
Feed: 25-round box magazine
Muzzle velocity: 750 metres per second

HELICOPTERS The SAS's main demand on helicopters is for the infiltration and extraction of teams at the beginning and end of operations, and the support of teams while they are conducting a mission. Helicopters are also used to sweep an area for signs of any escaping enemy forces after a successful SAS ambush.

Since the early 1960s, the Regiment has used helicopters in nearly all its operations, a notable example being the Pebble Island raid during the Falklands War, when D Squadron employed a number of S-61 Sea Kings as transport to the target. During the 1991 Gulf War, SAS teams were reportedly inserted deep behind Iraqi lines in CH-47 Chinook aircraft specially modified for night-time flying.

(SEE *AH-7; CH-47; Falkland Islands; Gulf War; Pebble Island; S-61; SA 330; Wessex*)

HERCULES
(SEE *C-130*)

'HIDE' SAS name for a covert observation post or lying-up position.
(SEE *OP*)

Below: Two jeeps of the 'Houndsworth' party on patrol near the town of Dijon. This operation led to 3000 Maquis being armed.

Above: 'Hides' come in all shapes and sizes according to the type of terrain.

HILL, LIEUTENANT MICHAEL SINCLAIR
Leader of a Malayan Scouts patrol in Malaya that stayed in the jungle for 103 days.
(SEE *Malaya; Malayan Scouts*)

HITLER'S COMMANDO ORDER
Issued in October 1942 by Adolf Hitler in response to raids undertaken by British Commando units in North Africa, including the SAS. This directive gave German commanders licence to execute any captured members from such units: 'I therefore order that from now on all opponents....in so-called Commando operations....are to be exterminated to the last man in battle or flight....Even should these, on their being discovered, make as if to surrender, all quarter is to be denied on principle.' Though General Rommel, the commander of the *Afrika Korps* in North Africa, disregarded this order, captured SAS personnel were executed during the later campaigns in France and Germany.
(SEE *Barkworth, Major Eric; Northwest Europe*)

HMG
Heavy machine gun
(SEE *Browning .5in*)

'HOT-BEDDING'
The sharing of one or two sleeping bags between the members of a four-man patrol, also

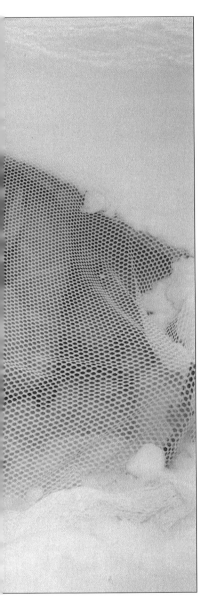

Fraser, was dropped into eastern France. His mission was to establish a base in the hilly, wooded country to the west of the town of Dijon, from where his men could disrupt enemy communications, sever railway lines and arm the local *Maquis*. By the end of June 'Houndsworth' totalled 144 men, nine jeeps and two 6-pounder anti-tank guns. In addition, a large quantity of arms had been given to the *Maquis*.

Covering a wide area, the SAS repeatedly cut the railway lines around Dijon. Such activity did not go unnoticed, however, and the Germans frequently carried out sweeps of the region. In one such operation in early July, the Germans captured a number of Resistance sympathizers in the small village of Montsauche. The SAS, alerted to this, ambushed the convoy containing the prisoners a short distance from the village. All the Germans were killed and the prisoners freed. Unfortunately, the Germans burned Montsauche in reprisal.

As the operations continued the SAS often moved camp because of poor *Maquis* security. On 3 August, a German attack on woods near Fraser's HQ was beaten off with the 6-pounders and 3-inch mortars. By early September the squadron was exhausted, having operated non-stop for three months. It was therefore decided to replace it with C Squadron. The switch was carried out on 6 September.

'Houndsworth' had been extremely successful: six trains derailed, 22 lines cut, 70 vehicles destroyed, 220 enemy personnel killed or wounded, and around 3000 *Maquis* armed.
(SEE *'Bulbasket', Operation; 'Cooney', Operation; 'Dingson', Operation; Fraser, Major Bill; Jeep; Maquis; Northwest Europe; 'Samwest', Operation*)

'HOUSE OF HORRORS' Building used by Delta Force, the American counter-terrorist unit, to sharpen its hostage-rescue and room-clearance drills. It is based on the SAS 'Killing House' and consists of four rooms: the first is a 'warm-up' room containing pop-up friend-or-foe targets; the second has entry and immediate engagement scenarios; the third is set up for night shooting and assaults; and the fourth is a mock-up of an aircraft cabin.
(SEE *Delta Force; 'Killing House'*)

'HOWARD', OPERATION Conducted by B and C Squadrons, 1 SAS, between 6 April and 6 May 1945. The jeep-mounted party, commanded by Lieutenant-Colonel 'Paddy' Mayne, left Tilbury on 6 April and arrived at Nijmegen, Holland, the next day. Mayne's mission was to recce ahead of the Canadian 4th Armoured Division towards Oldenburg, northwest Germany. The 40 jeeps travelled in two columns, though the terrain was far from ideal, being criss-crossed by dykes and waterways. They advanced 50km in three days, though B Squadron was caught in an ambush during which Mayne won his fourth DSO.

The SAS men soon discovered that their jeeps were no match for enemy ambush parties and so, after suffering a number of casualties, they pulled back to refit. Advancing once more, they reached Oldenburg on 3 May, before being ordered to move back to Belgium. Despite Mayne's bravery, 'Howard' was only a partial success and, though the SAS inflicted some damage, the party suffered heavy casualties.
(SEE *Germany; Jeep; Mayne, Lieutenant-Colonel 'Paddy' Blair; Northwest Europe*)

HYLANDS HALL Estate near Chelmsford in Essex and home of the SAS Brigade for much of the winter of 1944-45. After the successful mopping-up operation in Norway (May-August 1945), the brigade returned to Hylands where it was disbanded.
(SEE *'Apostle', Operation; Norway*)

called 'hot-bunking'. Usually employed inside an SAS observation post, where only two sleeping bags are required as two men are always on duty.
(SEE *Four-man Patrol; OP*)

'HOUNDSWORTH', OPERATION One of a number of operations undertaken by the SAS in support of the D-Day landings (6 June 1944). Between 6-21 June 1944, A Squadron, 1 SAS, under the command of Major Bill

I

IBAN TRIBESMEN Native inhabitants of the Sarawak region of Borneo, also called Sea Dyaks. Famed for their skill in warfare and tracking, Ibans were employed by the British in Malaya and Borneo, often working closely with SAS teams.
(SEE *Border Scouts; Cross-Border Scouts; Sarawak Rangers*)

'IBROX', OPERATION Cancelled raid by 10 men of 2 SAS to destroy a railway bridge in the vicinity of Trondheim, Norway, in March 1945.

INGRAM SUBMACHINE GUN The weapons invented by the American Gordon B. Ingram are all simple designs which fire at full-automatic only. The guns are very short, compact and solidly built and were, until the late 1970s, the primary weapons carried by SAS hostage-rescue teams. They can, in addition, be fitted with a detachable suppressor, and all models are equipped with a shoulder stock which pulls out for firing from the shoulder and pushes in for firing from the hip. Though currently used by the Regiment for counter-terrorist work, they are likely to be replaced by newer models such as the Glock 18 handgun and the Bushman IDW.

Ingram Model 10
  Type: submachine gun
  Calibre: 9mm
  Weight: 3.46kg
  Length: 269mm (stock telescoped); 548mm (stock extended)
  Effective range: 40m
  Rate of fire: 1145 rounds per minute (cyclic)
  Feed: 32-round magazine
  Muzzle velocity: 366 metres per second

Ingram Model 11
  Type: submachine gun
  Calibre: 9mm

  Weight: 2.1kg
  Length: 248mm (stock telescoped); 460mm (stock extended)
  Effective range: 40m
  Rate of fire: 1200 rounds per minute (cyclic)
  Feed: 16- or 32-round magazine
  Muzzle velocity: 293 metres per second
(SEE *Bushman IDW; Glock Handguns*)

INTELLIGENCE AND SECURITY GROUP British Army intelligence gathering unit which operates in Northern Ireland. Its recruits come from the Army on secondment and are trained in surveillance and intelligence gathering techniques by the SAS at Hereford.
(SEE *Northern Ireland*)

INTERNATIONAL LONG RANGE RECONNAISSANCE PATROL SCHOOL Located at Weingarten in Bavaria, Germany, the school provides instruction in all aspects of long-range reconnaissance patrol work including evasion techniques, signalling and survival skills. Students on the courses regularly include members of the SAS (including the two Territorial Army regiments), as well as soldiers from other NATO armies.

IPOH Major town in northern Malaya. During the Malayan Emergency (1948-60), armed communists openly paraded through its streets, and the jungle around the town also witnessed a high level of communist activity. Ipoh was the base for the Malayan Scouts' first operation, in November 1950. Its commander, Major 'Mad Mike' Calvert, devised a strategy whereby 14-man patrols would penetrate the jungle, establish a base camp with a radio, and despatch three- or four-man patrols to hunt down the terrorists. One such patrol remained in the jungle for 103 consecutive days.
(SEE *Calvert, Brigadier Mike; Communist Terrorist; Four-man Patrol; Malaya; Malayan Scouts*)

Above: An Iban tribesman guiding a patrol along a waterway in Borneo. These people taught SAS troopers the skills needed to operate in a jungle environment.

IRANIAN EMBASSY
(see *Princes Gate*)

IRAQ
(SEE *Gulf War*)

'IRIS' Name for the hand-held, infrared intruder detection device used by SAS soldiers on covert surveillance

operations, especially in Northern Ireland. Has an effective range of 5km.

(see *Northern Ireland*)

IRISH REPUBLICAN ARMY Irish nationalist group formed in 1919, dedicated to armed struggle in pursuit of its aims. In the latter years of the 1960s it exploited the civil rights demonstrations which were taking place in Northern Ireland. It is committed to violently ending British and Unionist rule in Ulster by the waging of guerrilla war.

In December 1969, the IRA split into two groups. The 'Officials', the old leadership based in Dublin, believed that a Marxist alliance between the Protestant and Catholic proletariats would bring about a united Ireland. The 'Provisionals', led by the hardliners from Belfast, believed the only way to achieve a free Ireland was to drive the British out by force. The 'Provos' soon gained the upper hand and drew support from the Catholics of Ulster, some of whom, although they had initially welcomed the arrival of British

troops, soon perceived the Army as a force of repression.

At the top of the IRA is the 12-strong Army Executive which elects the Army Council of seven members. Immediately below the Council is the 12-strong General Headquarters staff which implements the Council's decisions. Next in the chain of command are the IRA's Southern and Northern Commands which are in turn split into 'brigades', then battalions, companies and, the lowest operational body, the Active Service Unit (ASU). There are currently six IRA brigades:

bombing of the Grand Hotel in Brighton in October 1984, where Prime Minister Margaret Thatcher and many of her cabinet were staying at the time for the Conservative Party Conference. The deaths of 11 civilians at a Remembrance Day parade in Enniskillen in November 1987 resulted in a worldwide feeling of revulsion against the IRA. The SAS operation in Gibraltar five months later resulted in the movement recovering some sympathy. It seems likely that the IRA cannot be defeated and that the security forces in Northern Ireland can do little more than minimise its activities. The strength of the IRA lies in its permanent pool of recruits from the Catholic ghettos of Northern Ireland, and its tried and trusted structure. It can survive bad publicity because its taps into a rich vein of Catholic Irish nationalism. (SEE *Active Service Unit; Gibraltar; Northern Ireland*)

ITALY The SAS campaign in Italy during World War II can be characterised as being one of lost opportunities. The end of the war in North Africa witnessed a temporary decline in the overall effectiveness of the Special Air Service. This was caused by the capture of its founder, Lieutenant-Colonel David Stirling, and its general misuse during the subsequent liberation of Sicily and Italy.

The original SAS, 1 SAS, had been renamed the Special Raiding Squadron (SRS) and was placed under the command of Lieutenant-Colonel 'Paddy' Mayne. Lieutenant-Colonel William Stirling, David's brother, had formed 2 SAS in Algeria. Both would be employed in Sicily and Italy.

During the initial stages of Operation 'Husky', the invasion of Sicily, the SRS, under the overall control of the British XIII Corps, was tasked with conducting an amphibious assault and capturing an enemy gun battery on top of Capo Murro di Porco, which was achieved on 10 July

Above: IRA terrorists stop a vehicle at an illegal roadblock in Northern Ireland.

Belfast, Donegal, Londonderry, Tyrone-Monaghan, Armagh and Dublin.

For reasons of security, the IRA has no more than around 50 full-time 'soldiers' (bombers or gunmen) plus another 500 volunteers who provide logistical support for military operations. This reduced strength means that, in remote areas, a brigade usually comprises no more than one ASU, its controller, and a few volunteers. Only in Belfast is there a sizeable contingent, with four battalions each containing one ASU.

Nevertheless, the IRA's operatives are highly trained, well armed and

expertly organised. In addition, the movement has access to a continual flow of money to finance its operations, raised through robbery, extortion, donations from many sources (including NORAID in the US), moneylending and general fraud. This means that it can afford to purchase state-of-the-art weaponry and send its 'soldiers' on missions abroad.

The IRA has mounted operations not only in Northern Ireland but also in the Irish Republic, on the British mainland, and on the Continent. Significant actions include the deaths of 21 people in the Birmingham pub bombings in November 1974, and the

ITALY AND SICILY
1943—45

N

KEY

MAPLE: SAS Operations

0   50   100
Kilometres

SWITZERLAND

AUSTRIA

Brenner Pass
COLD COMFORT

Trieste

Milan   ITALY   Venice

Parma

Genoa   TOMBOLA
GALIA   Bologna   MAPLE   BAOBAB
SPEEDWELL
La Spezia   POMEGRANATE   Rimini   Ancona   YUGOSLAVIA

Florence   JONQUIL
CANDYTUFT   Ascoli
Siena   SAXIFRAGE

SLEEPY   *ADRIATIC SEA*
LAD   Pescara

CORSICA   ROME   Termoli

Anzio
NORTH AFRICA area—

SARDINIA   Naples   Bari
Salerno   Taranto

MARIGOLD

TYRRHENIAN SEA

Bagnara

CHESTNUT
SICILY   Catania

NORTH AFRICA   Augusta
Syracuse
SNAPDRAGON

Tunis   NARCISSUS

Pantelleria Island

1943. Two days later, the unit carried out another successful amphibious attack on the harbour of Augusta. On 3 September, the British Eighth Army crossed the Straits of Messina while, six days later, a combined British and American force landed farther north at Salerno.

The first SRS operation on the Italian mainland was the ill-fated raid on Bagnara (3 September 1943), which was compromised by the Royal Navy's incompetence. The unit's last action in Italy was around the port of Termoli in October 1943 in support of the Eighth Army's attempt to breach the so-called Termoli line north of Bari. The SRS, together with two Commandos and support detachments, was landed from the sea on the 2nd and quickly secured the town. By 5 October, troops from the 78th Division had reached Termoli,

together with elements of 2 SAS, and the SAS prepared to re-embark. However, on that day the Germans launched a counterattack, with the fighting continuing through the night and into the next day. The situation was eventually saved by the arrival of some Canadian Sherman tanks and the Royal Irish Rangers. After this fierce action the SRS was withdrawn south to rest. The unit remained in southern Italy until December 1943, when it was moved to Scotland to prepare for the 1944 invasion of France.

Bill Stirling's 2 SAS was more fully employed in Sicily and Italy, though Allied HQ still insisted on using all SAS units as shock troops, in the front line, or for standard reconnaissance duties. Those operations which were more along the lines envisaged by David Stirling were invariably

given inadequate logistical support, with the result that they were only partially successful.

During Operation 'Husky', 2 SAS was tasked with seizing strategic objectives and operating behind enemy lines to disrupt communications (though the latter often suffered from bad planning and some of the men were inexperienced in making group parachute jumps). Once on the Italian mainland, 2 SAS was mostly employed in advance of the main Allied forces, though usually not far enough behind enemy lines to maximise its effectiveness.

The unit assisted in the capture of Taranto, undertook numerous operations along Italy's Adriatic coast, supported the Allied landings at Anzio, as well as operating in northern Italy during the final stages of the war. The missions carried out by 2 SAS in Italy proved that small parties dropped behind enemy lines could inflict a large amount of damage on the enemy and operate for long periods among a friendly population. Italy also proved, however, that these parties needed to be well supported and equipped to be effective. There is no doubt that opportunities were lost.

Had around 100 parties been dropped behind German positions at Salerno, for example, then railway lines carrying reinforcements and supplies to the beachhead from the east and north could have been cut. Nevertheless, the Italian campaign did fulfil one important function: it proved that the SAS could operate in any theatre and not just the sandy wastes of North Africa.

(SEE *Bagnara; 'Baobab', Operation; 'Begonia', Operation; 'Candytuft', Operation; 'Chestnut', Operation; 'Jonquil', Operation; 'Maple', Operation; Mayne, Lieutenant-Colonel 'Paddy' Blair; 'Narcissus', Operation; 'Pomegranate', Operation; 'Saxifrage', Operation; 'Sleepy Lad', Operation; 'Speedwell', Operation; Stirling, Lieutenant-Colonel David; Stirling, Lieutenant-Colonel William; Termoli*)

Below: A soldier from 2 SAS liaising with two mounted partisans during the Italian campaign. In both France and Italy the SAS worked closely with the Resistance.

J–K

'JAGUAR', OPERATION Codename for the SAS-led assault on the Jebel Dhofar, Oman, in October 1971. It was a large-scale operation involving 800 men and was led by the SAS commander, Lieutenant-Colonel John Watts. His force comprised two squadrons of SAS, two companies of the Sultan's Armed Forces (SAF), five *firqats*, a pioneer platoon and a platoon of *askars* (armed tribesmen). Their mission was designed to drive the *adoo* off the jebel and established a government presence in their place.

The first part of the operation began on 2 October. One SAS squadron, two *firqats* and some *askars* assaulted and captured the old airstrip at Lympne, 6km east of Jibjat, after a gruelling march. Simultaneously, a small party under Captain Branson made a successful feint by climbing the jebel to the south. After Watts had taken Lympne, reinforcements were flown in. However, on 3 October he decided that the airstrip at Jibjat was better suited to his needs, and so ordered it to be taken. This was achieved after a sharp battle, and Watts then deployed his forces on the plateau, a move that resulted in five days of fierce fighting. Watts then divided the SAS into two separate groups, each one accompanied by *firqats*, and ordered them to advance down the western and eastern sides of the Wadi Darbat. The *adoo* were eventually cleared off the plateau and driven into the wadis.

However, it was at this point that the *firqats* decided they would stop

fighting and observe the religious festival of Ramadan, a period when Moslems are forbidden to eat or drink between dawn and dusk. This resulted in their military effectiveness being drastically reduced (the *firqats* had in fact been granted a dispensation by religious leaders and the Sultan). Watts, enraged, was forced to abandon some positions and re-group at a place called 'White City'. The *adoo* then launched a fierce counter-attack, which was eventually defeated. During the following month Watts set up three positions above the Jebel Khaftawt which became known as the Leopard line, though not before the *firqats* had again proved difficult. This time they demanded that their animals be brought off the jebel and transported to a government-organised market, or they would stop fighting (this was carried out, with jet fighters acting as escorts for the cattle).

'Jaguar' resulted in the Omani government establishing a presence on the Jebel Dhofar. It was also a significant defeat for the *adoo* which left the coastal plain and its towns all firmly under government control. In addition, government policies for improving agriculture, medicine and education were put into effect. The operation had also been a reminder that *firqat* units could, despite their good relations with the SAS, be headstrong and downright infuriating at times.
(SEE *Adoo; Askar; Firqat; Oman; Sultan's Armed Forces; Watts, Lieutenant-Colonel Johnny*)

JALO Forward base of the Long Range Desert Group (LRDG) in North Africa during World War II. Originally a French Foreign Legion outpost, it was captured from the Italians by the British on 25 November 1941. Situated some 240km south of Benghazi, it was well behind enemy lines and ideally suited to act as a base for the early SAS raids against enemy airfields around the Gulf of Sirte. The LRDG provided the transport to and from the targets during these early operations. Jalo was abandoned in January 1942 following General Rommel's offensive which drove the Eighth Army back to the Egyptian border.
(SEE *Benghazi; Long Range Desert Group; North Africa*)

JAVELIN Hand-held surface-to-air missile (SAM) anti-aircraft weapon currently in use with the British Army. Operation is relatively simple as guidance to target is by the semi-automatic command to line-of-sight (SACLOS) system. All the operator has to do is keep the aiming mark on the target. This weapon, like the US-made Stinger, provides portable air defence for small teams operating in hostile territory or isolated special forces bases.

Type: man-portable surface-to-air missile (SAM)
Length: 1400mm
Effective range: 4–5km
Maximum altitude: 2km
Maximum speed: Mach 1.7+
(SEE *Stinger*)

JEAPES, BRIGADIER TONY Originally of the Dorset Regiment, Tony Jeapes joined the SAS as a lieutenant in Malaya in 1958. He was to serve with the Regiment for the next 19 years, interrupted only by periods at the Army's Staff College and the National Defence College. In January 1959, Lieutenant Jeapes was with A Squadron during its assault on one of the peaks of the Jebel Akhdar. He led his troops up the rocky slopes and enagaged in savage hand-to-hand fighting, an action which won him the Military Cross.

His most influential period with the Regiment was during the war in Oman (1970-76). Arriving in the country in January 1971, the then Major Jeapes was instrumental in establishing the *firqat* units and implementing the SAS 'hearts and minds' campaign. He correctly perceived the way to victory in Oman: 'It was first and last a war about people, a war in which both sides concentrated upon winning the support of the civilians of the Djebel Dhofar and which was won in the end by civil development, with military action merely a means to that end.' His experiences in the war were summarised in his excellent

Below: Tony Jeapes was instrumental in establishing the firqat *units during the SAS campaign in Oman (1970-76).*

Above: Members of 22 SAS being briefed before their assault on the Jebel Akhdar, January 1959. The operation was another spectacular success for the Regiment.

book, *Operation Oman*. He commanded 22 SAS from 1974 to 1977, leading it on operational tours in both Oman and Northern Ireland.
(SEE Firqat, 'Hearts and Minds'; Jebel Akhdar, Oman)

JEBEL AKHDAR The inhospitable 'Green Mountain', situated in the north of Oman, was the scene of a daring SAS operation in 1959. The British, who had treaty obligations to the Sultan of Muscat and Oman, found themselves being drawn into a counter-insurgency campaign in Oman in the late 1950s. The Sultan's rule was being challenged by Sulaiman bin Himyar, chief of the Bani Riyam tribe, the Imam, Ghalib bin Ali, and Ghalib's brother, Talib. In 1957 Talib, together with an army of expatriate Omanis raised in Saudi Arabia, returned to the Jebel Akhdar

and declared the region independent of the Sultan.

Talib had the support of the two local tribes on the jebel, the Bani Himya and Bani Riyam, and quickly gained control of communications between the coast and Nizwa in the interior. The Sultan, having inadequate military resources to dislodge Talib, turned to the British for help. In 1957, the latter despatched an infantry brigade from Kenya to Oman which helped restore the Sultan's authority around Nizwa.

However, by mid-1958 Talib was still in a secure position on the jebel. The British decided that it would be useful if friendly forces could be positioned in the villages around the jebel, capture some rebels and persuade them to change sides. In this way forces could eventually be put on the jebel itself. The geography of the latter is imposing: the plateau has an area of 350 square kilometres and is surrounded by high mountain peaks. Access is via narrrow passes which are ideal for ambushes.

On 15 November 1958, Lieutenant-Colonel Deane-Drummond, 22 SAS's commander, ordered D Squadron into action. The 70 men under Major Johnny Watts arrived from Malaya three days later. The operation began immediately. On the northern side of the jebel Captain Rory Walker with two groups reached the top of the mountain later nicknamed 'Sabrina' and established sangars 2000m from rebel positions. A major attack on Walker's position in December was beaten off with heavy enemy losses.

The SAS had also been active on the southern side of the jebel. A rebel cave had been discovered which contained weapons and ammunition. It was assaulted by a group led by

Captain de la Billière, but, after a ferocious battle, he was forced to conduct a fighting withdrawal, the seasoned rebels putting in a professional performance.

In January 1959, it was decided to make a determined push against Talib's forces on the jebel. Aerial reconnaissance had revealed that there was a route from the village of Kamah between the Wadi Kamah and the Wadi Suwaiq. Though there was an enemy machine-gun post at the top, it was felt that it could be taken if surprise was achieved. The plan was for A Squadron under Major Cooper (which had arrived in Oman in January) to assault 'Sabrina' from the north, while D would remain at Tanuf in the south. A lie had been spread among the Arab donkey handlers that the main assault would come from the direction of Tanuf. This information quickly reached the

rebels, who began to concentrate their forces there.

At 0300 hours on 26 January, the attack was launched when Cooper's squadron assaulted 'Sabrina'. Three troops took it from the north side, though the rebels sent reinforcements from the vilage of Saiq to dislodge them. However, A Squadron left 'Sabrina' and headed down into Tanuf to link up with D. Cooper's men reached the village at 1800 hours and, together with most of D Squadron, were loaded onto trucks and taken to the assembly area at Kamah.

At 2030 hours, a diversionary attack was made from Tanuf by the SAS troop left there. Simultaneously, the two squadrons, heavily loaded, began their march up the jebel. Their three objectives were 'Vincent', 'Pyramid' and 'Beercan', the latter being the final summit. By 0500 hours on 27

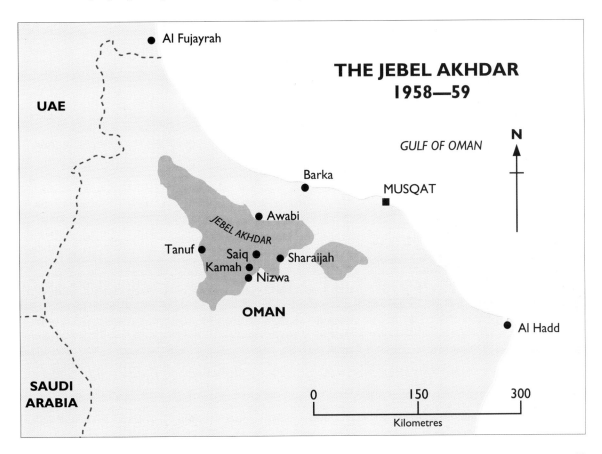

THE JEBEL AKHDAR
1958—59

January, D Squadron held 'Pyramid' and was poised to advance on 'Beercan'. Deane-Drummond and Watts decided to increase the chances of success by ordering the men to reduce their loads to just essential weapons and ammunition. They then ordered a dash to the summit; 90 minutes later, after a gruelling climb, the SAS men held 'Beercan'.

Soldiers from the British Life Guards and Sultan's Armed Forces were then brought in to secure the objective. The SAS then moved into the villages of Saiq and Sharaijah and began to disarm the rebels. Totally surprised, they put up only token resistance before surrendering. Their leaders, Talib, Ghalib and Sulaiman, fled into Saudi Arabia.

The assault on the Jebel Akhdar was testimony to what a small number of men could do against a strongly entrenched enemy if used with boldness and imagination. The difficult climb to the top was also indicative of the high level of fitness of each SAS soldier. By 5 February the jebel was firmly in SAS hands, the latter having lost only two men dead in the assault. They began an immediate, and ultimately successful, 'hearts and minds' campaign to turn the local inhabitants into supporters of the Sultan.
(SEE *Cooper, Lieutenant-Colonel Johnny; Deane-Drummond, Major-General Tony; de la Billière, General Sir Peter; 'Hearts and Minds'; Oman; Watts, Lieutenant-Colonel Johnny*)

JEDBURGH TEAMS Specially trained World War II units, each one having an American, a British and a French officer or noncommissioned officer.

Teams were dropped into France after D-Day to liaise with *Maquis* forces. Their tasks included organising local Resistance forces, arranging dropping zones and launching attacks on German troops heading for the Normandy beachhead. The 86 Jedburgh teams were controlled by Headquarters Special Forces and were frequently dropped with SAS parties into France.
(SEE *Maquis; Northwest Europe*)

JEEP During World War II the SAS made extensive use of modified American Willys jeeps. First used in the North African desert, they were equipped with twin Vickers 'K' guns mounted front and rear. These were often supplemented with a 0.5in Browning heavy machine gun. In the desert the jeeps carried water condensers, sand mats, radios, metal wheel channels and spare ammunition, in addition to a three-man crew.

Below: A World War II SAS jeep equipped with a Browning heavy machine gun and Vickers 'K' guns. Note the jerry cans which contained fuel and water.

Above: George Jellicoe (extreme right), commander of the Special Boat Squadron, at the unveiling of the memorial to the Greek Sacred Squadron in May 1944.

June 1942, he took part in the SAS raid on Crete. The party was taken to the island by submarine and reached the shore in rubber boats. Jellicoe and his companions managed to destroy 21 enemy aircraft at Heraklion airfield. Up to the end of the war in North Africa, Jellicoe took part in numerous other SAS actions. In March 1943, he was given command of the Special Boat Squadron (SBS), to be based at Athlit in Palestine, and effectively left the SAS. He commanded the SBS until January 1945, when he was sent to the Staff College. (SEE *Athlit; Crete; Special Boat Squadron*)

JOC Joint Operations Centre. Housed in the British Ministry of Defence in London, the JOC has the power to deploy the SAS at home and abroad. It includes representatives from the SAS, all the intelligence services, the Foreign Office, the Home Office, and the armed forces. It was the JOC which deployed the SAS to Gibraltar in March 1988. (SEE *Gibraltar*)

'JOCKWORTH', OPERATION Conducted between 15 August and 9 September 1944 by 57 men of 3 French Parachute Battalion (3 SAS) under the command of Captain Hourst. They were dropped in southeast France between the Rhône and Loire Rivers. Their mission was to disrupt enemy movements and organise local *Maquis* forces. 'Jockworth' was quite successful, with considerable damage and casualties inflicted on the Germans. The SAS troops were also the first Allied soldiers into Lyons, where they became involved in fierce house-to-house fighting. (SEE Maquis; *Northwest Europe*)

JOHORE Location of the base and first training camp for the Malayan Scouts. Situated in southern Malaya, all recruits to the Scouts underwent an eight-week course in jungle warfare techniques at Johore. However, the

The jeep had a top speed of approximately 100km/hr and a range of 450km, though this could be extended with the addition of extra fuel tanks. They were also fitted with armoured plate and bullet-proof glass to protect the driver and front gunner.

During operations in Europe (1943-45) SAS jeeps were often dropped by parachute to teams on the ground. The vehicles were packed into wooden crates, with air bags underneath to cushion the impact on landing. Each jeep, dropped from a four-engined Halifax, required four parachutes for a safe touchdown. (SEE *Browning .5in; Vickers 'K'*)

JELLICOE, EARL GEORGE The son of the famous World War I admiral, Captain George Jellicoe was one of the early members of the SAS. In

facilities left much to be desired. Live-firing exercises, for example, had to be conducted on football pitches and other areas around the camp! (SEE *Malaya; Malayan Scouts*)

JONES, LANCE-CORPORAL DAVID

One of the first SAS fatalities in Northern Ireland, and one which was to have a profound effect on the Regiment's tactics in dealing with armed terrorists. On 19 March 1978, Jones and Lance-Corporal Kevin Smyth, both SAS, were engaged on covert surveillance outside the village of Maghera, County Londonderry, when they spotted two armed men approaching their position. Thinking they were from the Ulster Defence Regiment (UDR), Jones stood up and issued a challenge. In fact the men were terrorists, who immediately shot at the SAS soldier. Jones and Smyth were both hit, though Jones himself managed to shoot one of the terrorists. A subsequent search resulted in the capture of the wounded man, identified as Francis Hughes, an Irish Republican Army member. Jones died the next day of his wounds.

The incident brought home what can happen when there is poor liaison between the Army, police and SAS. Subsequent operations were under much tighter control. Worse, Hughes had reacted faster than the two SAS soldiers. This too was rectified, with the result that in future contacts with terrorists SAS soldiers were better prepared. (SEE *Irish Republican Army; Northern Ireland*)

'JONQUIL', OPERATION

Mounted at the beginning of October 1943, 'Jonquil' was a complete disaster. It was intended as one of the operations to round up the large number of

Left: Jungle training in the forests of the Far East. Fighting in this type of environment, which is characterised by low light and poor visibility, is particularly tough on troops.

Allied prisoners of war (POWs) that were wandering around the Italian countryside following Italy's surrender. The plan called for four seaborne parties from B Squadron, 2 SAS, to land between Ancona and Pescara on Italy's Adriatic coast to act as guides for the POWs.

After assembling a number of civilian fishing vessels, the plan went immediately wrong. The Germans counterattacked at Termoli on 5 October, forcing the vessels to move back to Bari. In addition, there were enemy aircraft operating in the area and the Germans had impounded local fishing vessels which the SAS had hoped to used as cover for the operation.

Many POWs made it to the beaches but only a few were evacuated. Lack of communications resulted in the boats arriving when there were no POWs, and vice versa. The fact that the SAS was not involved in the planning of 'Jonquil' did nothing to mitigate against the feelings of deep disappointment about the whole affair. (SEE *'Begonia', Operation; Italy*)

JUNGLE TRAINING

Undertaken by prospective SAS recruits once they have completed Continuation Training. Lasts from four to six weeks and is held in the Far East, for example Brunei. All the students are taught basic jungle survival skills: constructing shelters, finding food and water, and jungle navigation. The course culminates in a final exercise which all the candidates must pass. They are split into four-man patrols and given a specific task which will test the skills they have learned over the preceding weeks. Failure means entry is denied to the SAS. All students who pass Jungle Training then go on to attend the static-line parachuting course. (SEE *Continuation Training; Static-line Parachuting Course*)

JUNGLE WARFARE SCHOOL

Located at Kota Tinggi in Malaya.

Used extensively by the SAS during, and after, its campaigns in the Far East. Also used by the New Zealand and Australian SAS. During the Vietnam War, for example, Australian instructors taught British SAS students the lessons they had learned in that conflict.

K

KABRIT

L Detachment's base camp and the SAS's first 'home'. Established in July 1941, Kabrit was located on the Suez Canal, Egypt. David Stirling initially had no tents or supplies for his new unit; these were stolen from a New Zealand camp nearby on one of the SAS's first 'missions'. Intensive training was carried out at Kabrit: night marches, physical exercises, map reading, route marches and parachute training. (SEE *L Detachment; North Africa*)

KEALY, MAJOR MIKE

As a captain in command of eight men from 8 (Mobility) Troop, 22 SAS, Kealy led the epic defence of the Omani coastal town of Mirbat on 19 July 1972. He was awarded the DSO for his part in the battle. Kealy had joined the SAS, via Sandhurst and the Queen's Surrey Regiment, in 1971. Tragically, he died of hypothermia whilst on a long-distance march across the Brecon Beacons in February 1979. (SEE *Mirbat*)

'KEENI MEENI'

Name given to the extremely dangerous British undercover work carried out in Aden from the mid-1960s. It is a Swahili phrase used to describe the sinuous movement of a snake in long grass. The SAS squads proved adept at 'Keeni Meeni' operations, particularly the Fijian members of the Regiment. (SEE *Aden*)

KENYA

SAS involvement in Kenya, a British crown colony from 1920 to

Above: SAS recruits undergoing training at Kabrit during World War II. David Stirling insisted on all his men being in top physical shape for missions in the desert.

1961, was slight during the 1950s and early 1960s. In 1953-54, teams from 22 SAS were deployed briefly to combat Mau Mau terrorist violence. In 1960, D Squadron, 22 SAS, was deployed briefly to the Aberdare mountains as a precaution against a hardcore of Mau Mau survivors who had taken refuge there.

'KEYSTONE', OPERATION Codename for the mission conducted by a jeep-mounted squadron of 2 SAS under the command of Major Druce. The objective was to interfere with enemy movements south of Ijsselmeer, Holland, and to capture bridges over the Apeldoorn Canal. On 3 April 1945, an advance party was landed to secure a dropping zone and link up with the Resistance. This was achieved, though the party's radio was smashed on landing. A second party, unable to identify the pre-arranged

reception signals, returned to Britain.

The main party and its jeeps were dropped on 11 April, though two subsequent attempts to drop men and vehicles were unsuccessful due to bad weather. A second jeep party under Druce was therefore tasked with driving north and linking up with the forward group. Though they had difficulty getting through German lines, Druce's team eventually joined the second group on 18 April. The united squadron then drove northeast to join the 'Archway' teams.

Though 'Keystone' inflicted damage and casualties on the enemy, the operation suffered because the SAS was used as a forward reconnaissance force and not as a deep-penetration unit. (SEE *'Archway', Operation; Druce, Captain Henry; Northwest Europe*)

'KILLING HOUSE' Name for the SAS Close Quarter Battle (CQB) building

at Stirling Lines in Hereford. Originally developed for perfecting bodyguard skills, it was later used to refine counter-terrorist tactics, specifically hostage-rescue drills (the US Delta Force has a similar building called the 'House of Horrors'). Students attend a six-week CQB shooting course at Hereford, during which time they expend a minimum of 5000 rounds a week, though the Special Projects Team on stand-by will shoot far more.

Techniques practised in the 'Killing House' include rapid magazine changes, malfunction clearance drills, shooting on the move and from unconventional positions, rapid target acquisition, exact shot placement, and head shots. The course ensures that all the above eventually become second nature to those under instruction.

The building used to contain a single room set up to represent a likely setting where hostages might be held. Inside the room were live 'hostages' (SAS men) and 'terrorist' dummies. To add to the realism the room was often in darkness. The SAS team would burst in and, in under four seconds, identify the hostages and terrorists and shoot the latter. Live ammunition was used to add extra realism. The system worked until 1986, when an SAS sergeant 'terrorist' moved at the wrong moment and was killed instantly by a head shot.

The 'Killing House' now has two rooms: one containing the 'terrorists' and 'hostages', and one which the assault team attacks. The rooms are connected by a sophisticated camera system which gives a 'real time' coverage of events taking place in one room to a life-size wraparound screen in the other, and vice versa. In this way the assault team can fire at the images of the terrorists projected onto the bullet-absorbent walls; the 'terrorists' can also fire at their screen. In addition, the whole sequence is recorded on video to allow debriefings and exercise appraisals afterwards.

(SEE *Delta Force; 'House of Horrors';
Special Projects Team; Stirling Lines*)

KILMARNOCK At the end of 1943, 1
SAS returned to Scotland for training
prior to D-Day and operations in
northern Europe. The Regiment
established a training base near the
remote village of Darvel to the east of
Kilmarnock, Scotland. At the end of
May 1944, 1 SAS was moved to
Fairford in Gloustershire.

'KIPLING', OPERATION Conducted
by 107 men and 46 jeeps of C
Squadron, 1 SAS, between 13 August
and 26 September 1944 in the area
west of Auxerre, central France. The
original aim of 'Kipling' was to aid
Allied airborne landings which were
due to take place in the Orleans Gap.
An advance party under Captain
Derrick Harrison was dropped on the
night of 13 August, with more men

and jeeps parachuted in on subsequent evenings. They were ordered to
establish a base, lie low and make
contacts with the *Maquis*. However,
the airborne operation was cancelled
and so the SAS was ordered to conduct aggressive patrolling.

The situation in the area at the time
was constantly changing: Patton's US
Third Army was driving towards
Reims, while other Allied forces were
advancing from the south after the
'Anvil' landings of early August. The
SAS took full advantage of this, often
engaging in heroics. On 23 August,
on hearing there were many Germans
in the village of Les Ormes, Harrison
decided to attack with two jeeps. The
party raced into the village square and
proceeded to shoot up the enemy and
their vehicles, setting the latter on
fire. The Germans, crack SS men,
began to fire back at the SAS and a
desperate battle ensued. Eventually

Harrison was forced to withdraw,
though he had to leave his damaged
jeep behind. For his bravery at Les
Ormes he was awarded the Military
Cross.

That night Major Marsh, the
squadron's commander, reached the
SAS camp with 20 jeeps. The next
day the squadron, leaving a troop
behind, drove to the Morvan area to
relieve A Squadron, 1 SAS. They
then conducted some very successful
patrolling, despite suffering from lack
of fuel due to supply drops being cancelled because of bad weather. Some
patrols joined up with the French
First Army which was advancing from
the south, assisting in the surrender of
3000 German soldiers at Autun. By
26 September the squadron had
moved back to Cosne to rest, effectively bringing the operation to an
end. By any measure 'Kipling' had
been a great success; the enemy had
been continually harassed and the
SAS had inflicted heavy casualties.
(SEE *Harrison, Captain Derrick;*
Maquis; *Northwest Europe*)

*Below: SAS troopers take a break during an operation against Mau Mau guerrillas
in Kenya. Such missions were often characterised by boredom. However, they did
provide an opportunity to brush up on jungle warfare skills.*

Above: Two SBS soldiers come ashore from their Klepper canoe. These small craft, though now rather old fashioned, are excellent for clandestine operations.

KLEPPER CANOE Two-man canoe used by the SAS and SBS. First introduced into service in the 1950s, the frame is constructed of hardwood Mountain Ash and Finnish Birch. The deck covering is self-sealing and self-drying cotton woven with hemp, while the hull material consists of a core of polyester cord surrounded by rubber. The skin is loose fitting until 'airsponsons' which run under each gunwale are inflated.
(SEE *Special Boat Section; Special Boat Squadron*)

KOREAN WAR A detachment of 21 SAS, the Territorial Army unit, was earmarked for service in the Korean conflict, which began on 25 June 1950. M Squadron, composed of volunteers with wartime experience, was raised and equipped to fight behind North Korean lines (General Douglas MacArthur, the United Nations supreme commander, had specifically requested the SAS). However, the entry of the Chinese into the war in November 1950 resulted in the British government considering the use of the SAS politically unacceptable for behind the lines operations. Nevertheless, the detachment was sent to Singapore, eventually linking up with the Malayan Scouts in Malaya, both units later becoming the joint founders of 22 SAS.
(SEE *Malayan Scouts; Special Air Service*)

'KREMLIN' Nickname for the SAS Operations Planning and Intelligence cell located at Stirling Lines, Hereford. The cell holds detailed information on prospective theatres of operations: climate, geography, political situation, social and economic factors, and any other intelligence which may be pertinent to an SAS mission overseas. This information is continually updated in response to the changing world situation.
(SEE *Special Air Service; Stirling Lines*)

KUFRA Oasis deep in the North African interior used as a staging post and rendezvous point by the SAS and Long Range Patrol Group.
(SEE *Long Range Desert Group*)

KUWAIT
(SEE *Gulf War*)

L

L2A3
(SEE *Sterling Submachine Gun*)

L34A1
(SEE *Sterling Submachine Gun*)

L42A1 This bolt-action sniper rifle, which is based on the venerable Lee Enfield .303, was used with great success by the SAS in Malaya, Aden, Oman, Northern Ireland and the Falklands, and was a very reliable weapon. The Regiment experimented with the Finnish Tikka M55 and the Austrian SSG 69 as replacements for the L42 in the 1980s, before adopting the Accuracy International L96A1 as the new SAS sniper rifle.

Below: The L42A1 sniper rifle.

Type: bolt-action sniper rifle
Designation: L42A1
Calibre: 7.62mm
Weight: 4.43kg
Length: 1181mm
Effective range: 800m
Feed: 10-round box magazine
Muzzle velocity: 838 metres per second
(SEE *Accuracy International PM; Tikka M55; SSG 69*)

L96A1
(SEE *Accuracy International PM*)

LABALABA, CORPORAL Fijian member of 22 SAS who played a distinguished part in the Battle of Mirbat, July 1972, during which he was killed. Labalaba, a veteran of 'Keeni Meeni'

operations in Aden and missions in Borneo, was Mentioned in Despatches for his efforts at Mirbat.
(SEE *'Keeni Meeni'; Mirbat*)

LAND ROVER The SAS has used Land Rover vehicles for over 40 years. Their general ruggedness, reliability, manoeuvrability and ease of maintenance has made them ideal for special forces operations. The famous SAS 'Pink Panther', for example, is a Land Rover model.

To list all the variants available would be impossible. Nevertheless, a brief summary can be given of some of the accessories which can be fitted to long-range versions. Weapon-mounting facilities have increased from the fixed variety to power-

Above: Two examples of Land Rovers designed for special forces use. The SAS will continue to employ these vehicles well into the twenty-first century.

assisted mounts with adjustable swivel seats which are capable of carrying weapons ranging from single 7.62mm machine guns to light cannon. The vehicles usually have a three-man crew, with space for water, rations, radio and navigation equipment, and enough fuel to give an operational range of 650km.

The choice of weapons available includes the 7.62mm GPMG, the 7.62mm M60 machine gun, the 0.5in Browning machine gun, the 7.62mm chain gun, or 20 and 30mm cannon. There is a GPMG mounting in front of the commander's seat, next to the driver. In addition, twin GPMGs or a single heavier calibre gun can be mounted on the back of the vehicle.

A camouflage netting roll is strapped to the front end of the bonnet and the side, allowing the vehicle to be rapidly covered. All vehicles are fitted with a special belly plate beneath the cab for protection against mine attack. Sand channels and spare wheels are mounted on the side and back of the

vehicle. All Land Rovers can be fitted inside the fuselage of C-130 Hercules aircraft or slung beneath a medium-lift helicopter.

The following data applies to the current Remote Area Patrol Vehicle variant.

Length: 4.43m
Width: 1.79m
Height: 2m
Ground clearance: 215mm
Wheelbase: 2.79m
Maximum road speed: 120km/hr
Engine: Rover V-8 petrol 3.5 litre, 134bhp at 5000rpm
Transmission: manual, 5 forward, 1 reverse

(SEE *C-130; 'Pink Panther'*)

LANE, CORPORAL MICHAEL 'BRONCO' SAS soldier who, along with Sergeant John 'Brummie' Stokes, reached the summit of Mount Everest in late April 1976. Both men suffered grievously during their descent from the peak, losing several toes through frostbite. Lane went on to serve in

Northern Ireland where he was awarded a Military Medal.

'LARKSWOOD', OPERATION Conducted by two squadrons of the Belgian Independent Parachute Company (5 SAS), commanded by Captain Blondeel, between 3 April and 8 May 1945. The Belgians were used as reconnaissance troops, initially by Canadian II Corps and, later, by the Polish Armoured Division. As the Canadians advanced into northeast Holland, the SAS, mounted on 40 jeeps, raced ahead. However, the terrain was hard-going for jeeps as it was criss-crossed by dykes and canals. Nevertheless, the SAS did manage to capture several bridges and relieve some of the 'Amherst' parties which had not been reached by the Canadians. The Belgians, in the face of determined resistance, took heavy casualties.

Pushing on into Germany, the Belgians then acted as spearhead troops for the Polish Armoured Division up to the end of the war in Europe. Though 'Larkswood' was moderately successful, it was indicative of how higher Allied command often misused the SAS as forward reconnaissance forces rather than as raiders hitting targets deep behind the lines.

(SEE *'Amherst', Operation; Blondeel, Captain; Northwest Europe*)

LASER AIMING SYSTEMS Mounted on weapons and for use in low and artificial light conditions, these systems work by bringing a laser spot to bear on to the desired point of aim. The SAS employ such devices for counter-terrorist work, especially hostage-rescue operations, which often require firing from the hip against fleeting targets in low light conditions, and in the field for night fighting.

Visible laser aiming systems, in which the operator does not have to wear night vision goggles or other infra-red sensitive equipment, are used by assault team members during hostage-rescue operations. There are many models available, most of which can be fitted to handguns, rifles, sub-machine guns and shotguns. The Imatronic LS45 laser sight, for example, can be fitted to a Remington 870 pump-action shotgun. All the firer has to do is sight the laser spot on the target. Hensoldt's aiming point projector throws a narrow beam of light on to the target. In the middle of the beam is a small black area which resembles a black dot, the aiming mark. More traditional aiming devices include the Law Enforcement International LE-100 laser aiming sight which focuses a red aiming dot on to the target. Visible to the naked eye, the dot has a 60mm diameter at a 50m range and can be fitted to Heckler & Koch submachine guns.

Non-visible laser beam sights, usually employed by counter-terrorist snipers and for field use, include Optic Electric Corporation's AN/PAQ-4 laser aiming light. Designed for anti-terrorist work, special forces and jungle warfare, it can only be used with night vision goggles or other infra-red sensitive equipment.

The same is true of Pilkington's Laser Target Indicator which projects a spot of light out to ranges of up to 500m. The operator must be wearing image intensifying goggles to see the beam. International Technologies' AIM-1DLR long-range laser aiming light projects a beam up to a range of 3km. Designed to be used on long-range light weapons, it too requires the operator to be wearing night vision goggles.

(SEE *Sniper Sights*)

LASSEN, MAJOR ANDERS Danish member of the SAS and the Special Boat Squadron during World War II. Lassen joined the British Army at the outbreak of hostilities and underwent commando training before joining the Small Scale Raiding Force. In May 1943, he transferred to the Middle East as a member of D Squadron, 1 SAS, which became part of the Special Boat Squadron. The Dane quickly gained a reputation as a tough, hard-fighting type and was present at many classic SBS opera-

tions, including the June 1943 raids on the Greek islands of Crete and Simi. In 1944 Lassen was involved in missions in Italy, the Adriatic and Greece. The following year he was again in action in Italy when he was killed in action as he attempted to destroy a series of German pill-boxes alongside the waters of Lake Comacchio (April 1945). It was for his bravery at Comacchio that Lassen won the VC.

(SEE *Special Boat Squadron*)

'LAST LIGHT' SAS term meaning dusk or sundown.

LAW Light anti-armour weapon.
(SEE *LAW 80; M72*)

LAW 80 Designed as a replacement for the M72, LAW 80 is a one-shot short-range British light anti-tank weapon (LAW). Though designed primarily for use by conventional infantry against armoured vehicles in a large-scale battle scenario, LAW 80, because of its weight and lethality,

Below: Major Anders Lassen (standing) was awarded a posthumous VC for his actions at Lake Comacchio in April 1945. Though mortally wounded by small-arms fire, Lassen still managed to throw grenades to cover his comrades' retreat.

will be used by the SAS.
  Calibre: 94mm
  Weight: 10kg
  Length: 1m (folded); 1.5m
  (extended)
  Effective range: 20-500m
  Armour penetration: in excess of
  700mm
(SEE *M72*)

LAYCOCK, BRIGADIER ROBERT
(SEE *Layforce*)

LAYFORCE A Commando brigade
assigned to General Wavell's Middle
Eastern Army in 1941. Commanded
and named after Brigadier Robert
Laycock, it was tasked with exploiting
the success of Major-General
O'Connor's North African offensive
against the Italian Tenth Army
(December 1940 to February 1941) by
seizing the island of Rhodes. Layforce
was composed of three Commandos,
including No 8 which contained
David Stirling, the SAS's founder,
and numbered 2000 men.

  It was, however, hampered by a
chronic shortage of manpower and
equipment and, following Rommel's
appearance in North Africa in
February 1941 and the German offensive in the Balkans, Layforce was split
up. One part under Laycock fought in
Crete, another was based around
Tobruk and the third – including No
8 Commando – was sent to Syria.
The latter was used to mount raids on
the Cyrenaican coast. Three large-
scale operations were launched but
only one was successful. The failure
of the operations prompted David
Stirling to devise new ways of hitting
enemy rear areas without committing
great numbers of ships or men – these
ideas would lead directly to the establishment of the SAS. Layforce itself
was disbanded because its men and
ships were needed elsewhere.
(SEE *North Africa; Stirling, Lieutenant-
Colonel David*)

L DETACHMENT The Special Air
Service started life in July 1941 as L

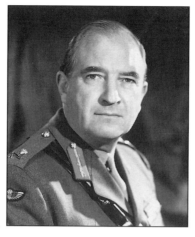

*Above: Lieutenant-General George Lea
led the SAS in Malaya from 1955.*

Detachment, SAS Brigade. HQ
Middle East devised this name in an
attempt to deceive German intelligence into thinking that a whole new
airborne brigade had been formed. In
fact, the 'brigade' numbered 67 men
who had been recruited from
Layforce.
(SEE *Layforce; North Africa; Special
Air Service*)

LEA, LIEUTENANT-GENERAL
GEORGE Commander of 22 SAS in
Malaya. Lea took charge of the
Regiment in January 1955, instilling a
new sense of professionalism and
gathering together a cadre of experienced or dynamic young officers.
Later, Lea was the overall Director of
Operations in Borneo, where he was
able to renew his acquaintance with
the Regiment during the final stages
of the campaign.
(SEE *Borneo; Malaya*)

LEAD SCOUT The soldier responsible
for taking the 'point' (lead) at the
front of an SAS four-man patrol's line
of advance. 'Point' requires great skill
and alertness as the individual has to
navigate while at the same time move
like lightning in the event of a surprise contact with enemy forces. Traditionally lead scouts have been armed

*Above: The Longline Light Strike
Vehicle saw service with the SAS during the 1991 Gulf War. Unconfirmed
reports state that several vehicles suffered mechanical faults.*

with weapons that allow them to lay
down heavy suppressive fire if
required, such as semi-automatic shotguns (specially useful in jungle terrain), rifles fitted with grenade
launchers, or light machine guns.
(SEE *Head-on Contact Drill*)

LEWES BOMB Named after its inventor, Lieutenant 'Jock' Lewes, the Lewes bomb was a simple, effective way of destroying enemy aircraft on the ground. It consisted of half a kilo of plastic explosive rolled in a mixture of thermite from an incendiary bomb and old engine oil. It was detonated by means of a time pencil and detonator which were carried separately on the approach to the target. The time pencil consisted of different strengths of acid, which ate through a wire connected to the plunger of the detonator at different rates. This gave a time delay of anything from 10 minutes to two hours or longer. Lewes bombs were employed to great effect by the SAS in North Africa.

(SEE *Lewes, Lieutenant John Steel 'Jock'; North Africa*)

LEWES, LIEUTENANT JOHN STEEL 'JOCK' Stalwart of L Detachment in the early days of the campaign in North Africa during World War II, after he volunteered for the SAS while serving in Layforce's No 8 Commando. Lewes took part in the Detachment's early actions: the first disastrous jump in November 1941, the raid on Agheila (14 December) and Nofilia (26 December). During the latter operation, Lewes was killed during a strafing run by Italian aircraft. His death was a great loss. Lewes was an able and practical officer: he was able to 'acquire' parachutes for early SAS training

101

Above: The Light Support Weapon is essentially a heavy-barrelled version of the SA-80. A replacement for the GPMG, it has now entered British Army service.

programmes, he invented the highly practical Lewes bomb and he had a cool head in action.
(SEE *Agheila; Layforce; L Detachment; Lewes bomb; Nofilia*)

LIGHT STRIKE VEHICLE Fast attack vehicle designed and built by the British company Longline. Used by the SAS during the 1991 Gulf War, the Light Strike Vehicle (LSV) is a high mobility vehicle designed for special forces operations in hostile environments. The 'dune buggy' design has several attributes which make it attractive for clandestine missions: it is easy to conceal; it can use small tracks and access points unlike larger vehicles such as the Land Rover; and it can be manhandled by its crew if it gets stuck. In addition, its open frame construction and low silhouette give it a reduced radar and thermal signature. The LSV also presents a harder target to hit than the larger, slower special forces jeeps. It can be equipped with a number of armaments as it has a weapon mounting platform which can accommodate all calibres up to a 20mm cannon. Future variants will also be equipped with anti-tank weapon firing mounts

for Milan or TOW systems.
Crew: two
Range: 200km
Payload: 500kg
Passengers: none, though an additional load of up to 12 troops can be carried in emergencies
(SEE *Gulf War*)

LIGHT SUPPORT WEAPON Designed as a replacement for the GPMG, the LSW is both lighter and has a higher muzzle velocity. In addition, 80 per cent of its parts are interchangeable with the SA-80 (as the LSW is essentially a heavy-barrelled version) and both weapons can take the same magazines. These qualities make the LSW attractive for long-range Special Air Service missions.
Type: machine gun
Designation: L86A1
Calibre: 5.56mm
Weight: 6.58kg
Length: 900mm
Effective range: 1000m
Rate of fire: 700-850 rounds per minute (cyclic)
Feed: 30-round box magazine
Muzzle velocity: 970 metres per second
(SEE *GPMG*)

Above: North Africa, World War II. Long Range Patrol Group trucks prepare to move out. The LRDG and SAS worked together during 1941-42.

LILLICO, SERGEANT EDDIE 'GEORDIE' Renowned jungle fighter who played a prominent part in SAS 'Claret' cross-border raids during the war in Borneo. On one patrol in February 1965, Lillico and his party from D Squadron, 22 SAS, were ambushed and he was badly wounded in the legs. Lillico spent the next two days avoiding the enemy as he crawled to a helicopter rendezvous. For his coolness under fire, Lillico was awarded the Military Medal.
(SEE *Borneo; 'Claret' Operations*)

LLOYD-OWEN, CAPTAIN DAVID

During the early stages of the war in North Africa, Lloyd-Owen commanded B Squadron of the Long Range Desert Group (LRDG), and it was during one mission that he met the founder of the SAS, David Stirling (who had just returned from the SAS's failed first mission). In discussions, the two men worked out a system by which the LRDG would transport the SAS teams to and from their targets, thereby doing away with the dangerous and frequently inaccurate parachute drops that the SAS had employed.

(SEE *'Crusader', Operation; Long Range Desert Group; North Africa; Stirling, Lieutenant-Colonel David*)

LMG Light machine gun.

(SEE *Bren Gun; Light Support Weapon*)

'LONG DRAG' Another name for 'Fan Dance'.

(SEE *'Fan Dance'*)

LONG RANGE DESERT GROUP

British reconnaissance and intelligence gathering unit raised on 3 July 1940 which had its antecedents in the inter-war period. During World War I, the British Army in the Middle East employed Light Car Patrols against Senussi tribesmen, and Major Ralph Bagnold of the Royal Corps of Signals, with some colleagues, had undertaken a series of desert journeys throughout the 1920s and 1930s

which had solved most of the problems of living and travelling in the desert. Bagnold wrote a paper on the possible use of a desert reconnaissance force, though GHQ Middle East initially rejected the idea.

When Italy declared war on 10 June 1940, the British Army's most pressing need in North Africa was for intelligence concerning the enemy's intentions. Bagnold was given his chance. The Provisional War Establishment of the Long Range Desert Group (LRDG), authorised in July 1940, called for a unit of 11 officers and 76 men. However, in November 1940 it was decided to double the strength of the group to 21 officers and 271 men, divided between headquarters and two squadrons. Each squadron consisted of three patrols transported in 10 vehicles (open-topped Chevrolet trucks). By March 1942 the LRDG numbered 25 officers and 324 other ranks.

The LRDG's activities varied, but were mostly concerned with recon-naissance, intelligence gathering, pathfinding and courier work. Operations might include elements of all of these tasks, and every mission

tended to be characterised by long periods of boredom punctuated by short bursts of violent action. Reconnaissance and intelligence gath-ering were vital tasks, involving long cross-country drives to pinpoint enemy bases and positions, or 'road watches' to monitor the movement of enemy units. Direct action against the enemy caused the Italians a great deal of anxiety in areas they believed to be secure from attack. The LRDG also

weakened the Italian war effort by forcing the enemy to divert men and aircraft from the front.

The SAS used LRDG transpor-tation to and from enemy targets dur-ing late 1941 and early 1942. This was a consequence of a meeting between David Stirling, the SAS's founder, and Captain David Lloyd-Owen, an LRDG patrol commander, after the disastrous Special Air Service opera-tion in the Gazala area in mid-

November 1941. The relationship blossomed, though SAS activities provoked a greater enemy reaction and made the LRDG's task more difficult.

In March 1943, the LRDG was withdrawn to Cairo to re-equip for operations in Greece, Italy and Yugoslavia. When the war in Europe ended Lloyd-Owen, now the LRDG's commander, made a plea for the unit not to be disbanded. However, the Long Range Desert Group, which

Left: The RUC station at Loughall photographed after the SAS ambush.

had turned in five splendid years of service, officially ceased to exist in June 1945.

(SEE *Lloyd-Owen, Captain David; North Africa*)

'LOST', OPERATION Conducted between 23 June and 18 July 1944 by seven men of 4 French Parachute Battalion (4 SAS) commanded by Major Carey Elwes. They were parachuted into Brittany, France, to establish contact with the 'Dingson' party, also from 4 SAS. Contact was made on 30 June. The subsequent large-scale operations conducted in the Brittany area resulted in large numbers of *Maquis* being armed and over 2000 casualties being inflicted on the enemy. More importantly, the Germans were forced to divert large numbers of troops against the French and away from the main Allied forces in Normandy.

(SEE *'Dingson', Operation;* Maquis; *Northwest Europe*)

LOUGHALL Location of a successful SAS ambush in May 1987 in which eight Irish Republican Army (IRA) terrorists were killed. The IRA had, in late 1986 and early 1987, intensified their campaign against the security forces in Northern Ireland. This had resulted in the security forces themselves being put on a higher state of alert. Surveillance was increased on known and suspected terrorists, and the intelligence agencies in Ulster were searching for any sensitive information that would indicate possible future targets. Attacks on police stations had been a favourite terrorist tactic (there had been 22 such attacks prior to Loughall).

In 1986, a mechanical digger with a large bomb in its bucket had been used in an attack on a Royal Ulster Constabulary (RUC) station at The Birches, County Armagh. In April 1987, another JCB was stolen in East

Tyrone, indicating another such attack was being planned. The digger was subsequently discovered at a derelict farm 16km from Loughall. It was put under immediate observation by the RUC's surveillance unit, E4A, who witnessed explosives being taken to the farm. The security forces had seemingly identified the vehicle and the probable target, but had no idea of the date. The latter was supplied by the IRA itself, as the RUC intercepted a phonecall made by one of their operatives concerning the timing of the attack: 8 May.

SAS soldiers and RUC snipers moved into the deserted police station, and other SAS men were deployed in the surrounding countryside to prevent the escape of any of the terrorists. The plan was to spring a box-type ambush on the IRA. Once the latter were in the trap there would be no way out.

The terrorists, two Active Service Units of the East Tyrone Brigade – eight men in all – had carefully thought out their plan. There were three men on the JCB as it lumbered into Loughall from the Portadown side, a driver and two armed guards. The large bomb was situated in its bucket. The terrorists had stolen a blue Toyota van earlier in the day, this too would be used in the attack.

At 1920 hours, the digger crashed through the perimeter fence of the police station. The occupants of the van had already piled out and were spraying rifle and machine-gun fire into the building. The three men on the digger made a run for the van which was waiting on the road. The SAS and RUC opened fire on the van and the terrorists almost immediately. The bomb then detonated, demolishing a large part of the building and throwing debris over the surrounding area. The terrorists, all dressed in blue boilersuits, were surprised by the ambush and attempted to escape in the van. Four were killed in the van and four more in the open; the action was over in seconds.

Meanwhile, a white Citroen car with two brothers inside inadvertently drove into the area of the ambush. The SAS cover squad, seeing their blue boilersuits and believing them to be terrorists, opened fire, killing one and seriously injuring the other. Anthony Hughes, the dead motorist, had no links with the IRA.

Immediately after the ambush was triggered, British Army helicopters and RUC roadblocks were activated to scour the area around Loughall for any surviving terrorists. The SAS soldiers themselves, after ensuring there was no longer a threat, were evacuated by helicopter. The Special Air Service had just completed its most successful operation to date in Northern Ireland.

The IRA was stunned by this blow. Eight of its top operatives had been killed on one mission, it was its worst defeat since the 1920s. The months that followed Loughall indicated that the Republican movement was reeling. The IRA suspected a mole in its ranks and, though this was never proved, the organisation was riven with doubt and suspicion. In addition, Sinn Fein, the political wing of the IRA, suffered badly in the British general election held in June 1987, gaining no more than 11 per cent of the vote (it fared much worse in the February elections in Eire).

However, on Remembrance Day 1987, the IRA reached its lowest ebb. One of its bombs exploded during the ceremony in the town of Enniskillen, Northern Ireland, killing many innocent civilians. It was an atrocity that attracted worldwide condemnation. After this outrage the IRA desperately needed a victory against the British government. Its attention eventually focused on Gibraltar, a 'soft' target which was regarded as a symbol of British imperialism. Therefore preparations were made to form an Active Service Unit to undertake a bombing mission. The plans were conducted in the utmost secrecy; this time there would be no mistakes. What the IRA

did not realise was that the British were alert to the possibility of revenge for Loughall. The next meeting between the IRA and the SAS would result in another victory for the latter. (SEE *Active Service Unit; E4A; Gibraltar; Irish Republican Army; Northern Ireland*)

'LOYTON', OPERATION Codename for an operation carried out by 91 men of 2 SAS in the Vosges, eastern France. Tasked by Supreme Headquarters Allied Expeditionary Force (SHAEF) to gather intelligence on enemy road and rail movements, attack enemy installations and cooperate with the local *Maquis*, an advance SAS party, accompanied by a Phantom patrol and a Jedburgh team, parachuted in on 12 August. More drops took place in the days following, including the leader of the party, Lieutenant-Colonel Franks.

The timing of the operation was, however, unfortunate. The Germans at the time had abandoned the idea of making a stand west of Paris and had decided to hold the crests of the Vosges and the east bank of the River Moselle. Consequently, the area that the SAS dropped into was swarming with enemy troops. Worse, the Germans had two Gestapo HQs in the area, at Nancy and Strasbourg, each with its own anti-partisan unit.

Once on the ground the SAS teams met with varying success. Although they did cause some damage to the enemy, the large number of German forces in the area limited their freedom. The local *Maquis* units were also a cause for concern as they contained many traitors. The local population, on the other hand, proved friendly and helpful, though they paid for their cooperation. The village of Moussey, for example, was occupied by a large force of Germans, who rounded up all the men between 16 and 60 years of age and took them to concentration camps. Of the 210 taken, only 70 returned after the war.

Franks terminated the operation on

9 October as the party was short of supplies and the weather had closed in, making aerial supply impossible. He ordered his men to make their way back to Allied lines. For limited results 'Loyton' cost the SAS two dead and 31 captured, all of whom were executed by the Gestapo. (SEE *Franks, Lieutenant-Colonel Brian; Jedburgh Teams;* Maquis; *Northwest Europe; Phantom*)

LRRP Long-range reconnaissance patrol. LRRP troops, such as the SAS and US Rangers, are trained to operate for long periods with little or no support. They work in small groups of between four and six men mostly behind enemy lines, and are equipped with long-range communications equipment. Their task is to provide a continuous and accurate stream of intelligence on enemy movements, strengths, locations of HQs, supply depots and airfields. They are not primarily combat troops, rather they are observers who are highly skilled in fieldcraft. Their skill is in avoiding the enemy while at the same time collecting their intelligence.

LS Landing site. Generally used by the SAS to indicate an aircraft landing strip.

LUP Lying-up position. General term applied to any position occupied by a patrol either prior to an operation, or for sleeping overnight. SAS LUPs are always well concealed.

'LURPS' Term for long-range reconnaissance troops. (SEE *LRRP*)

LUTTENSEE (SEE *Mountain and Winter Warfare School*)

LYNX (SEE *AH-7*)

LZ Landing zone. Used by the SAS to indicate a helicopter landing area.

M

M16 One of the most successful assault rifles ever built. Used extensively by the SAS in Borneo, the Middle East, Northern Ireland and the Falklands, as well as in the 1991 Gulf War. Capable of semi- or full-automatic fire as well as three-round bursts, an additional advantage of the weapon is that an M203 grenade launcher can be fitted beneath the barrel. This results in a significant force multiplier. M16s and M203s were used to devastating effect during the SAS raid upon the Argentinian air base on Pebble Island during the 1982 Falklands War.

Type: assault rifle
Designation: M16A2
Calibre: 5.56mm
Weight: 3.72kg
Effective range: 500m
Rate of fire: 950 rounds per minute (cyclic)
Feed: 20- or 30-round box magazine
Muzzle velocity: 991 metres per second
(SEE *Falkland Islands; Gulf War; M203; Pebble Island*)

M72 A lightweight, one man, throwaway light anti-tank weapon (LAW). Easy to sight and fire, the high explosive anti-tank (HEAT) warhead is

Below: The M16, one of the most successful assault rifles ever built.

Above: Lightweight and compact, the M72 LAW packs a powerful punch.

extremely effective against most tanks and soft-skinned vehicles. Because of its size, the M72 is particularly favoured by the SAS for raids and sabotage missions.

Type: one-shot anti-tank weapon
Designation: M72A2
Calibre: 66mm
Weight: 2.36kg (complete assembly)
Length: 655mm (closed); 893mm (extended)
Effective range: 150mm (moving targets); 300m (stationary targets)
Feed: single-shot and discard
Muzzle velocity: 145 metres per second
Armour penetration: up to 300mm

M79 This US-made single-shot, breech-loading, break-open, shoulder-fired grenade launcher was widely used by SAS soldiers during the 1960s, before being replaced by the M203 in the early 1970s.

Type: grenade launcher
Calibre: 40mm
Weight: 2.95kg (loaded); 2.72kg (unloaded)
Length: 737mm

Right: The M203 grenade launcher, seen here attached to an M16 rifle.

Effective range: 350m (area targets); 150m (point targets)
Muzzle velocity: 76 metres per second
(SEE *M203*)

M203 The M203 is a lightweight, single-shot, breech-loaded, shoulder-fired weapon designed for attachment to the M16 rifle. A replacement for the M79, it fulfils the requirement for

an effective rifle/grenade launcher package. The firepower thus encompassed in one weapon makes it extremely attractive for special forces operations. The M16/M203 combination was used by the SAS during the Pebble Island raid in the Falklands.

Type: grenade launcher
Calibre: 40mm
Weight: 1.36kg (unloaded); 1.63kg (loaded)
Length: 394mm
Effective range: 350m
Feed: breech-loading, sliding barrel
Muzzle velocity: 75 metres per second
(SEE *M79; Pebble Island*)

MACLEAN, CAPTAIN FITZROY On the outbreak of war, Maclean resigned as an MP, joined the Cameron Highlanders and ended up in the Middle East where he was persuaded by David Stirling to join the SAS. In late May 1942, Maclean took part in an unsuccessful attempt to attack enemy shipping in Benghazi harbour and was badly injured returning from the mission. In late 1942, he left the SAS to lead a special operation in Persia: the kidnap of a pro-Axis general. Maclean succeeded in his task and was recalled to the Middle East,

where he joined the Special Boat Squadron in March 1943. In July of that year, however, he was chosen to head the Allied Military Mission to Yugoslavia where he helped coordinate the operations of Tito's partisans. (SEE *Benghazi; M Detachment; Special Air Service; Special Boat Squadron; Stirling, Lieutenant-Colonel David*)

MCLEAN, TROOPER TOM Member of 22 SAS who rowed singlehanded across the Atlantic in 1969. In 1982, he established another record by sailing across the Atlantic in the smallest recorded vessel, the 3m-long *Giltspur*.

MCLEOD, GENERAL RODERICK 'RODDY' Took charge of the SAS Brigade for operations in northwest Europe in January 1944, just prior to D-Day. McLeod did much to turn the brigade into an efficient and effective force, but was frequently at loggerheads with his superiors who did not understand the true military role of the SAS, i.e. its role was strategic not tactical. McLeod had to fight to identify suitable missions for the brigade and prevent its premature disbandment. In March 1945, he left to become Director of Military Operations in India; his replacement was Brigadier Mike Calvert.

Below: Fitzroy Maclean was honorary colonel of 23 SAS between 1984-88.

Above Tom McLean conquered the Atlantic Ocean in 1969.

(SEE *Calvert, Brigadier Mike; Northwest Europe; Special Air Service*)

MALAYA Prior to World War II, the British-dominated Malay peninsula had been divided into the Straits Settlements, the Federated Malay States and a group of unfederated but protected states on the Thai border. The Japanese occupation (1942-45) stimulated nationalist sentiment in the region which the British tried to accommodate in 1948 by setting up a 'Federation of Malaya'. This composed Johore, Kedah, Kelantan, Labuan, Malacca, Negeri Sembilan, Penang, Perlis, and Selangor and Trengganu (Singapore enjoyed separate status). In 1940, the population of the peninsula consisted of some 2,600,000 Malays, 2,100,000 Chinese, 602,000 Indians and a few thousand whites.

The Chinese minority resented Malay dominance of the Federation and some Chinese communists turned to violence in an attempt to right their grievances. Attacks on estate owners and rubber planters by the Malayan Races Liberation Army (MRLA) began in June 1948. The British authorities, in reply, proclaimed a state of emergency and organised a military response.

At the beginning of the campaign, the MRLA's bases were situated only a few hours' walking distance from the Chinese settlements which provided the bulk of the movement's recruits and food. When the 'Briggs Plan' was put into effect (General Sir Harold Briggs was the Director of Operations) – relocating villagers to more easily defendable positions – the MRLA bases were effectively cut off from their supply sources. The Communist Terrorists (CTs) were thus forced to retreat into the jungle interior and grow their own food in clearings. They were pursued by British Army and Commonwealth units, assisted by Iban trackers who had been brought in from Borneo. However, as the CTs retreated ever deeper into the jungle, it became apparent that a deep-penetration unit was needed which could remain in the jungle for longer than three weeks at a time (the maximum period thought possible for regular troops).

In 1950, Lieutenant-Colonel 'Mad' Mike Calvert, a veteran of the Chindit campaigns in Burma who had ended the war in Europe as commander of the SAS Brigade, was commissioned by General Harding, Commander-in-Chief Far East Land Forces, to write a report on all aspects of the war in Malaya. After six months of working with police and Army units, and conducting lone reconnaissance marches, he submitted his report. The study formed the basis of the 'Briggs Plan', but it also recommended the formation of a special counter-insurgency force which would live, move and fight the guerrillas in the jungle. Later that year, the Malayan Scouts was formed under the command of Calvert himself. He established a training base at Johore and set up an Intelligence Section under the leadership of Major John Woodhouse.

Calvert's plans envisaged his unit winning over the Aborigines who inhabited the jungle. This was the beginning of the SAS's 'hearts and minds' concept, although the phrase

Above: SAS troops conducting a search for MRLA guerrillas in the Trengganu region of eastern Malaya.

itself was first used by General Templer, who became British High Commissioner in 1952. He stated: 'The answer lies not in pouring more soldiers into the jungle, but rests in the hearts and minds of the Malayan people.' By November 1950, the Scouts were operating against the CTs in the Ipoh area, with three- or four-man patrols laying ambushes and giving medical aid to the Aborigines when possible. One patrol spent 103 consecutive days in the jungle, fully vindicating Calvert's beliefs. The patrolling, often involving other Army and colonial units, continued into 1951.

In June 1951, the Scouts were operating in the Johore area, working with the security forces on the edge of the jungle. Calvert was invalided home in November 1951 and replaced by Lieutenant-Colonel John Sloane. The Scouts were then assigned a more regular mission: assisting the Malay Police Force in defending the jungle forts which had been built to protect the relocated villagers.

The Scouts were back in the jungle again in February 1952, after the art of 'tree-jumping' had been devised. This involved troopers parachuting into the jungle canopy and then descending by rope to the jungle floor. A total of 54 men jumped into the jungle as part of an operation against CTs in the Belum Valley near the Thai border. It was a combined operation involving Gurkhas, Royal Marines, two SAS squadrons and police units. Although this particular mission was not successful, the deep-penetration patrols continued. Between November and December 1952, numerous patrols were conducted in Negri Sembilan in cooperation with Gurkha and Fijian infantry, resulting in the deaths of 16 terrorists.

In 1952, 22 SAS was formed in Malaya from the Malayan Scouts, and consisted of an HQ and four squadrons. In the autumn Woodhouse returned to Britain to establish a base at the Airborne Forces Depot, Aldershot, which would train replacements for the SAS. In late 1955 he returned to Malaya with a new squadron. Led by Major Dudley Coventry, it was made up of men drawn from the three regular battalions of the Parachute Regiment. In December the Rhodesian Squadron, the volunteers that had comprised C Squadron, Malayan Scouts, returned home, to be replaced by a New Zealand Squadron. A third of the latter were Maoris who were adept at establishing contact with the Aborigines.

As the jungle patrols continued, the SAS began to acquire the necessary skills to survive in the hostile terrain. Life on operations was invariably grim; clothes were always soaked with rain or sweat, and it was mostly dark and damp below the jungle canopy. As well as the ever-present threat of enemy ambush or booby traps, the patrols had to contend with hostile wildlife: tigers, elephants, snakes, water buffalo, hornets and mosquitoes. In addition, leeches were everywhere, although they were particularly dense in the Kerbau Valley. On active service each man usually carried field dressings, maps, a compass, rifle, grenades, machete and

water bottle. SAS patrols were trained to move through the jungle at a very slow speed, so as not to miss any signs of the enemy. Though they employed Iban trackers brought in from Borneo, some SAS soldiers themselves became expert trackers, men such as Sergeant Turnbull, who spoke fluent Malay and who once tracked a group of terrorists for 14 weeks. Others included Sergeant McFarland, Sergeant Hawkins and Sergeant Creighton.

The SAS soon learnt to avoid jungle tracks which could be mined or ambushed. They acquired the skills to navigate accurately through the dark-ened jungle and, most importantly, they earned the trust of the Aborigines. The 'hearts and minds' policy effectively cut the terrorists off from their sources of food and intelligence. The troopers treated the natives, many of whom had never seen a white man, with respect and caution. In particular, they stayed well clear of the native women. As Major Dare Newell stated: 'When dealing with guerrillas ignore their women folk like poison; the women might not appreciate it but the men will.'

Aircraft, both the fixed-wing variety and helicopters, were invaluable to the SAS in Malaya. RAF Valettas and

Beverleys dropped supplies and men, and S51 helicopters evacuated wounded troops. By 1956, 22 SAS had a strength of 560 men, divided between A, B, D, the New Zealand and Parachute Squadrons and a Regiment HQ.

From April 1956, the New Zealand Squadron undertook two 13-week operations on the Perak-Kelantan border which resulted in the destruction of the communist *Asa* (Aborigine) Organisation and the death of the gang's notorious leader, Ah Ming. In May, B Squadron commenced a 14-week operation which resulted in the location of a large store of enemy crops. Later, in August, a patrol of 17 Troop, D Squadron, killed four terrorists in the Perak-Kelantan border area. One of the patrol, Sergeant Turnbull, was awarded the Military Medal for his gallantry.

By 1958 the conflict had almost been won. The last major SAS operation, conducted in the spring of 1958, was by D Squadron, led by Major H. Thompson, in the swamp near Telok Anson. The targets were two groups of CTs under the leadership of Ah Hoi, nicknamed 'Baby Killer'. Two troops of the squadron were parachuted in west of the swamp while the other two and the small HQ were ready to act once the terrorists were located. For 10 days the SAS troopers patrolled the stinking swamp, immersed all day in water as they searched. They eventually found an enemy camp six kilometres into the swamp, then radioed Thompson to put the other two troops in from the east. A cordon was placed around the area, but it took another 10 days before the trap was sprung. Eventually 10 CTs, including Ah Hoi himself, surrendered. The operation was an excellent example of SAS tracking skills.

Earlier, in 1957, the Regiment was affected by the British Army reforms, being reduced to just two squadrons and an HQ. However, in 1958 the Army Council had stated that there

was a long-term future for the SAS. The unit had not won the war (more than 100,000 British soldiers served in Malaya), but it had made a significant contribution. Templer's 'hearts and minds' campaign in the towns and villages had been won by the administration and security forces, in the jungle it was won by the SAS. The latter had also trained Aborigines, four sections being formed at the end of 1956. Within a year the *Senoi Pra'ak* (Fighting People) had three squadrons, each with 12 five-man sections. In helping to win the war in Malaya, the SAS had also assured its own future.

(SEE *Ah Hoi; Ah Poy; Beverley; 'Briggs Plan'; Calvert, Brigadier Mike; Communist Terrorist; Coventry, Major Dudley; 'Hearts and Minds'; Johore; Malayan Races Liberation Army; Malayan Scouts; Newell, Major Dare; 'Tree-jumping'; Valetta; Woodhouse, Lieutenant-Colonel John*)

MALAYAN RACES LIBERATION ARMY

Military wing of the mainly Chinese Malayan Communist Party (MCP). Conducted a terrorist campaign against the British in Malaya (1948-60). During World War II, the British had encouraged and armed the MCP's Malayan People's Anti-Japanese Army (MPAJA) to fight the Japanese occupiers. After the war many weapons were hidden in secret caches, later to be unearthed and used against the British.

The MRLA, led by Chin Peng, wanted an end to British rule in Malaya and to redress the balance of power in the country in favour of the Chinese. The guerrillas operated from camps on the fringes of the thick jungle which covered three-quarters of the country. At its height in 1951, the MRLA had 8000 guerrillas supported by around 60,000 *Min Yuen* (People's Movement) who operated in the villages and squatter camps. They provided food, money and intelligence for the guerrillas. Further support, given freely or under duress, was provided

by the approximately 500,000 rural Chinese.

Following the successful implementation of the 'Briggs Plan', the guerrillas, called Communist Terrorists (CTs), moved ever-deeper into the jungle, pursued by regular and SAS units. Because of the operations conducted by the security forces, including the SAS, and the social and economic policies of the British administration – not least the plans for accelerated independence – the MRLA had, by mid-1958, been reduced to around 1000 men. Though they were determined fighters, the guerrillas failed to convince the mainly non-Chinese villagers that they would benefit under Chinese communist rule. The 'hearts and minds' campaign waged by the administration in the urban areas and the SAS in the jungle encouraged this belief and was to lead to the eventual British victory over the MRLA.

(SEE *Chin Peng; Communist Terrorist; 'Briggs Plan'; 'Hearts and Minds'; Malaya*)

MALAYAN SCOUTS

British military unit raised by Lieutenant-Colonel Mike Calvert in 1950 to fight communist guerrillas in Malaya. The Scouts were a special counter-insurgency force trained to live and fight in the jungle in small groups of three or four men. As Calvert stated: 'The fewer you are, the more frightened you are, therefore, the more cautious you are and, therefore, the more silent you are. You are more likely to see the enemy before he will be able to see you.'

The unit had an original strength of 100 men, with Calvert selecting the officers personally. Training was to emphasise self-reliance, initiative and self-confidence, as well as winning over the Aborigines who lived in the jungle. A Squadron was formed from local volunteers, some of whom had seen service in World War II with SOE or Force 136. The training base was at Johore, though the Scouts were

Above: On patrol in Malaya. The Malayan Scouts and, later, the SAS were to prove that British soldiers could operate in the jungle for long periods.

called upon almost immediately to fight in the Ipoh area, 450km to the north. They were sent into the jungle to lay ambushes and direct RAF bomb strikes. Although they achieved some success, their general indiscipline and raucous behaviour left much to be desired. This was a consequence of the extremely short training period, three weeks in some cases. Nevertheless, the foundations of an effective unit had been laid.

B Squadron was made up of members of 21 SAS and reservists from other World War II special forces units who had come together in a temporary unit called M Squadron. Originally earmarked for service in

the Korean War, they were despatched to Singapore, then to Malaya. These men, unlike A Squadron, were extremely well disciplined. C Squadron was formed from Rhodesian volunteers after Calvert had made a quick visit to the country.

After Calvert left Malaya in 1951, his successor, Lieutenant-Colonel John Sloane, with help from John Woodhouse and Dare Newell, tightened up discipline in the Malayan Scouts, a move which led to the force becoming more professional. By 1952 the success of the Scouts had paved the way for the creation of 22 SAS.
(SEE *Calvert, Brigadier Mike; Force 136; Korean War; Newell, Major*

Dare; Malaya; Sloane, Lieutenant-Colonel John; SOE; Woodhouse, Lieutenant-Colonel John)

MALVERN Until 1960, the location of the main barracks of 22 SAS in Britain. Called Bradbury Lines, it was located at Merebrook Camp, Malvern, Worcestershire. It was then moved to Hereford.
(SEE *Bradbury Lines; Stirling Lines*)

'MAPLE', OPERATION Codename for a mission undertaken by several parties from 2 SAS in support of the Allied landings at Anzio in Italy (22 January 1944). The intention was to cut rail communications north of Rome and on the Italian east coast. The mission was divided into two groups: 'Thistledown' involved four

Above: A patrol takes a break during an operation in Malaya. As well as the constant threat of enemy ambush, soldiers had to be on guard against exhaustion.

parties of four men assigned to sever railway lines around Terni and Orvieto; 'Driftwood' was composed of two four-man parties with orders to cut the Urbino-Fabriano and Ancona-Rimini lines.

The parties were parachuted in on 7 January. All of 'Thistledown's' targets were successfully attacked (although the RAF had already bombed one of the lines). However, all the men were subsequently captured. The fate of the 'Driftwood' parties remains a mystery as none of the men turned up at a beach evacuation rendezvous. It has been surmised that they either drowned or were captured and shot. It had been intended to send a reinforcement party by sea to link up with

the 'Driftwood' party, but bad weather prevented this and so the party, codenamed 'Baobab', was sent at the end of January.
(SEE *'Baobab', Operation; Italy*)

MAQUIS Corsican word meaning scrub or bush. When the Germans introduced compulsory labour services in the occupied countries of western Europe in 1942, many men fled their homes to live in makeshift camps in the forests and woods. The French called these escapees *Maquis*.

Before the D-Day landings (6 June 1944), the British Special Operations Executive (SOE) and, to a lesser extent, the American Office of Strategic Studies (OSS) endeavoured

to organise the *Maquis* to undertake sabotage missions behind German lines. After D-Day the SAS worked closely with the *Maquis*, many parties parachuting into France to link up with Resistance groups and establish operating bases.

The SAS encountered a number of problems with the *Maquis*. First, they were split between the supporters of General de Gaulle's Free French and the communists. The latter regarded de Gaulle as nothing more than a British and American stooge, to be used and later discarded. Many *Maquis* seemed more interested in storing weapons for after the war to battle de Gaulle's supporters rather than killing Germans. Second, SOE saw *Maquis* groups as its own concern, and did not approve of the SAS arming and organising Resistance groups as it had its own Jedburgh teams to carry out the same tasks.

After D-Day there was a high level of cooperation between the SAS and *Maquis*. Generally the SAS found the latter were well organised and motivated, and their local knowledge proved invaluable for planning raids. However, there were traitors in the ranks of the Resistance, who also had a habit of gathering in large, noisy groups, thus often compromising secrecy. On the whole SAS commanders preferred to operate separately from the *Maquis*, though there were joint operations. During 'Houndsworth', for example, the SAS helped to beat off an attack on a Resistance camp, and Operation 'Wallace' saw the *Maquis* and SAS launch a joint assault on German forces at Chatillon. (SEE *'Houndsworth', Operation; Jedburgh Teams; Northwest Europe; SOE; 'Wallace', Operation*)

MARBLE ARCH Axis airfield in North Africa during World War II. Its name was derived from the nearby large arch erected by Benito Mussolini in the desert to mark the border of Tripolitania. The airfield was raided by an SAS party, commanded by Major Bill Fraser, on 24 December 1941. However, on reaching the airfield they found it deserted. They made their way back to the rendezvous with the Long Range Desert Group (LRDG) and waited. In fact, a LRDG patrol was despatched to pick them up but went to the wrong rendezvous point. After seven days of waiting, Fraser and his four men decided to walk back to the British lines. They therefore set off on what turned out to be an epic eight-day journey across the blistering desert, during which time they ran short of water, hijacked a German staff car and walked a total of 320km. (SEE *Fraser, Major Bill; Long Range Desert Group; North Africa*)

'MARIGOLD', OPERATION An unsuccessful mission mounted by a joint SAS/Special Boat Section (SBS) party. The plan was to land on Sardinia to snatch a prisoner. The eight SAS and three SBS men landed by submarine on the night of 30 May 1943. However, as soon as they were on the beach the enemy were alerted to their presence and began shooting at them. After a brief firefight all of the party managed to escape back to the submarine in their dinghies. (SEE *Special Boat Section*)

MARS AND MINERVA Regimental journal of the SAS. Mars was the Roman god of war, while Minerva was the Roman goddess of wisdom.

'MARSHALL', OPERATION Extremely successful mission conducted by 32 men of 3 French Parachute Battalion (3 SAS) who were parachuted into the Correze area of France.

Conducted between 11 and 24 August 1944, the purpose of the raid was to interfere with enemy troop movements and stiffen the local Resistance. The party, commanded by Captain Wauthier, carried out a number of daring attacks on the Germans, including a 300-strong SS unit. (SEE *Northwest Europe*)

'MAROON MACHINE' SAS name, and general British Army term, for the Parachute Regiment. The name is derived from the colour of the berets worn by the paras.

MARTUBA Axis airfield in North Africa during World War II. The SAS planned to attack it on the night of 13 June 1942 as part of a larger Special Air Service operation to support a British convoy attempting to reach Malta. The party, Free French volunteers driven by Special Interrogation Group personnel disguised as Germans and driving captured enemy vehicles, was betrayed by an ex-*Afrika Korps* soldier in the group (which was also going to attack Derna airfield). All but two of the party were captured.

(SEE *Crete; Derna; Free French SAS; North Africa; Special Interrogation Group*)

MAYNE, LIEUTENANT-COLONEL 'PADDY' BLAIR One of the legendary figures of the Special Air Service. Originally a member of 11 Scottish Commando, Mayne was one of the first recruits to David Stirling's new desert unit. Blair Mayne was a big Irishman who, before the war, had been an accomplished rugby international and a boxer. Usually of a quiet disposition, he could be dangerous when roused. More importantly, he had superb leadership qualities, probably greater than those of David Stirling himself. At the end of 1941 Mayne, a captain, took part in the first SAS operation, a parachute jump into the desert to attack airfields in the Tmimi/Gazala area. The operation was a complete disaster, although subsequent missions were to prove more fruitful.

Over the next year Mayne participated in many raids against enemy airfields, for example Tamit, Berka, around Benghazi, Bagoush, Fuka and Sidi Haneish. His actions were invariably characterised by often reckless bravery, and in North Africa he personally accounted for over 100 enemy aircraft. It was his idea for the SAS to use its own transport to reach targets, as opposed to relying on the Long Range Desert Group, and so the SAS jeep was born. By August 1942, Mayne was a major and had acquired a reputation as a superb leader and raider. In March 1943, he was given command of the Special Raiding Squadron (1 SAS renamed) and led it through the Sicilian and Italian campaigns as a lieutenant-colonel. He later led 1 SAS during the campaign in northwest Europe (1944-45).

There are so many examples of the personal bravery displayed by 'Paddy' Mayne throughout the war, but one will suffice to illustrate the kind of soldier he was. On 9 April 1945, two columns of SAS jeeps were moving

Above: 'Paddy' Mayne caught in a reflective mood. Volatile, courageous and a born leader of men, Mayne is one of the most famous figures to have worn a beige beret.

towards Oldenburg, Germany, to create a path for Canadian armour which was heading for Wilhelmshaven.

Enemy troops in the area included the crack 1 Parachute Division, and very soon one of the columns came under accurate and intensive fire. The occupants of the three leading jeeps were forced to leave their vehicles and take cover in a ditch by the side of

the road, where they were pinned down. Thus the column ground to a halt. Mayne was informed by radio of the situation and rushed to the scene. On arrival he armed himself with a Bren gun and walked up the road to conduct a reconnaissance of the scene. Returning, he deduced that the Germans had fortified one of the houses by the side of the road and

had placed a rocket team in the woods behind them. He asked for a volunteer – Lieutenant John Scott stepped forward – and then jumped into one of the jeeps. Mayne drove the vehicle up the road, manning the Browning heavy machine gun, with Scott in the rear with the twin Vickers guns. The latter fired into the woods as the jeep stopped at the head of the column, next to the men in the ditch. The two men leapt out, Scott manning one of the guns in an abandoned jeep. The Germans, meanwhile, were shooting at the SAS men, with Scott returning fire. The latter continued to fire as Mayne evacuated the trapped men, and then drove the whole party back to the rear of the column. For his bravery Mayne was awarded his fourth DSO. The only mystery concerning 'Paddy' Mayne, which survives to this day, is why he was never awarded a VC during the war. He survived the war by 10 years, being killed in a car crash in 1955, aged 40. (SEE *Bagoush; Benghazi; Berka; Fuka; Germany; Italy; Long Range Desert Group; North Africa; Northwest Europe; Sicily; Sidi Haneish; Special Air Service; Stirling, Lieutenant-Colonel David; Tamit*)

MCR I Nicknamed the 'Biscuit Receiver', the MCR 1 was an extremely lightweight radio transmitter used by SAS parties in northwest Europe after the D-Day landings to relay valuable intelligence back to Allied headquarters in England. Weighing only one kilo, it fitted into a Huntley & Palmers biscuit tin and contained three batteries and five miniature valves. Although it sent out very weak signals, these could be picked up by the Phantom centre in Britain.
(SEE *Phantom*)

M DETACHMENT Formed in the autumn of 1942, it consisted of 150 volunteers from the Special Boat Section led by Captain Fitzroy Maclean who were trained in

parachuting and other infiltration techniques. General Headquarters Persia and Iraq feared that the Germans would break through to Persia to seize its vital oilfields and, therefore, decided to create an SAS-type force to disrupt their supply lines. However, M Detachment's first task was the successful kidnapping of General Zahidi, a Persian officer who was in contact with the Germans and planning a pro-Axis coup. With their defeats at El Alamein and Stalingrad, however, the enemy threat to Persia receded. M Detachment was therefore moved to Athlit, Palestine, to train with the Special Boat Squadron before moving to the Lebanon. The unit saw no further action and Maclean was selected to lead a Military Mission to aid Tito's Yugoslavian partisans.
(SEE *Athlit; Maclean, Captain Fitzroy; Special Boat Section; Special Boat Squadron*)

MELOT, MAJOR BOB An early recruit to the SAS in World War II, Melot was involved with British Intelligence and was a fluent speaker of Arabic. He took part in raids on Benghazi in North Africa in September 1942, where he was wounded. Later he fought with the Special Raiding Squadron at Termoli in Italy and, as 2 SAS's intelligence officer, coordinated operations in northwest Europe.
(SEE *Benghazi; North Africa; Termoli*)

MFF Military Freefall. Parachuting technique employed by the SAS and other special forces in which a man's parachute is not opened automatically on exiting from the aircraft. Rather, it is the soldier himself who pulls the rip-cord to open the 'chute.
(SEE *HAHO; HALO*)

MI5 Military Intelligence, Department 5. British counter-intelligence organisation, now called the Security Service. MI5 works closely with the SAS in Northern Ireland, providing back-up information for surveillance or ambush operations, and requests SAS assistance in the collection of intelligence. In Ulster since 1973, MI5 runs agents, conducts psychological missions and undercover 'operations, all with varying degrees of success. It has representatives on all the British intelligence bodies including the Joint Operations Centre, which despatched an SAS team to Gibraltar in March 1988 to arrest three IRA terrorists. MI5 also deployed its own surveillance team for this particular operation.
(SEE *Gibraltar; JOC; Northern Ireland*)

MI6 Military Intelligence, Department 6. British intelligence gathering organisation known as the

Below: A freefall parachutist comes in to land. Note the kit suspended below him.

Above: Milan is one of the most effective anti-armour weapons in the world. The SAS employed it against Argentinian bunkers in the Falklands.

Secret Intelligence Service (SIS). Liaises with the SAS on all matters concerning Northern Ireland, where it has been deployed since 1971. The delineation of responsibility between MI5 and MI6 has resulted in a great deal of bickering between the two, a situation which has aided no one but the IRA. In the Irish Republic MI6 runs a covert intelligence gathering network.

(SEE *Northern Ireland*)

MICRO-UZI

(SEE *Uzi Submachine Gun*)

MILAN

An effective anti-tank weapon. All troopers within the Regiment are fully trained in its use. It was deployed in the Falklands War, when 60 men from D Squadron, equipped with GPMGs, mortars and Milans, landed near Goose Green to act as a diversion for the main British landings at San Carlos.

Type: wire-guided anti-tank weapon
Calibre: 90mm
Weight: 23.08kg
Length: 770mm
Effective range: 25-2000m
Muzzle velocity: 75 metres per second (at launch); 200 metres per second (at 2km)
Armour penetration: up to 352mm

'MINDING'

(SEE *Bodyguarding*)

MINI-UZI

(SEE *Uzi Submachine Gun*)

MIRBAT

Small coastal town in Oman, located 65km east of Salalah. Scene of an epic battle between a handful of SAS men and their Omani allies, and 250 enemy guerrillas on 19 July 1972. Following the deployment of SAS units (called British Army Training Teams) to the country in 1970, the implementation of their 'hearts and minds' policy, and the recruiting of *firqat* units, the *adoo* (enemy guerrillas) were losing ground. The attack and brief capture of Mirbat was designed to show *firqat* units the continuing power of the *adoo* (an SAS BATT had been training *firqats* in the town).

The timing of the attack was well-chosen: the *adoo* believed that the rainy period would ensure that the Sultan of Oman's Air Force (SOAF) would be unable to provide air cover because of the low cloud (though in fact the SOAF did fly during the battle). The *adoo* had collected 250 men for the assault, all armed with automatic rifles, 75mm recoilless rifles and one Carl Gustav rocket launcher.

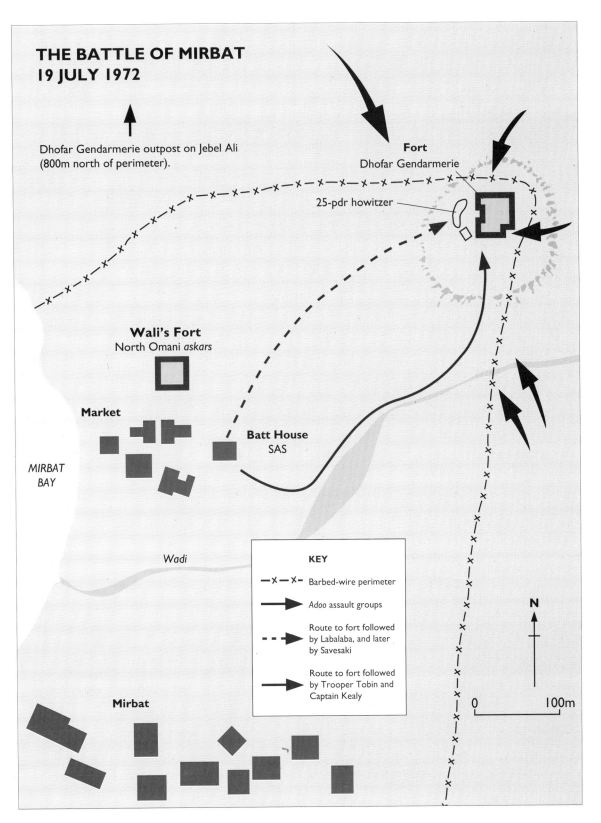

THE BATTLE OF MIRBAT
19 JULY 1972

↑

Dhofar Gendarmerie outpost on Jebel Ali
(800m north of perimeter).

Fort
Dhofar Gendarmerie

25-pdr howitzer

Wali's Fort
North Omani *askars*

Market

Batt House
SAS

*MIRBAT
BAY*

Wadi

KEY

—x—x— Barbed-wire perimeter

⟶ *Adoo* assault groups

- - -► Route to fort followed
by Labalaba, and later
by Savesaki

⟶ Route to fort followed
by Trooper Tobin and
Captain Kealy

N

0   100m

Mirbat

To weaken the garrison, a group of *adoo* had deliberately allowed themselves to be spotted by a mountain escarpment nearby, thus prompting a 60-strong *firqat* to be despatched to investigate. On the night of 18 July, the attackers surrounded the town and its fortified perimeter.

The defenders were heavily outnumbered. There was a nine-man BATT in Mirbat, all from 8 Troop, B Squadron, 22 SAS. The commander was Captain Mike Kealy, only 23 years old. His men included Corporal Bob Bradshaw, Trooper Labalaba (a Fijian), Corporal Pete Wignall, Corporal Roger Chapman, Lance-Corporal Harris, Trooper Savesaki (a Fijian), and Trooper Tobin. In addition, there were 30 *askars* holding the Wali Fort and 25 gendarmes occupying the Gendarmerie Fort, beside which was an old World War II 25-pounder howitzer in a gun-pit.

At around 0500 hours, shots were heard from the Gendarmerie Fort as the *adoo* cautiously approached the perimeter, giving the defenders notice of their presence. Then the support weapons opened up – the Battle of Mirbat had begun. Captain Kealy rushed to the roof of the 'Batthouse' (the BATT headquarters) to assess the situation.

Labalaba was already in the gun-pit, firing the 25-pounder. With Kealy on the roof were Wignall and Chapman, firing the GPMG and the 0.5in Browning heavy machine gun at the waves of *adoo* that were threatening to engulf their positions. Lance-Corporal Harris, meanwhile, was operating a mortar from the pit at the base of the 'Batthouse'.

The key to the action was the Gendarmerie Fort, especially the 25-pounder. If that fell the *adoo* would win, but if it could be held then the SAS would stand a chance. Savesaki, manning the short-range radio, relayed to Kealy that Labalaba had been wounded and that the fort was in danger. Savesaki asked permission to get medical aid to him by running

over the bullet-swept ground between the 'Batthouse' and the Fort. Kealy agreed. Savesaki set off, running at speed across the exposed ground, dodging the hail of bullets that greeted his attempt. He fell panting but unharmed into the gun-pit. The 25-pounder continued to fire.

However, the *adoo* were now concentrating most of their fire on the Gendarmerie Fort itself and were attempting to cross the barbed wire that blocked their path. Bradshaw, Wignall and Chapman laid down a murderous barrage of fire, but the enemy kept on coming. Nevertheless, by 0700 hours the first crisis of the battle had passed.

As the fighting continued the gun-pit failed to respond to Kealy's radio calls. Deciding to investigate himself, he left Bradshaw in command and, taking Tobin with him, headed for the Gendarmerie Fort. Taking a more circuitous route than Savesaki, they too reached the fort safely.

Labalaba, badly wounded, explained that Savesaki, though hit in the back, was covering the left-hand side of the fort. However, at that moment the guerrillas breached the wire and started to advance towards the fort. The second crisis of the battle had arrived. Despite his wounds, Labalaba continued to man the 25-pounder, loading shell after shell into the breech. However, he was hit by a second bullet and died instantly. Tobin took over, but only briefly, before he too received a fatal wound.

Kealy radioed to the 'Batthouse' to direct mortar and machine-gun fire at the Gendarmerie Fort in an effort to beat off the hordes of *adoo* who were closing in. Bradshaw obeyed his orders and also told Kealy that Omani Air Force jets were on their way. Kealy's relief was short-lived, however, as at that moment a grenade rolled over the lip of the gun-pit. He braced himself for certain death, but, miraculously, it failed to go off. Moments later Strikemaster jets streaked overhead, pouring cannon

fire into the *adoo*. The latter started to pull back as Kealy and Bradshaw directed the aircraft attacks. By this time the *firqat* who had stayed in the town were in action against the *adoo*.

Though the situation was still serious, reinforcements had arrived. Helicopters had landed 23 men of G Squadron, 22 SAS, on the shore southeast of Mirbat. Laying down a barrage of fire, they advanced towards the battle, forcing the *adoo* to retreat. Mirbat had been relieved.

The SAS lost two men at Mirbat: Labalaba and Tobin. Another two were seriously wounded. Over 30 *adoo* dead were found on the battlefield, although many more later died of their wounds. Mirbat was a turning point in the war, as its successful defence proved the worth of Sultan Qaboos's policies and led to violent disagreements within the guerrilla movement. It was also a supreme example of SAS and skill at arms. (SEE Adoo; Askar; *British Army Training Team*; Firqat; *GPMG*; 'Hearts and Minds'; Kealy, Major Mike; Oman; Qaboos, Sultan; Sultan of Oman's Air Force)

MOBILITY TROOP One of the four troops that comprise an SAS squadron. Members of Mobility Troops are trained in the use of special forces vehicles: Land Rovers, fast attack vehicles and motorbikes. (SEE *Air Troop; Boat Troop; Land Rover; Light Strike Vehicle; Mountain Troop; Troop Skills*)

MOGADISHU Scene of a spectacular hostage-rescue operation carried out by the elite German counter-terrorist group GSG 9 and two SAS soldiers. On 13 October 1977, four Palestinian terrorists hijacked a Lufthansa Boeing 737 aircraft en route from the Balearic Islands to Germany. Their leader was

Right: SAS Mobility Troops employ a wide variety of vehicles and motorbikes. All models are thoroughly tested by the Regiment before they enter service.

Above: Her three comrades dead, Suhaila Sayeh, gravely wounded but still defiant, is taken to hospital. She was the only terrorist to survive GSG 9's assault on the hijacked Boeing 737 at Mogadishu.

the notorious terrorist Zohair Youssef Akache, the self-styled 'Captain Mahmoud', who demanded the immediate release of 11 Baader-Meinhof terrorists in jail in Germany. On board the aircraft were five crew and 86 passengers.

After landing and taking off from various places, the aircraft eventually set down at Mogadishu airport, Somalia. It was quickly followed by a 30-strong GSG 9 team headed by Ulrich Wegener, the unit's commander. Also with the Germans were two SAS soldiers, Major Alastair Morrison and Sergeant Barry Davies, who had brought along a number of stun grenades and were ready to give general advice on tactics (the actual assault was planned by the two men from Hereford).

On 16 October, 'Mahmoud' murdered the captain of the aircraft and threw his body onto the tarmac. Conditions inside the aircraft were deteriorating and 'Mahmoud' was becoming increasingly irrational. He set a deadline of 0245 hours, 18 October, to release all the terrorists or he would blow up the plane. GSG 9, with the two SAS men, decided to assault the aircraft.

At 0205 hours, Somali soldiers lit a diversionary fire on the runway ahead of the aircraft. Two of the hijackers went to the cockpit to assess its significance. At 0207 hours, the aircraft's emergency doors over the wings, and the doors front and rear, were blown open and stun grenades thrown inside the fuselage. There was a blinding flash and a loud bang, then

the four GSG 9 assault teams led by Wegener stormed the aircraft. For the next five minutes there was an intense battle as the soldiers encountered and shot each terrorist. 'Mahmoud' appeared in the doorway of the flight-deck and was hit by a hail of bullets, but he still managed to throw two grenades before being scythed down by a burst from a Heckler & Koch MP5 submachine gun (fortunately the grenades rolled under some seats where they exploded harmlessly). Wegener himself killed one of the terrorists with a head shot. Three terrorists were killed, the fourth being seriously wounded. Three hostages had been hurt but none was killed. The operation had been a stunning success.

The SAS's involvement was admitted to immediately after the assault by the British Prime Minister, James Callaghan. Mogadishu was to have major consequences for the SAS as

the decision was taken to conduct Counter Revolutionary Warfare (CRW) training for each 'Sabre' Squadron on rotation, ensuring that Britain would have a counter-terrorist unit on 24-hour standby.
(SEE *Counter Revolutionary Warfare; GSG 9; Heckler & Koch MP5 Submachine Gun; 'Sabre'; Stun Grenade*)

MOOR PARK Located in a suburb of northwest London, this was the home of the SAS Brigade's HQ during operations in northwest Europe in 1944.

MORRISON, MAJOR ALASTAIR
(SEE *Mogadishu*)

MORTARS The SAS has used a variety of mortars in its campaigns since World War II. These weapons have, in the main, been those that were in British Army use at the time. The most popular mortars used by the Regiment since 1941 have been: the 2-inch (50mm) mortar, which weighed just under 10kg and could fire a 1kg load of high explosive; the 3-inch (76.2mm) mortar, which weighed 40kg and had a range of 450-2560m; and the giant 4.2-inch (100.6mm) mortar, which weighed an incredible 116kg and had a range in excess of 3000m. All these weapons are now obsolete.

The two mortars in current service with the Regiment are the 51mm light mortar and the 81mm M16, which are both also in service with the British Army. The 81mm model was used with great success by the Special Air Service during D Squadron's Pebble Island raid (14 May 1982) during the war to retake the Falkland Islands.

51mm light mortar
  Calibre: 51mm
  Weight: 6.275kg
  Length: 750mm
  Effective range: 750m
  Rate of fire: eight rounds per minute (rapid)

81mm mortar
  Designation: L16 ML
  Calibre: 81mm
  Weight: 14.08kg (including base plate)
  Length: 1280mm
  Effective range: 5800m
  Rate of fire: 15 rounds per minute (rapid)
(SEE *Falkland Islands; Pebble Island*)

'MOSES', OPERATION Very successful mission conducted between 3 August and 5 October 1944 by 47 men of 3 French Parachute Battalion (3 SAS) under the command of Captain Simon. The party, which included four jeeps, was tasked with disrupting enemy communications in the area around Poitiers, southwestern France. 'Moses' resulted in significant casualties and damage being inflicted on the enemy. In one particular incident, for example, intelligence relayed back resulted in one target being attacked by Allied aircraft which destroyed over 400 enemy vehicles.
(SEE *Northwest Europe*)

MOUNTAIN AND WINTER WARFARE SCHOOL German military establishment located at Luttensee, near Mittenwald in Bavaria. Instructs German and foreign students – members of 22 SAS are regular attendees – in all aspects of mountain and arctic warfare: rock training, ice climbing, skiing, mountain warfare operations, high altitude medicine and mountain rescue. Members of 22 SAS who attend the school are qualified to train the Regiment's Mountain Troops.
(SEE *Mountain Troop*)

MOUNTAIN TROOP One of the four troops that comprise an SAS squadron. Members of Mountain Troops are trained in all aspects of mountain and arctic warfare, special climbing techniques and high altitude movement. Exercises are conducted in Norway, the Arctic and in Scotland, frequently with units such as the British Royal Marines.

(SEE *Air Troop; Boat Troop; Mobility Troop; Troop Skills*)

MOUNT KENT
(SEE *Falkland Islands*)

MUNICH OLYMPICS 1972 The massacre of 11 Israeli athletes at the Munich Olympics by the Palestinian group 'Black September' was a turning point in the history of Western counter-terrorism. This one act prompted many western European nations – as well as Israel itself – to substantially upgrade their counter-terrorist/hostage-rescue capability. In France and Germany the massacre was to lead to the establishment of crack anti-terrorist units, and in Britain it would result in the refinement of SAS counter-terrorist training and tactics. What the Munich massacre made clear was that local police forces, no matter how well trained, did not possess the expertise or experience to deal with a full-blown terrorist attack.

After Munich Western governments realised that their countries had become soft targets for extremist terrorist groups, which viewed liberal democracy with disdain. They were therfore forced to muster the political will to create what were in effect units which existed in the twilight world between civil police forces and the military. Nevertheless, by and large these counter-terrorist squads have been remarkably successful. The victories at Mogadishu (1977) and Princes Gate (1980) have not only demonstrated the effectiveness of counter-terrorist training and equipment, they also highlighted the West's determination to defeat terrorism.
(SEE *Counter Revolutionary Warfare; GIGN; GSG 9; 'Killing House'; Mogadishu; Princes Gate*)

Overleaf: The L16 ML 81mm mortar. Though the weapon is too bulky for long-range reconnaissance missions, it is ideal for actions such as the SAS's Pebble Island raid.

N

Above: Captain Robert Nairac, killed by the IRA in May 1977.

NAIRAC, CAPTAIN ROBERT Alleged by some commentators to have been a member of 22 SAS and by others to have been working for the 14th Intelligence Unit, Nairac was certainly operating undercover in Northern Ireland in the 1970s. In May 1977, his cover was blown while drinking in the Three Steps Inn near the village of Dromintee in South Armagh. Nairac was abducted by the IRA, brutally interrogated and then murdered. His body has never been found and the precise details of his mission in the Province have never been disclosed by the British authorities.
(SEE *14th Intelligence Unit; Irish Republican Army; Northern Ireland; South Armagh*)

'NARCISSUS', OPERATION Undertaken by a 40-man detachment of A Squadron, 2 SAS, on 10 July 1943. The party landed on the southeast coast of Sicily to seize a lighthouse where, it was suspected, there were enemy artillery pieces which would interfere with the Allied invasion of the island (Operation 'Husky'). The party was transported to the beach by landing craft and then climbed up to the lighthouse, only to find it deserted. Having achieved their objective without any loss, the 40 men were ordered to return to the *Royal Scotsman* lying offshore.
(SEE *Italy*)

NATIONAL LIBERATION FRONT Arab nationalist group which fought the British in Aden during the 1960s. Formed in late 1963, its guerrillas conducted a highly effective hit-and-run campaign against British forces. As the British withdrawal neared, NLF guerrillas also fought with members of the Front for the Liberation of Occupied South Yemen, whom NLF fighters regarded as a tool of Egypt. Following Britain's withdrawal, the NLF took control of the country and established the Marxist and pro-Russian People's Democratic Republic of Yemen.
(SEE *Aden; Front for the Liberation of Occupied South Yemen*)

'NELSON', OPERATION Codename for a planned operation in the Orleans Gap area of France in July 1944 which never materialised.

NEWELL, MAJOR DARE A long-serving member of the SAS, Newell joined the Malayan Scouts in the early 1950s during the campaign in Malaya, bringing with him a wealth of wartime experience of jungle fighting that he had gained against the Japanese. Later, he became the SAS's regimental adjutant and Secretary of the SAS Regimental Association.
(SEE *Malaya; Malayan Scouts*)

'NEWTON', OPERATION Successful mission undertaken by 57 men of 3 French Parachute Battalion (3 SAS), commanded by Lieutenant de Roquebrune, between 19 August and 11 September 1944. Operating in the Champagne/Burgundy area of central France, the jeep-mounted party was tasked with reinforcing existing SAS bases to increase the pressure on retreating German forces. The party inflicted numerous casualties on the enemy, often operating in conjunction with advancing US troops.
(SEE *Northwest Europe*)

NEW ZEALAND SAS The New Zealand SAS (NZSAS) was originally formed in 1954 as part of that country's contribution to the British Commonwealth Strategic Reserve in Southeast Asia. From the start the training at Waiouru, New Zealand, emphasised physical and mental stamina. The selection process was extremely tough and many recruits failed. However, in June 1955 the company-sized Independent New Zealand SAS Squadron was formed, its first commander being Major F. Rennie. The unit was deployed operationally in December, six months after its creation. The stringent selection process was to reap substantial dividends, for the NZSAS performed well in the jungles of Malaya.

Trained to conduct small unit, long-range patrols, the NZSAS, which contained many Maoris, soon gained the trust of the local Aborigines. Two 13-week operations in the Fort Brooke area on the Perak-Kelantan border resulted in the removal of the terrorists working there. The unit's last of three long missions was in the hilly area of Negri Sembilan. The results were impressive: eight terrorists killed, including their leader Li-Hak-Chi, two wounded and 19 surrendered. During the whole campaign the NZSAS lost only two men killed, testimony to their skill in jungle warfare techniques.

The unit was disbanded in December 1957, only to be reactivated as a troop in December 1959 under the command of Captain J.A. Mace. The next year it was expanded into a squadron and received instruction from the Australian SAS. The new unit was tasked with conducting standard SAS-type missions: long-range, small-unit operations behind enemy lines; intelligence gathering, ambushing and sabotage; and general reconnaissance. In 1961, a territorial (reserve) troop was formed.

A 30-man NZSAS detachment was sent to Thailand in May 1962, along with US Green Berets, to train Thai soldiers in counter-insurgency warfare (the situation along Thailand's northern border at the time gave rise to fears that a guerrilla war was about to break out). In 1963, the unit was redesignated 1st Ranger Squadron, NZSAS, to commemorate two units of New Zealand's Maori Wars: the Forest Rangers and Taranaki Rangers.

Between February 1965 and November 1966, detachments from the squadron were rotated to Borneo during the 'Confrontation' with Indonesia. The New Zealanders next saw service in Vietnam, where, between November 1968 and February 1971, they were based at Nui Dat, Phuoc Tuy Province, under the command of the Australian Task Force. As in their previous campaigns, the NZSAS proved themselves adept at jungle fighting.

Currently the NZSAS Squadron has five troops, a headquarters and a training establishment at Papakura Military Base. As well as being tasked to support the New Zealand armed forces in times of war, the squadron also has a major counter-terrorist responsibility. The NZSAS maintains contact with other SAS units in Britain and Australia to aid general training and tactics, especially hostage-rescue drills. The great strengths of the New Zealand SAS are the high standards of selection and training that ensure a constant pool of highly skilled soldiers. Like its British counterpart, the NZSAS wears the beige beret and famous winged dagger badge.
(SEE *Borneo; Fort Brooke; Malaya*)

'NIMROD', OPERATION Codename for the SAS assault on the Iranian Embassy in May 1980.
(SEE *Princes Gate*)

'9-MILLY' SAS nickname for the Browning High Power handgun.
(SEE *Browning High Power*)

'NOAH', OPERATION Highly successful mission which began on 16 August 1944. A party of 41 men from the Belgian Independent Parachute Company (5 SAS), commanded by Captain Blondeel, was parachuted into the French Ardennes to gather intelligence concerning the enemy's circumstances in the area. Close liaison was established with the *Maquis* and some first-class intelligence was transmitted back to HQ. In addition, the party inflicted damage on the retreating Germans. The operation was completed by 13 September 1944.
(SEE *Blondeel, Captain;* Maquis; *Northwest Europe*)

NOFILIA World War II Axis airfield in North Africa. Raided by an SAS party led by Lieutenant 'Jock' Lewes on 26 December 1941. The attack was unsuccessful, only two aircraft were destroyed before the party was forced to retire because of the large number of enemy troops alerted by the attack. On the way back to the Long Range Desert Group rendezvous, the party was attacked by an Italian aircraft and Lewes killed.

Below: An SAS jeep in typical North African terrain during World War II.

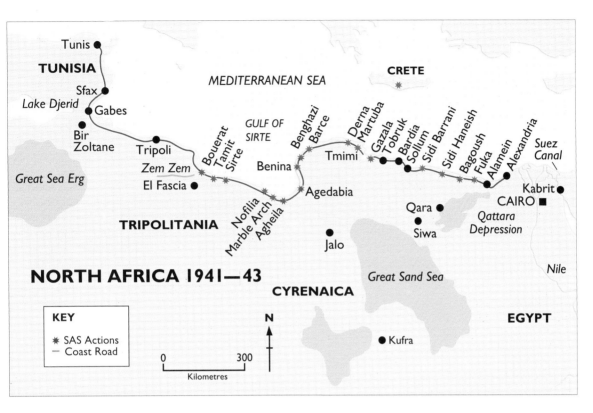

NORTH AFRICA 1941—43

KEY
* SAS Actions
— Coast Road

0   300
Kilometres

N

(SEE *Lewes, Lieutenant John Steel 'Jock'; Long Range Desert Group; Marble Arch; North Africa; Sirte; Tamit*)

NORTH AFRICA The war in the North African desert (1940-43) was dominated by supply lines. The few roads were mostly situated near the coast and the armies were reliant upon supply depots, airfields and ports to keep them in the field. As an army moved farther from these installations, its supply lines became longer and thus more vulnerable.

David Stirling, a young Scots Guards lieutenant, had taken part in a number of unsuccessful large-scale raids against enemy targets along the Cyrenaican coast. He saw the wisdom of hitting targets behind enemy lines, but believed that small parties of men stood a better chance of achieving surprise. Their chances would be increased still further if they were trained to reach the targets by land, sea or air. He succeeded in bringing

his ideas to the attention of General Sir Claude Auchinleck, Commander-in-Chief Middle East, and Major-General Sir Neil Ritchie, Auchinleck's Chief of Staff. Stirling was given permission to raise his unit, which began life as L Detachment, Special Air Service Brigade (though in July 1941 it contained only 65 men).

Its first raid was a complete disaster. The parties were dropped by parachute to attack the enemy airfields in the Gazala/Tmimi area in November 1941. However, they were scattered on landing and never reached their targets. This debacle convinced Stirling that parachute insertion was too risky for SAS missions. Instead he secured an agreement with the Long Range Desert Group (LRDG) to use its vehicles and drivers to transport his men to and from their targets. The first successful SAS/LRDG operations were in December, when different parties raided the airfields at Sirte, Agheila, Tamit, Agedabia, Nofilia and at

Marble Arch. They were to support the forthcoming Eighth Army attack on Benghazi (which in fact never materialised). This was an early indication of Stirling's insistence that the SAS must not be used tactically but strategically to be effective, a point not always adhered to by Allied commanders later in the war. It is estimated that the raids carried out in December resulted in 97 enemy aircraft being destroyed.

The new year saw a number of SAS actions. The port and area around Benghazi was hit three times, in March, June and September, Tobruk was also raided, along with other airfields, shipping and supply dumps. By the summer of 1942, General Rommel, the German commander, was holding the Gazala line prior to his offensive and Auchinleck, the British Commander-in-Chief, did not feel strong enough to launch an attack to drive the Germans back (the enemy also held the airfields of Cyrenaica, which were being used to launch

Above: A group of tired but cheerful SAS soldiers return to base after a mission in early 1943. Note the varied headdress worn.

attacks on British convoys attempting to reach Malta).

Stirling therefore planned a number of raids on them which took place in the middle of June (raids were also mounted on Axis airfields on Crete). The SAS destroyed a total of 50 aircraft on the ground. However, fresh disasters overtook the British as Rommel attacked and advanced into Egypt. The SAS, which by this time had been equipped with its own jeeps, continued to operate behind enemy lines. At Bagoush one party drove its jeeps onto the tarmac and raked the enemy aircraft with machine-gun fire; 40 aircraft were destroyed at Sidi Haneish at the end of July.

In September 1942, the SAS was officially placed on the roll of regiments in the British Army, and was listed as the 1st Special Air Service Regiment. Stirling was promoted to the rank of lieutenant-colonel.

Although taking no part in the Battle of El Alamein in November, Stirling was determined to assist in General Montgomery's advance to Tripoli. He therefore devised a plan whereby his men would launch at least two raids a week on the stretch of land between Agheila and Tripoli,

concentrating on the roads being used by the retreating Germans and Italians. The Allied landings in the French North African colonies (Operation 'Torch'), also in November, resulted in Axis forces retreating into Tunisia. Though the SAS had been quite successful during the Eighth Army's advance, the Tunisian countryside was not as suitable for their operations as Libya had been. The terrain consisted of scrub-covered hills and cultivated valleys, and the population was also more pro-Axis. This resulted in SAS operations having rather mixed fortunes. Many men were captured, including David Stirling himself.

Nevertheless, the Regiment's future seemed assured. By January 1943, 1 SAS had an establishment of 47 officers and 532 other ranks. Lieutenant-Colonel William Stirling, David's brother, had also formed 2 SAS and was with the British First Army. Though there was uncertainty at the end of the campaign in North Africa (May 1943) concerning the SAS's future, the invasion of Sicily meant its skills were again needed. (SEE *individual entries on personalities, locations and operations*)

NORTHERN IRELAND The SAS has been involved in the 'Troubles' in Northern Ireland, on and off, since 1969. It is an involvement the Regiment neither sought or desired, but it seems certain that the SAS will remain in the Province until the conflict is resolved militarily or politically (both of which seem unlikely).

The British government established a separate parliament and executive administration for the six counties of Ulster (Londonderry, Antrim, Down, Armagh, Fermanagh and Tyrone) in 1921. Thus Northern Ireland remained part of the United Kingdom, returning Members of Parliament to the House of Commons at Westminster. However, the electoral laws in the Province were manipulated to the disadvantage of the Catholic working class minority because they favoured owners of property, who were mostly Protestant (Protestant immigrants had been settling in the north of Ireland in some numbers since the seventeenth century). Major civil rights disturbances erupted in late 1968, leading, in April 1969, to the Belfast government's request for troops to be sent to the Province to keep order. The disturbances, or 'Troubles' as they have since been known, were manipulated by the Irish Republican Army (IRA), which seeks to drive the British out of Ireland by force, for its own ends. There followed a rapid increase in sectarian violence which threatened to engulf the Province.

British troops were despatched to Ulster in August 1969 to prevent inter-communal violence. The Catholic population at first welcomed their presence, but rapidly began to view them as a force of oppression, especially when they were seen to use unnecessary violence to disperse crowds and mount raids on Catholic areas in the search for arms. 'Bloody Sunday' in 1972, when 13 Catholics were shot dead by British paratroopers, seemed to confirm the 'bias' of the British Army. Political loyalties

Above: A patrol is extracted by helicopter following an operation in Northern Ireland. The SAS's main role in Ulster is one of intelligence gathering.

were split between the Unionists (Loyalists) and the Nationalists (Republicans). The former, consisting of Protestants, although in the majority in Northern Ireland, realised that, if Ulster were ever allowed to join the Irish Republic, they would become an insignificant minority in a Catholic land. This they have sought to prevent, by violence if necessary. An atmosphere of intransigence and mistrust soon established itself, and any thoughts of compromise quickly evaporated. The growth of terrorist groups fed on this feeling of mutual historical antagonism. On the Republican side there was the nationalist IRA, and the smaller, Marxist-orientated Irish National Liberation Army (INLA).

Loyalist paramilitary groups include the Ulster Volunteer Force (UVF), the Ulster Freedom Fighters (UFF) and the Ulster Defence Association (UDA). In the middle, attempting to keep the peace, is the British Army, the Royal Ulster Constabulary (RUC) and the locally raised, overwhelmingly Protestant, Ulster Defence Regiment (UDR). The situation is further complicated by the fact that some members of the RUC and UDR have supplied information and liaised with the Protestant paramilitaries, facts which have alienated the Catholic population further, making the job of the security forces more difficult.

The SAS was first deployed to the Province in 1969, when members of

D Squadron, openly wearing uniform, complete with beige berets and winged dagger badges, were engaged in the countryside searching for Protestant weapons. This mission largely proved fruitless, although the opportunity was not missed to lay a wreath on the grave on 'Paddy' Mayne.

The war in Oman (1970-76) meant the Regiment did not have the manpower to maintain a sizeable presence in the Province, although individual officers and NCOs were posted there to conduct military intelligence tasks. In 1976, the British government announced that the SAS was being deployed to the Province. Individual Special Air Service members had always been in Ulster, but the statement marked the beginning of a squadron presence in Northern

Above: British paras in Northern Ireland. There is close cooperation between the Army, RUC and SAS in Ulster, though the latter does not patrol overtly as here.

Ireland. SAS squadrons are now rotated there on a regular basis.

The Regiment was first deployed to South Armagh to counter the increase in IRA activity in the area. By 1977 there were two squadrons in situ, with the result that the terrorist threat temporarily declined. In one spectacular incident, Peter Cleary, a senior officer in the IRA, was captured near Forkhill, South Armagh, although he was killed trying to escape. However, the IRA quickly recovered and the SAS was faced with the prospect of a long war in Northern Ireland.

Despite the mystique which has grown around the Regiment in the Province, partly cultivated by the British Army to intimidate the IRA and reassure the Loyalists, the SAS role in Ulster is relatively simple, if highly dangerous: it runs agents, con-ducts surveillance and intelligence gathering missions, and carries out ambush operations. Contrary to popular opinion, the SAS does not operate a shoot-to-kill policy. It adheres to the British Army's rules of engagement. However, when attempting to arrest an armed terrorist, the subsequent firefight frequently results in the death of the suspect.

In theory, all the military and intelligence agencies in the Province work with each other to combat the terrorist threat. In reality, the different bodies are sometimes antagonistic towards each other. MI6, for example, often prevents the RUC's Special Branch from seeing certain classified material. The RUC, in turn, withholds its own intelligence. The SAS often found itself given the cold shoulder by the Army and the RUC as both felt that

the Regiment's presence implied that their efforts had failed. Nevertheless, the SAS campaign went on.

Throughout the 1970s, the patient observation post work in the rural areas, coupled with the plain clothes work in the towns and cities, began to pay off. There was a steady stream of successes; numerous IRA units were ambushed and their members killed or arrested. Between 1976 and 1989, for example, 37 IRA and INLA terrorists were killed in gun battles with the SAS, including the ambush at Loughall and the operation at Gibraltar. However, in the same period the SAS lost four men: Lance-Corporal David Jones, Captain Richard Westmacott, Sergeant Paul Oram and Lance-Corporal Alistair Slater.

The Regiment also conducted controversial cross-border raids to arrest wanted terrorists, such as the capture of Sean McKenna, Kevin Byrne and Patrick Mooney in 1976. In the same year eight members of the Regiment were arrested in the Republic. After a highly embarrassing trial, they were fined for possessing unlicenced weapons and released. The SAS has also made other mistakes in the Province which, though understandable in the context of an undercover war, have brought unwanted attention down upon the Regiment and the British government.

In addition, despite being carefully arranged, several SAS ambush operations have resulted in the deaths of several innocent people. In particular, John Boyle, a 16-year-old schoolboy, was shot dead in July 1978 in the mistaken belief that he was an armed terrorist. There have been others – James Taylor, a County Tyrone wildfowler, was accidentally shot dead in the same year.

Despite these setbacks, the SAS has made a significant contribution to the war in Northern Ireland, not least in training the covert 14th Intelligence Unit. The conflict provides no scope for the implementation of a 'hearts

and minds' policy, as nothing short of the full withdrawal of British forces and rule from the Republic will satisfy those sections of the Catholic population which supports the IRA and INLA. This being the case, it is unlikely that the SAS will ever be able to repeat the success it achieved in Borneo or Oman.
(SEE *Coagh Shooting; Dunloy Shooting; 14th Intelligence Unit; Gibraltar; 'Hearts and Minds'; Irish Republican Army; Loughall; Nairac, Captain Robert; Westmacott, Captain Richard*)

NORTHWEST EUROPE The SAS campaign in France, the Low Countries and Germany in 1944-45 was one of the most spectacular periods in the unit's history. In January 1944, authority was granted for the formation of an SAS Brigade under

the command of Brigadier Roderick McLeod which would consist of 1 and 2 SAS, two French units (3 and 4 SAS) and a Belgian detachment (5 SAS). In addition, F Squadron GHQ Reconnaissance Regiment (Phantom), was attached as a brigade signals unit. The total brigade strength was around 2500 men.

The subsequent operations in France broadly fell into two categories. First, to provide small-scale, tactical support for General Montgomery's 21st Army Group. This involved cutting enemy lines of communication and providing intelligence concerning the movement and dispositions of German forces. In the period immediately following D-Day, the SAS was ordered to prevent enemy reinforcements from reaching the vulnerable beachhead. Second,

parties were inserted by air deep behind enemy lines to establish a base, link up with local *Maquis* forces, and disrupt enemy logistics. These parties sometimes operated for periods of up to three months.

The reconnaissance operations, such as 'Houndsworth', 'Samwest', 'Dingson', and 'Bulbasket', were carried out some 80km ahead of Allied forces in Normandy. The SAS had been somewhat restricted initially because 21st Army Group insisted that no parties were to be dropped before D-Day (though immediately after the landings almost half the brigade was delayed in England because of a shortage of air transport).

The procedure for inserting an SAS party was as follows: an advance group, normally accompanied by a Phantom signals section, would be parachuted in, establish contact with the local *Maquis* and then select suitable dropping zones for the main

Below: A column of SAS jeeps operating in northwest Europe, 1945. Note the armoured shields and bullet-proof windscreens to protect the driver and front gunner.

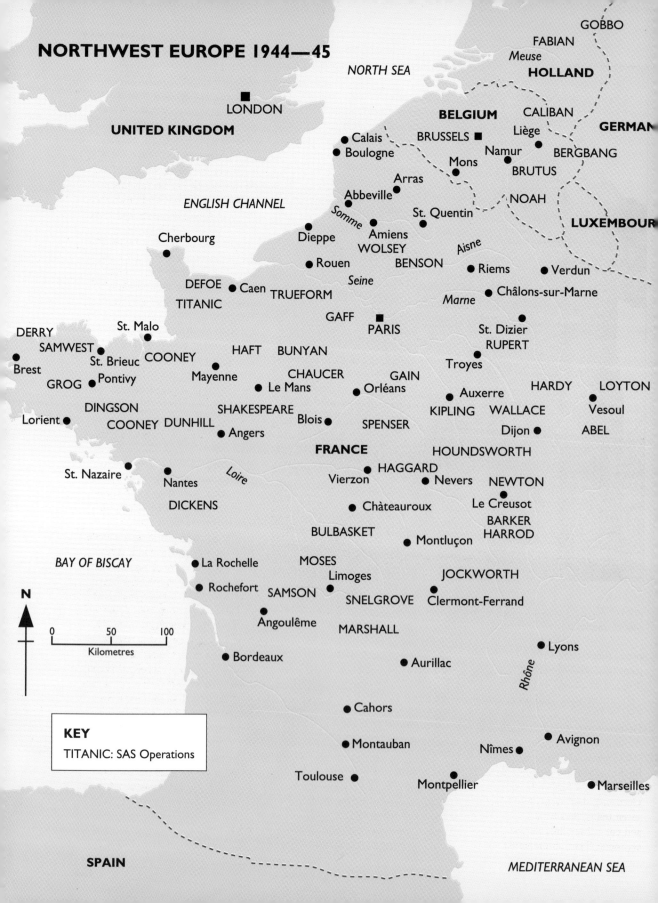

NORTHWEST EUROPE 1944—45

NORTH SEA

GOBBO
FABIAN
Meuse
HOLLAND

LONDON ■

UNITED KINGDOM

BELGIUM
BRUSSELS ■

CALIBAN
Liège
GERMAN

Calais
Boulogne
Mons
Namur
BERGBANG
BRUTUS

Arras
Abbeville
St. Quentin
NOAH
LUXEMBOUR

ENGLISH CHANNEL

Cherbourg

Dieppe
Somme
Amiens
WOLSEY
Aisne

Rouen
BENSON
Riems
Verdun

Seine
DEFOE
Caen
TRUEFORM
Marne
Châlons-sur-Marne

TITANIC
GAFF
PARIS ■
St. Dizier
RUPERT

DERRY
St. Malo
Troyes

SAMWEST
HAFT
BUNYAN

Brest
St. Brieuc
COONEY
GAIN
Auxerre
HARDY
LOYTON

GROG
Pontivy
Mayenne
CHAUCER
Orléans
KIPLING
WALLACE
Vesoul

Lorient
DINGSON
SHAKESPEARE
SPENSER
Dijon
ABEL

COONEY
DUNHILL
Blois

Angers
FRANCE
HOUNDSWORTH

St. Nazaire
Loire
HAGGARD
NEWTON

Nantes
Vierzon
Nevers

DICKENS
Châteauroux
Le Creusot
BARKER
HARROD

BULBASKET
Montluçon

BAY OF BISCAY
La Rochelle
MOSES
JOCKWORTH

N
Rochefort
Limoges
Clermont-Ferrand

SAMSON
SNELGROVE

0   50   100
Angoulême
MARSHALL

Kilometres
Bordeaux
Aurillac
Lyons

Cahors

Rhône

KEY
Montauban
Avignon

TITANIC: SAS Operations
Nîmes

Toulouse
Montpellier
Marseilles

SPAIN
MEDITERRANEAN SEA

Above: The SAS helped hunt down Nazi sympathisers in northwest Europe. Here, a soldier searches a civilian for concealed weapons and incriminating papers.

party. Subsequent reinforcements of jeeps, men and equipment would be dropped by the RAF.

By any measure SAS operations in France, Belgium, Holland and Germany were very successful. Around 2000 men killed or wounded 7733 enemy soldiers and captured a further 4784 (they also negotiated the surrender of a further 18,000 Germans), destroyed 700 vehicles, seven trains, derailed a further 33, and cut railway lines on 164 separate occasions. They also reported a host

of bombing targets to the RAF. This list omits the wealth of valuable intelligence which was continually relayed back to England. There was, of course, a price to pay for this success – the SAS sustained 330 casualties, and many French civilians and *Maquis* fighters were shot by the Germans for assisting the SAS (the latter, if captured, also suffered the same fate on many occasions, despite the fact that they operated in uniform at all times). (SEE *individual entries on personalities and operations*)

NORTH YEMEN The Yemen was the scene of two covert operations involving men from the SAS, both led by Lieutenant-Colonel Johnny Cooper, an SAS veteran. On 26 September 1962, Imam Mohammed al-Badr, North Yemen's ruler, was toppled in a military coup by Colonel Abdullah Sallal. Badr fled to the mountains and organised an army. Sallal proclaimed the Yemen Arab Republic and started to receive substantial backing from Egypt's ruler, President Nasser. The British and French, alarmed at the spread of what they saw as Arab nationalism in the Gulf, decided to despatch a clandestine party to North Yemen to discover the scale of Egyptian involvement before they recognised the new regime.

The man picked to lead the party was Cooper, at the time second-in-command of the Omani Muscat Regiment. In June 1963, the mixed French/SAS eight-man party, consisting of three regulars from 22 SAS – Sergeant Dorman, Corporal Chigley and Trooper Richardson – entered the country and linked up with royalist forces near Sana. They trained royalist tribesmen, supplied them with weapons, and collected intelligence which confirmed that Sallal's regime relied on Egyptian support. After nearly three months, the party had to depart the country, though Cooper returned to collect more intelligence and arrange air drops to the royalists.

He worked alone for the next 11 months. However, just before the air drops Cooper was joined by two SAS personnel, Cyril Weavers and David Bailey. There were nine drops undertaken by aircraft of the Israeli Air Force, although this was kept from the Arab guerrillas. In all, Cooper spent three years in North Yemen, gathering information on Egyptian forces and training royalist soldiers. (SEE *Aden; Cooper, Lieutenant-Colonel Johnny*)

NORWAY
(SEE *'Apostle', Operation; Bergen*)

O

'O GROUP' Orders group. SAS term for a pre-action briefing.

'OGs' Olive-greens. SAS and general British Army term for standard-issue military clothing (in the late 1950s and early 1960s, the term 'OGs' referred to tropical military clothing which was manufactured in India).

OMAGH AMBUSH. This operation, conducted by the SAS in August 1988 in County Tyrone, Northern Ireland, is a good example of the difficulties facing the Regiment in the Province. In June of that year, British intelligence collected a vital clue concerning a forthcoming Irish Republican Army (IRA) operation. The information pointed to the assassination of a former Ulster Defence Regiment (UDR) officer who was working in Omagh. The terrorists' arms dump, recently discovered by British Army troops, was put under surveillance. The SAS, working with the Army, intelligence agencies and the Royal Ulster Constabulary (RUC), decided to set up an ambush to capture the terrorists before the assassination attempt.

The identity of the local IRA members was well known to the security forces. They were Martin and Gerald Harte and Brian Mullen, who together formed the Mid-Tyrone Brigade. The intended victim was informed of the IRA's plans, and he agreed to continue driving his Leyland truck to work along his regular route, thus establishing a movement pattern which would be observed by the terrorists.

As soon as the IRA team was in position to spring the ambush, the truck would 'break down'. SAS soldiers would then lie in wait around it and spring their own ambush when the IRA arrived. However, unknown to the security forces, the IRA team was planning another operation. On 20 August 1988, a bomb destroyed a bus on the A5 road carrying a party of young British soldiers to their barracks in Omagh. Eight members of the 1st Battalion, The Light Infantry, were killed, and many more wounded. An outraged British government announced a whole series of measures to combat terrorism in the Province, one of which was to send more SAS soldiers to Ulster.

The surveillance operation, meanwhile, went on. On 29 August, the terrorists returned to their arms cache. Very early the next day, a disguised SAS trooper took the place of the IRA target and drove the Leyland truck to the ambush point. Simultaneously, a three-man SAS party left the barracks in Omagh and walked to a derelict farmhouse near the village of Drumnakilly. It members carried Browning High Power handguns and Heckler & Koch MP5 submachine

Left: Before any action an 'O Group' will ensure all members of the unit are fully informed of their role in the forthcoming operation.
Below: 'OGs' are hard-wearing items of clothing worn throughout the British Army.

Above: While an SLR-armed trooper looks on, SAS soldiers unload military supplies from the rear of a Beverley transport aircraft in Oman in the early 1970s.

guns. One man took cover in a barn while the other two hid in hedgerows on either side of the road.

At 0900 hours, the Leyland truck stopped outside the farmhouse. The 'driver' alighted from the cab and unloaded the spare tyre and tools to give the impression he was changing a flat tyre. The IRA, who were planning to ambush the truck, soon got word of its whereabouts. The three terrorists, wearing black balaklavas, blue boilersuits and gloves and armed with AK-47 assault rifles and Webley revolvers, stole a Fiat car at 1430 hours and made a reconnaissance of the immediate area. Shortly afterwards, at 1530 hours, they stole another car, a white Sierra, and returned to the truck.

The security forces had been trailing the terrorists, but had called off the

surveillance when one of their cars was spotted by a local youth as the IRA team was stealing the Fiat. The police car sped off, fearing the operation would be compromised. The SAS were now blind. The SAS soldier standing by the truck did not realise who was in the Ford Sierra as it sped towards him, however his sixth sense, borne of years of experience with the Regiment, told him something was wrong. He immediately sprinted to a nearby wall for cover just as the terrorists opened up with their automatic weapons. With 7.62mm bullets tearing up the earth around him, the SAS man reached the wall and dived behind it unhurt. The Sierra raced past him, but suddenly screeched to a halt as the IRA terrorists prepared to jump out and finish him off.

At that moment a hail of 9mm bullets tore through the bodywork of the Sierra as the hidden SAS soldiers opened fire. The terrorists were killed instantly. The man in the barn radioed for a Lynx helicopter to take them back to Omagh barracks as RUC and British Army units sealed off the immediate area.

This stunning operation, which must rank beside the Loughall ambush for sheer daring, had unfortunate repercussions. Although the Regiment had achieved a military success, it was to suffer a political defeat. The British government remained silent on the action as the media made implications that the ambush was a revenge killing for the bus bombing. The security forces, particularly the SAS, were horrified that no-one contradicted these claims. The question of a shoot-to-kill policy was again raised, to be only belatedly denied by the Defence Secretary, Tom King.

The end result was a propaganda victory for the IRA and its supporters. (SEE *Loughall; Northern Ireland*)

OMAN The campaign in Oman stands as a testimony to the SAS's ability to conduct a lengthy counter-insurgency war and bring it to a successful conclusion.

The Sultanate of Muscat and Oman had long-standing treaties of friendship and cooperation with Britain. The country remains strategically important as it is situated on the southeast corner of the Arabian peninsula. A hostile regime in Oman could interrupt the flow of oil to the West. The country is dominated by mountain ranges: in the north the highest point is the Jebel Akhdar (scene of a successful SAS campaign in 1958-59); in the southwest lies the province of Dhofar, location of the massive Jebel Dhofar. The west of the country is desert which borders on the Empty Quarter and the east comprises a coastal strip which, in many places, is

extremely narrow. Most of the population of 500,000 lived in abject poverty, made worse by the repressive regime of Sultan Said bin Taimur.

The reactionary regime of the Sultan in Dhofar – whose people are culturally and ethnically different from the population in the north – eventually led to the outbreak of rebellion in 1962, albeit on a small scale at first. The rebels formed a political party, the Dhofar Liberation Front (DLF), which demanded improvements in the quality of life of the Dhofaris. The Sultan's Armed Forces (SAF), comprising the Muscat and Northern Frontier Regiments, were initially able to contain the rebellion, deploying around 1000 men in Dhofar. However, the DLF was gradually subsumed into the more radical People's Front for the Liberation of the Occupied Arabian Gulf (PFLOAG), a communist group backed by the recently-formed People's Democratic Republic of Yemen (PDRY), the Soviet Union

and, until 1972, China. This tipped the scales in favour of the rebels, or *adoo*, and the regime of Said bin Taimur began to fall apart. The Sultan's forces did not have the manpower or training to wage an effective counter-insurgency war.

The situation was saved by Qaboos, the Sultan's son, who, in 1970, mounted a bloodless palace coup which removed his father. He immediately declared a general amnesty for any *adoo* who wanted to surrender and implemented plans for social development in Dhofar. The amnesty brought some rebels over to the government, though the communist hardliners merely intensified their efforts.

The commanding officer of 22 SAS at the time, Lieutenant-Colonel Johnny Watts, saw the possibilities of mounting a counter-insurgency operation in Oman, but realised that it would be ineffective while Said bin Taimur still ruled the country; his removal radically reversed the situation. An SAS troop had been in

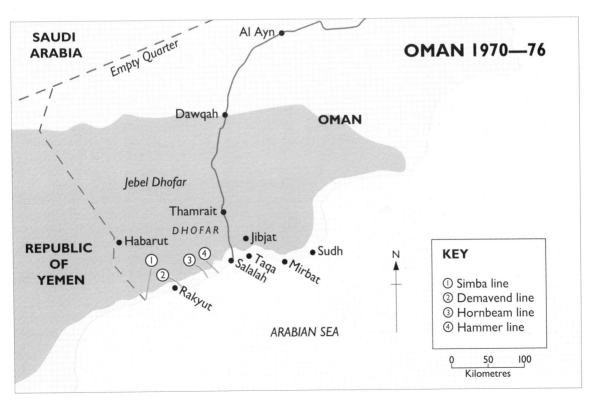

OMAN 1970—76

SAUDI ARABIA

Empty Quarter

Al Ayn

Dawqah

OMAN

Jebel Dhofar

Thamrait

DHOFAR

Habarut

Jibjat

REPUBLIC OF YEMEN

Taqa

Salalah

Mirbat

Sudh

Rakyut

ARABIAN SEA

N

KEY

① Simba line
② Demavend line
③ Hornbeam line
④ Hammer line

0   50   100
Kilometres

Above: An SAS Land Rover (foreground) with firqat *troops in Dhofar. The* firqat *proved effective, if occasionally unreliable, allies.*

Oman training the Sultan's forces since December 1969, and within hours of the coup an SAS team arrived in Dhofar. It was officially known as a British Army Training Team (BATT), so it could be denied that any British troops were actively engaged in Oman. The first two training teams were based at Taqa and Mirbat.

By 1970 Dhofar was on the verge of collapse; the Sultan's forces had been driven from the mountains near the coast and were restricted to Salalah, Rayzut, Taqa and Mirbat. Watts realised that the key to the war was winning back the Dhofaris. He therefore devised his famous 'Five Fronts' campaign which stated that any SAS role in Dhofar should be waged on five fronts: an intelligence cell, an information team, medical expertise for the local inhabitants, a veterinary officer for their livestock, and, where

possible, the enlistment of Dhofaris as soldiers to fight for the Sultan. This was the basis for the 'hearts and minds' campaign that was to prove crucial during the next six years of war.

The SAS team at Salalah, headed by Corporal John Lane, conveyed the Sultan's amnesty in the late summer of 1970. The task of the team was to disseminate the truth, not mindless propaganda. In September a full SAS squadron arrived in Oman, so the work of the BATTs could be stepped up. In the same month, a hard core of guerrillas led by Salim Mubarak, alienated by hard-liners of PFLOAG, fought their way off the Jebel Dhofar and surrendered. In January 1971, Major Tony Jeapes arrived in Oman, to be later followed by his squadron (he was to command a squadron in Dhofar 1971-72, and between 1974 and 1976 led the Regiment itself).

Mubarak visited him and suggested the idea of forming a *firqat* (company) to fight for the Sultan from his band of men. Jeapes took the idea to the British brigadier in Muscat, proposing that the SAS train these men and provide radio communications for them in the field. The Sultan agreed to this plan and the *firqats* were born.

The SAS civil aid programme continued in Dhofar. The teams established clinics for the people and their animals (the gossip picked up from these places often provided invaluable intelligence), and advanced drilling equipment was brought in from the UK to bore new wells or open up old ones which had been sealed on the orders of Said bin Taimur. The SAS fight against disease and ignorance was conducted on the understanding that the Omanis would themselves take over the tasks started by the British, a move which helped convince the Dhofaris that their government was sincere in its wishes to aid them.

Between September 1970 and March 1971, 200 *adoo* surrendered to the government. The SAS formed them into *firqat* units. Their first action was the successful taking of Sudh, 30km east of Mirbat, on 24 February 1971. Watts decided to launch an offensive on to the Jebel Dhofar itself, therefore in March the SAS and *firqat* mounted a probing operation during which 'Eagle's Nest', a position of caves and ridges on the edge of the plateau, was taken despite heavy enemy attacks which lasted for a week.

Watts realised that if civil aid was to be brought to the jebel itself, firm bases would have to be established there. Therefore, in October Operation 'Jaguar' was launched. Commanded by Watts, a force consisting of 100 SAS, 250 SAF, a few Baluchis and five *firqat* (300 men) was prepared. Two positions, Jibjat and 'White City', were secured in addition to the creation of the Leopard line, a barrier consisting of barbed wire, booby traps, mines and ground sensors designed to cut off guerrilla supplies coming into Dhofar from PDRY (others SAS barriers were the Hornbeam line, Demavend line and Simba line). Despite some problems with the *firqats*, who had refused to fight at one point because of the festival of Ramadan, 'Jaguar' was a success. Other operations were 'Leopard' in the west of the jebel, and 'Simba' in the south, on the border with Yemen.

By the end of 1971, the government had made substantial gains: it had a presence on the jebel, there were 700 Dhofaris fighting in *firqats*, and the coastal plain and towns were under government control. In response, the guerrillas decided to mount an operation which would give them a great victory, one which would show those wavering Dhofaris that the government's cause was lost. They opted to capture the small town of Mirbat.

The attack by 250 *adoo* on Mirbat in July 1972 and its successful defence by a nine-man BATT, supported by a few Omanis, was the turning point of the war in Dhofar. Though there would be another four years of fighting, PFLOAG was thereafter waging a losing battle. After Mirbat, government agencies started to take over duties from the BATTs. The civil aid programme continued apace, the Dhofaris began defecting to the government's cause in ever-greater numbers, and the SAS continued to take the war to the enemy. In 1973, operating with the Iranians – an Iranian special forces battalion had been sent to man the Hornbeam line – the SAS cleared the area between Salalah and the Thamrait road. The next year seven SAS teams were deployed in the northeast of the jebel with several *firqat* units, and the enemy was finally cleared from all the valleys in central Dhofar.

By 1975 the rebels were being pushed back to the Yemeni border. They lost Rakyut and, on 1 December, Dhalqut was taken by SAS forces. The Yemenis had withdrawn all their regular troops, who had been assisting the rebels, in October. In September 1976, the SAS squadrons were withdrawn from Oman, signalling the successful end of the war. Though individual SAS units had fought extremely well during the campaign, Mirbat being a case in point, the Regiment's 'hearts and minds' campaign, which had been patiently conducted by four-man teams throughout Dhofar, had been the key to victory. The ability of individual troopers to converse with the Dhofaris in their own tongue, to treat their sick and their livestock, and the subsequent bond formed between civilians and soldiers, had laid the basis for military victory.
(SEE *Baluchis; British Army Training Team; Dhofar Liberation Front;* Firqat*; 'Five Fronts' Campaign; 'Hearts and Minds'; 'Jaguar', Operation; Jeapes, Brigadier Tony; Jebel Akhdar; Mirbat; People's Front for the Liberation of the Occupied* Arabian Gulf; Qaboos, Sultan; Said bin Taimur, Sultan; Watts, Lieutenant-Colonel Johnny*)

I SAS
(SEE *Special Air Service*)

ONE-TIME PAD Used by the SAS in their campaigns from World War II to the Falklands, it is a signals method used to defeat enemy direction-finding equipment. The sender and receiver each possess an identical set of grids of letters from which an indecipherable random choice of code letters can be transmitted. Once the transmission has been completed the sender destroys his copy. In World War II, for example, some 600 four-letter messages were devised; AOAO meant 'All containers safely received'. Each four-letter group would be encoded with the rest of the message from a one-time pad.

OP Observation post. SAS skill in establishing covert OPs, or 'hides', is legendary and has been practised in Northern Ireland, the Falklands and the 1991 Gulf War.

The most important part of any OP work is choosing a suitable site for the 'hide'. This involves close scrutiny of maps and other visual intelligence sources such as aerial reconnaissance photographs. An excellent field of vision is obviously of paramount importance, as is a location with a concealed route for entry and exit. Therefore, most OPs are dug into the earth and situated on high ground.

The rules for construction of an OP are simple: an unlikely spot is chosen as this will arouse the least suspicion (the enemy will be aware that high ground affords a good field of view, therefore an SAS patrol will steer well clear of ridge lines); the OP is always constructed at night; and it is extremely well camouflaged. Its construction is, of necessity, simple: waterproof sheets or ponchos, locally available materials, plastic sheets and camouflage netting.

Above: Unlike this British para OP, SAS observation posts are almost invariably covert. OP work is demanding and unglamorous, though vitally important.

The two OP shapes favoured by the SAS are the star formation, in which each member of the four-man patrol lays in one 'arm', or the rectangular shape, where the members lay side-by-side or two at each end. OPs are usually equipped with binoculars, telescopes, night vision aids, cameras, radio equipment, clothing, weapons, food and sleeping bags. They are always very uncomfortable and cramped, and usually the men have to stay in them for long periods and eat rations of cheese, biscuits and chocolate during the day, with the only hot meal being soup cooked on a hexamine stove at night. One on Beaver Ridge during the Falklands War, for example, was maintained for 26 days. This means that the men must get on with each other extremely well, and clearly there is no distinction between officers and men in a 'hide'. Each man has to urinate and defecate in the presence of the other occupants of the OP (this can have unfortunate consequences: both functions are carried out in diferent bags which are then sealed together in a plastic bag; do both in the same bag and it is likely to explode, discharging the contents over everyone).

The OPs established in urban areas are often more vulnerable to discovery than those set up behind enemy lines because of the number of people living in the area. SAS 'hides' in the towns and cities of Northern Ireland, for example, have been located underneath garden sheds, in the roofs of terraced houses, and on building sites.

The success of SAS observation work is not due to sophisticated surveillance devices, but rather to the calibre of the Regiment's soldiers.
(SEE *Falkland Islands; Northern Ireland*)

OSBORNE, LIEUTENANT-COLONEL MIKE Commander of 22 SAS for a short time in Malaya between the departure of Oliver Brooke and the arrival of Lieutenant-Colonel George Lea.
(SEE *Brooke, Lieutenant-Colonel Oliver; Lea, Lieutenant-Colonel George; Malaya*)

OWEN SUBMACHINE GUN The Australian Owen was favoured by SAS units, especially lead scouts, operating in the jungles of Malaya during the 1950s. Extremely reliable and rugged, it was well suited to jungle fighting. Its most distinctive feature was its top-mounted magazine.
Type: submachine gun
Designation: Machine carbine, 9mm Owen
Calibre: 9mm
Weight: 4.21kg (unloaded)
Length: 813mm
Effective range: 150m
Rate of fire: 700 rounds per minute (cyclic)
Feed: 33-round box magazine
Muzzle velocity: 381 metres per second

P–R

'PAGODA' TROOP Codename for the SAS assault group which stormed the Iranian Embassy in 1980. (SEE *Princes Gate*)

PARACHUTES During World War II the SAS used the Irvin X-Type parachute, a reliable if somewhat crude device for reaching the ground safely. This model was in use until the 1960s before being replaced by the Irvin PX1 Mk 4, the current British Army static-line parachute. During training SAS students are introduced to the PX1 Mk 4 and PX Mk 5, and the PR7 reserve.

The parachute used by the SAS for high altitude, low opening (HALO) descents is the Tactical Assault Parachute Mk 4 with the PR3 reserve. The rig is fitted with an Irvin Hitefinder barometric altimeter device which pulls the ripcord of the main 'chute automatically at an altitude of around 460m. The parachute used for high altitude, high opening (HAHO) descents is the GQ 360 nine-cell flat ramair canopy which allows the trooper to drift silently for great distances. (SEE *HAHO; HALO; Static-line Parachuting Course*)

PARANG Long jungle knife used by the SAS.

'PARAQUET', OPERATION Codename for the recapture of South Georgia by

Right: The Irvin main parachute, as used by the Special Air Service.

the British during the Falklands War in 1982.
(SEE *Falkland Islands; Fortuna Glacier; South Georgia*)

PATROL SKILLS Each member of an SAS four-man patrol has his own special patrol skill. This is either signalling, demolitions, medicine or languages. The four-man patrol is a self-contained unit in which the combination of these skills allows it to operate at its maximum effectiveness.

Communications skills ensure that the patrol is able to keep in constant touch with its HQ. Language skills are extremely important for cultivating links between the patrol and the local population, and are a crucial part of the SAS's 'hearts and minds' policy. In Malaya, for example, many troopers spoke the language of the jungle Aborigines. Demolitions expertise is essential for sabotage operations behind enemy lines, such as those carried out during World War II.

Finally, medicine is useful not only in the treatment of the other patrol members, but also for a 'hearts and minds' campaign. In Oman the work of the medics made a great contribution to the winning of the war. Most members of a four-man patrol have more than one patrol skill as the SAS place great emphasis on cross-training.
(SEE *Four-man Patrol; 'Five Fronts' Campaign; 'Hearts and Minds'; Malaya; Oman; Patrol Skills*)

PEBBLE ISLAND During the 1982 Falklands War, the Argentinians established an airstrip on Pebble Island off the north coast of West Falkland. There were a number of ground-attack aircraft based there that could have posed a major threat to British ground forces once they had landed on East Falkland. The SAS was therefore tasked with destroying them. The ships involved were the carrier HMS *Hermes*, *Broadsword* (an air defence ship for *Hermes*) and *Glamorgan* (which was tasked with bombarding the shore).

Members of D Squadron's Boat Troop landed by canoe on the island before the raid and carried out a reconnaissance of the airstrip. Originally the SAS had been ordered to destroy the aircraft, their ground crews and the garrison on the island. However, because of strong headwinds *Hermes* took longer to reach the flying-off point than expected. This meant that the SAS had only 30 minutes, not the original 90, to carry out the tasks. The aircraft thus became the main priority target. The helicopters used to transport the men to the airstrip had to be back on *Hermes* before full daylight, as she and her escorts had to be well to the east of the island to minimise the threat from the Argentinian Air Force.

On the night of 14 May 1982, the Sea King helicopters of 846 Squadron carrying 45 members of D Squadron took off from *Hermes*. Also on board was a Royal Naval gunfire observation team. The helicopters landed approximately 6km from the airstrip. Mountain Troop was tasked with attacking the aircraft while the other two troops sealed off the approaches to the airstrip and formed a reserve. As the party moved off, over 100 bombs for the 81mm mortar, explosive charges and 66mm LAW rockets were offloaded from the helicopters.

The party, each man carrying two mortar rounds, was guided to the target by a member of Boat Troop, while other soldiers from the latter formed a protective screen for the mortar team. The attack on the airstrip was led by Captain John Hamilton. When the troops reached the perimeter they opened fire with small arms, M203 grenade launchers and 66mm LAWs. Para-flares from *Glamorgan* illuminated the whole area as the SAS men placed their explosive charges on the aircraft. The Argentinians, caught totally by surprise, managed to return inaccurate fire, causing only one minor casualty.

When the party withdrew, six Pucaras, four Turbo-Mentors and a

Skyvan transport aircraft lay destroyed on the grass. In addition, the SAS had destroyed a large quantity of Argentinian ammunition. More importantly, the Argentinians were denied the use of the airstrip. The raid on Pebble Island was a classic SAS action, reminiscent of the type undertaken in World War II.
(SEE *Falkland Islands; Hamilton, Captain John*)

PEN-Y-FAN Highest peak in the Brecon Beacons range of hills in south Wales. Pen-y-Fan plays an important part in SAS Selection Training.
(SEE *'Fan Dance'; Selection Training*)

PEOPLE'S FRONT FOR THE LIBERATION OF OMAN
(SEE *People's Front for the Liberation of the Occupied Arabian Gulf*)

PEOPLE'S FRONT FOR THE LIBERATION OF THE OCCUPIED ARABIAN GULF Communist Arab group based in the People's Democratic Republic of Yemen (PDRY) which fought the SAS during the campaign in Oman (1970-76). PFLOAG received substantial backing from the Soviet Union and China in the form of money, weapons and training. During the 1960s the movement suggested merger with the less radical Dhofar Liberation Front (DLF) which was waging a guerrilla war against the forces of the Omani government headed by the repressive Sultan Said bin Taimur. The DLF was at first lukewarm about the proposal, finding little merit in the PFLOAG's atheist ideology. However, its members finally agreed, won over by PFLOAG'S modern weapons and money. The well-organised communists quickly established cells on the Jebel Dhofar and started to disseminate propaganda.

PFLOAG also endeavoured to destroy the Dhofaris' tribal structure: children were forcibly taken from their parents and sent for schooling in the PDRY, old men were tortured for

Above: The 'Pink Panther' Land Rover was used by the SAS during the 1991 Gulf War. Its pink camouflage allows it to blend into the desert background.

refusing to deny their God, and young men were sent to China and Russia for training in guerrilla warfare. People's courts were established to oversee what were often pre-judged trials. By 1970 PFLOAG had control of the whole jebel.

However, its techniques had alienated many of the local population. Dhofar, like the rest of Oman, is strongly Moslem. The communists' denial of the existence of God offended many and played into the hands of the government. It also aided the SAS in its attempts to win over the guerrillas. In September 1970, a hard core of the DLF fought their way off the jebel and surrendered to the Omani government after PFLOAG had ordered the disarming of the DLF. They were to become a *firqat* unit, trained and led by the SAS. Whereas PFLOAG lost the support of the majority of Dhofaris because of its methods, the SAS gained support through its 'hearts and minds' policy. Nevertheless, at its height PFLOAG had around 200 full-time soldiers and a 3000-strong militia. After the British had totally withdrawn from the Gulf, PFLOAG changed its name to the People's Front for the Liberation of Oman. (SEE *Dhofar Liberation Front;* Firqat; *'Hearts and Minds'; Oman; Said bin Taimur, Sultan*)

PETERHEAD PRISON Located in Aberdeen, Scotland. In October 1987, an SAS team was used to free a warden being held at knife-point by a prisoner. The troopers abseiled down the outside walls and, under cover of darkness, stormed the building. The operation was over in minutes and the warden was freed unharmed. The prisoner received only minor injuries.

PHANTOM Name given to F Squadron, GHQ Liaison Regiment, which was attached as a general signals section to the SAS Brigade in World War II. The men of Phantom operated with SAS parties, obtaining intelligence from the forward positions and relaying it back to England by wireless. Phantom consisted of a headquarters and four patrols, all under the command of Major J.J. Astor. Two patrols were attached to 1 SAS and two to 2 SAS. Phantom's task was extremely important as its operatives relayed a constant stream of information back to England from SAS bases in France after D-Day. (SEE *Special Air Service*)

'PHANTOM MAJOR' Nickname given by the Germans to David Stirling, the

founder of the Special Air Service, on account of his unit's elusiveness during the North African campaign.
(SEE *North Africa; Stirling, Lieutenant-Colonel David*)

'PINK PANTHER' SAS desert Land Rovers are known as 'Pink Panthers' because of their camouflage. Experience has shown that pink makes them less visible to the enemy.
(SEE *Land Rover*)

'PISTOL', OPERATION Conducted by 51 men of 2 SAS who were dropped into the Alsace/Lorraine region of eastern France on the night of 15 September 1944. Their mission was to cut enemy road and rail communications between the River Rhine and the River Moselle. The group, divided into four parties, was dropped blind, although one party failed to jump due to fog over the target area.

The operation was carried out in terrible weather conditions, and the local population was generally unfriendly because of the area's proximity to the German border (many were of German origin). Nevertheless, four trains were derailed, one locomotive destroyed and one railway line cut. In addition, some vehicles were destroyed. On the debit side, several SAS soldiers were captured and at least two were murdered by the Gestapo. The operation was ended on 3 October, by which time the soldiers had linked up with advancing US forces.
(SEE *Northwest Europe*)

POAT, MAJOR HARRY Joined 1 SAS in North Africa and took part in operations in Tunisia before winning a Military Cross for his part in the landings in Sicily. Became second-in-command of 1 SAS in 1944 and led A and D Squadrons in Operation 'Archway' in 1945.
(SEE *'Archway' Operation*)

'POMEGRANATE', OPERATION This was the only SAS attempt during the

Above: The PRC 319 communications set is ideal for special forces operations. It is designed to take a lot of punishment and still be able to transmit messages.

Italian campaign to destroy aircraft on the ground. On the night of 12 January 1944, Major Widdrington, Lieutenant Hughes and four others from 2 SAS were dropped in central Italy to raid the airfield at San Egidio where a number of German reconnaissance aircraft were based. This was designed to support the Anzio landings (22 January 1944). After the drop the party advanced to the target, but were forced to split up when challenged by a German guard. Widdrington and Hughes went on alone, the others making it back to Allied lines. On the night of 17

January, the two officers got onto the airfield and planted Lewes bombs on seven aircraft. As they were making the bombs they hadn't used safe, one exploded, killing Widdrington and injuring Hughes. The latter was taken to a German hospital, but eventually escaped his captors and made it back to Allied lines in March.
(SEE *Lewes bomb; Italy*)

POPSKI'S PRIVATE ARMY Like the SAS and the Long Range Desert Group (LRDG), this unit was one of a number of 'freelance armies' which sprang up during World War II. The

Russian Vladimir Peniakoff, nick-named 'Popski', initially served in the Libyan Arab Force before joining a number of LRDG patrols. He proposed the formation of a small independent unit to work alongside the LRDG which would specialise in carrying out sabotage behind enemy lines.

In October 1942, Popski was given command of No 1 Demolition Squadron, consisting of 23 men all ranks (it would never exceed 80 men during its career). It was nicknamed Popski's Private Army by Lieutenant-Colonel Shan Hackett, who was at that time coordinator of special forces. The unit became operational in early 1943 and assisted in the German defeat in North Africa, most notably during the outflanking of the Mareth line in Tunisia. With the end of the war in North Africa, the unit seemed destined for disbandment. However, Popski's excellent contacts within the Eighth Army ensured its survival, and it went on to serve as a jeep-mounted reconnaissance and raiding force in Italy up to the end of the war. (SEE *Long Range Desert Group; North Africa*)

'PORTIA', OPERATION Original codename for Operation 'Gobbo'. (SEE *'Gobbo', Operation*)

PRC 319 This state-of-the-art lightweight radio system produced by Thorn EMI is currently in service with the SAS. Specifically designed for use with long-range reconnaissance forces, the PRC 319 transmits at 50 watts (or lower power) in burst data, voice and continuous wave modes. Antennas for sky-wave transmissions can also be attached to the system if required. The set can withstand salt contamination, dust, rain, immersion in water, and can be dropped by parachute.

Frequency range: 1.5 to 40 MHz
Weight: 3.4kg
Facilities: detachable fast Antenna Tuning Unit; detachable Burst Data

Above: The scene at the front of Iranian Embassy on 5 May 1980 as black-clad SAS soldiers armed with Heckler & Koch MP5 submachine guns storm the building.

Device; ancillary Narrow Band Secure Voice Unit; detachable battery; integral modem for burst transmission; and 20 stored channels (10 each for receiver and transmitter Battery life: 500 hours (standby mode)
(SEE *Communications*)

PRINCES GATE Of all the operations carried out by the Special Air Service since World War II, it is the ending of the siege at the Iranian Embassy in 1980 which has most caught the pub-

lic imagination. The image of the black-clad soldiers entering the smoke-filled building created a mysterious aura about the Regiment which endures still.

On the morning of 30 April 1980, six armed terrorists of the Democratic Revolutionary Front for the Liberation of Arabistan (a region of Iran) burst into the Iranian Embassy in Princes Gate, London, and seized 26 hostages, including PC Trevor Lock from Scotland Yard's Diplomatic Protection Group. Within

Above: The SAS storm the embassy.

minutes the five-storey, 50-room building was surrounded by the police. Very soon more specialist units arrived: 'Blue Beret' D11 police marksmen, C13 anti-terrorist officers, members of the Special Patrol Group and C7, Scotland Yard's Technical Support Branch. In addition, SAS plain clothes men arrived during the afternoon to assess the situation.

The terrorists demanded the immediate release of 91 Arabs being held in Iranian jails and their transfer to Britain, and made a request for Arab ambassadors to mediate on their behalf with the British government. The deadline for these demands to be met was set at midday the next day, otherwise the embassy would be destroyed and the hostages killed. Police negotiators started working on the terrorists, who by the evening of 1 May had abandoned their call for the release of the prisoners, though they still threatened the hostages with death if their demands were not broadcast over the radio. The demand for the mediators was broadcast over the radio later, though they failed to materialise.

While negotiations were going on, an SAS Special Projects Team had been deployed to the area as part of Operation 'Nimrod'. They were put on stand-by on the orders of Prime Minister Margaret Thatcher, who had consulted with members of the Ministry of Defence (MOD), MI5, MI6 and the SAS, known collectively as the Cabinet Office Briefing Room (COBRA). COBRA'S recommendations were then passed to the Joint Operations Centre (JOC) within the MOD – the Special Projects Team had then been deployed.

At a barracks in Regents Park the SAS soldiers studied a model of the building. Intelligence was also gathered and passed on by C7, which had placed a number of microphones and surveillance devices in the chimneys and walls of adjoining buildings. Thermal imagers were also used to determine which rooms were occupied. The SAS plan was quite simple:

one four-man team would abseil down the rear of the building to the ground and first floors. Another team would enter the building at the front. The teams would use frame charges to effect entry and then lob in stun grenades immediately beforehand to disorientate the terrorists. All team members would be dressed in black one-piece suits, bullet-proof jackets, respirators, and would carry Browning High Power handguns and Heckler & Koch MP5 submachine guns.

By the morning of 5 May, the situation inside the embassy was rapidly deteriorating. The government's refusal to make concessions had resulted in the terrorists losing confidence in the police negotiators. At 1850 hours, they shot an embassy press officer and dumped his body on the pavement at the front of the building. The negotiators made immediate contact with the leader of the terrorists and promised safe conduct for him and his group and an aircraft to take them out of the country. However, while these talks were going on 'Pagoda' Troop, the code-name for the SAS party, stormed the building.

One pair of SAS soldiers abseiled down to the first-floor balcony while another pair reached the ground. The men on the balcony were unable to detonate their frame charge because one of their comrades was dangling above them, entangled in his rope. Both teams were forced to use sledge-hammers to gain entry. Stun grenades were thrown in and then the men went inside the building. At the front of the building, the SAS team blew in the window with frame charges, threw in stun and CS grenades, and then went inside. The electric power to the embassy had been cut immediately before the assault to aid the counter-terrorist soldiers. The building quickly filled with smoke and tear gas.

The terrorist leader was killed on the first-floor landing as the SAS sol-diers made their way to the second-floor telex room where, thanks to C7

Above: The pulk, *such as these in use with the Royal Marines, is ideal for pulling heavy loads over snow and ice. They were used by the SAS on Fortuna Glacier.*

surveillance, they knew the hostages were being held. The three terrorists guarding the hostages killed one of their captives and wounded two oth-ers before the SAS burst into the room and stopped the slaughter. Two terrorists were killed and the third captured. All six had been accounted for, as one had been killed in the hall-way near the front door and another was killed in an office at the back of the building. The operation was over in 17 minutes. The hostages and one remaining terrorist were quickly evac-uated from the burning building. The SAS soldiers, who had suffered no

casualties, left the area in two vans. Operation 'Nimrod' was over.
(SEE *Counter Revolutionary Warfare; Counter Revolutionary Warfare Equipment; Counter Revolutionary Warfare Wing; Frame Charge; JOC; MI5; MI6; Special Projects Team; Stun Grenade*)

PULK Hand-drawn sledge used by the SAS and other British Army units to haul heavy loads over snow and ice.
(SEE *Fortuna Glacier*)

PUMA
(SEE *SA 330*)

Above: Sultan Qaboos, the ruler of Oman since 1970, gave his support to the SAS raising firqat *units in Oman.*

Q

QABOOS, SULTAN Ruler of Oman since 1970. Qaboos' reign saw the deployment of the SAS to his country, where the Regiment fought one of its most effective campaigns. Born on 18 November 1940, Qaboos received extensive education in Britain before undertaking military training at the Royal Military Academy Sandhurst and being commissioned into a British regiment, the Cameronians, as a second lieutenant. He was also sent on a fact-finding mission around Britain, a period which involved him sitting on council committees, industrial boards and the like to enable him to understand the intricacies of running a nation state. When he returned to Oman, however, he was placed under virtual house arrest. His father, the autocratic Sultan Said Taimur, believed he had become too westernised and that his moderate ideas for reform were too radical.

Qaboos endured his imprisonment for seven years. Meanwhile Oman, under the reactionary rule of his father, was falling apart. In the southwest the inhabitants of Dhofar province rebelled against their miserable living conditions, which could have been improved if the Sultan had not refused to spend any of the oil revenues on the social betterment of his people. Qaboos decided to act; on 23 July 1970, with the aid of Sheikh Baraik Bin Hamood, he mounted a palace coup which removed his father.

Within days the new Sultan, protected by SAS bodyguards, announced a general amnesty and plans for civil development in Oman. These measures greatly aided the SAS 'hearts and minds' policy which was launched in the same year as they convinced many Omanis that their lot would improve under Qaboos. In addition, Qaboos's enthusiasm for the formation of *firqat* units was another boost for the SAS campaign. Though the rule of Sultan Qaboos was, and is, autocratic, the living standards of Omanis have improved. More impor-

tantly perhaps, Oman also remains a pro-Western state in a sensitive, oil-rich region.

(SEE *Firqat; 'Hearts and Minds'; Oman; Said bin Taimur, Sultan*)

QATTARA DEPRESSION Located in Egypt, the Qattara Depression is a geographical feature 240km long and 120km wide with a salt-pan floor. It has steep sides and only a few hard crossing points which can carry vehicles. In July 1942, it formed the southern end of the British so-called El Alamein line, the northern end of which rested on the North African coast. To support the proposed offensive of the Commander-in-Chief Middle East, General Sir Claude Auchinleck, David Stirling, the commander of the SAS, wanted to mount a series of raids on several forward Axis airfields: Sidi Haneish, Bagoush, Fuka, El Daba and Sidi Barrani. Stirling was determined to establish a forward operating base from where

Below: SAS jeeps such as these made the crossing of the Qattara Depression in July 1942. As was usual for vehicles operating in the North African desert, the jeeps suffered many punctures and overheated engines. Despite this, all completed the journey.

parties could be sent out on raids. In early July an SAS column consisting of jeeps and trucks and 100 men set off from Cairo and headed south, skirting the edge of the Depression before reaching open desert. After two weeks of operations a party had to be sent back to Kabrit to pick up fresh supplies.

However, by this time the Germans had cut off the original route and so the column had to cross the Depression. The journey was extremely tough: trucks often had to be dug out of the sand and the heat was so intense that petrol vaporised in fuel pipes. Nevertheless, in true SAS style, all the vehicles made it and the supplies were transported back to those who had been left behind at the forward base 100km north of Qara. (SEE *Bagoush; El Daba; Fuka; Kabrit; North Africa; Sidi Barrani; Sidi Haneish; Stirling, Lieutenant-Colonel David*)

Queen Elizabeth II A luxury cruise liner owned by the British company Cunard. In May 1972, an anonymous caller rang Cunard's American office and disclosed that six bombs had been planted on the ship which, at the time, was en route from the USA to Britain, and that they would be detonated unless a demand for a large sum of money was met. The ship was in mid-Atlantic and the captain, William Law, ordered an immediate search of the vessel. London was informed and an RAF Nimrod aircraft was stationed over the liner to act as a communications centre.

Lieutenant-Colonel George Styles, at the time in charge of Explosive Ordnance Disposal, was ordered to deal with the threat. He immediately sent a team which was to be dropped by parachute from a transport aircraft near the liner. The four men were Captain Robert Whelms, a bomb disposal expert, Sergeant Clifford Oliver, 22 SAS, Lieutenant Richard Clifford and Corporal Thomas Jones, both of the Special Boat Squadron. They took

Above: British troops on patrol in the Radfan. Intensely hot during the day and freezing cold at night, the region was a soldier's nightmare.

off from RAF Lyneham in a C-130 and were dropped by parachute into the Atlantic a short distance from the ship.

Davies and his team examined the suspicious objects which had been discovered by the vessel's engine-room staff. Pronouncing them harmless, the team then made a thorough search of the ship but found nothing. The emergency had been a hoax. Shortly afterwards a man was arrested by the FBI in America and charged with demanding money with menaces from Cunard.

Though the incident had come to nothing, it did highlight the versatility and preparedness of Britain's special forces units.
(SEE *C-130; Special Boat Squadron*)

R

RADFAN Inhospitable mountainous region in the north of the Republic of Yemen. During the British involvement in Aden in the 1960s, the Radfan was the scene of several SAS operations. By 1964 the fiercely independent inhabitants of the region were conducting guerrilla attacks against the British, having been trained by the North Yemenis and armed by the Egyptians. In May of that year A Squadron, 22 SAS, arrived at Thumier, 50km from the Yemeni border. This would be the main SAS base during its involvement in the region.

Above: The Habilayn airstrip. Aircraft flown from here were used to support SAS operations in the Radfan (1964-67). The Regiment had a base at nearby Thumier.

In the same month the British assembled Radforce, made up of Royal Marines, members of the Parachute Regiment, Royal Horse Artillery, East Anglian Regiment and units of Aden's Federal Regular Army. Its task was to re-establish British authority over the area and stop the flow of weapons to the rebel Quteibi tribesmen. The first operation, which was spearheaded by a nine-man patrol from 3 Troop, A Squadron, was launched at the end of April and was designed to capture two strategic positions named 'Cap Badge' and 'Rice Bowl'. The SAS patrol, led by Captain Robin Edwards, was tasked with capturing 'Cap Badge' which was to be be used as a dropping zone for paratroopers. However, during the next 30 hours the patrol encountered hostile tribesmen and was forced to retire. Edwards and

Warburton, his signaller, were killed and their heads later displayed in public.

Despite this inauspicious beginning, the SAS quickly settled into a routine in the Radfan. Small teams would be inserted into enemy territory at night to establish concealed observation posts (OPs) high on the rocky slopes, from where they directed air and artillery strikes against rebel tribesmen moving through the passes. The Regiment maintained a presence in the Radfan until Britain's withdrawal from Aden in 1967. The area's hostile environment was attested to by A Squadron's commander, Peter de la Billière, who stated: 'A further interesting aspect is the manner in which the tough conditions out here have sorted out the weak and the strong individuals in the squadron. The mental and combined physical strain

here are never approached in Borneo, and an average man can bumble along quite happily out there. Here, however, a man has to be master of self-discipline and of his job, or he will start to waver.'
(SEE *Aden; de la Billière, General Sir Peter; Edwards, Captain Robin; North Yemen; OP; Thumier*)

RAPPELLING
(SEE *Abseiling*)

RECCE SAS and British Army abbreviation of reconnaissance.

REDDY, TROOPER 'RIP' Ill-fated member of an SAS mission to Oman's northern province in 1970. Reddy, along with other members of one of the Regiment's recce troops, made a night-time freefall parachute drop from a height of 3000m but fell to his death. Nevertheless, the remainder of the troop managed to link up with other SAS personnel and

Above: Rhodesian SAS soldiers on patrol in the bush. The unit was prominent in the long fight against black nationalism in what is now Zimbabwe.

carry out sweeps for dissidents operating in the area.

'REGAN', OPERATION This operation, conducted by 5 SAS during World War II, was later renamed Operation 'Fabian'.
(SEE *'Fabian', Operation*)

'REGENT', OPERATION Conducted by the whole of the Belgian Independent Parachute Company (5 SAS) between 27 December 1944 and 15 January 1945. The jeep-mounted party, commanded by Captain Blondeel, was tasked with supporting British armoured units in preventing a German breakthrough in the Ardennes during the 'Battle of the Bulge'. The Belgians, operating in the St Hubert/Burl area, were used as assault troops in the wooded terrain and not for reconnaissance.
(SEE *Ardennes; Blondeel, Captain; Northwest Europe*)

REID-DALY, COLONEL RONALD Commander of the Rhodesian unit, the Selous Scouts, and, before that, a member of the Malayan Scouts.
(SEE *Malayan Scouts; Selous Scouts*)

REMINGTON 870 Pump-action shotgun which is used by the Regiment for counter-terrorist work, specifically blowing door hinges prior to a forced entry into a building or room during a hostage-rescue operation. It has been widely employed in this role in Northern Ireland.

Type: pump-action shotgun
Designation: Remington 870
Calibre: 12-gauge
Weight: 3.6kg
Length: 1060mm

Effective range: 40m
Feed: seven-shot tubular magazine

RENNIE, MAJOR FRANK The first commander of the New Zealand SAS, Rennie was responsible for establishing the stringent entry requirements which resulted in the unit performing so well in Malaya.
(SEE *Malaya; New Zealand SAS*)

RHODES, COMPANY SERGEANT-MAJOR 'DUSTY' One of the team of SAS men who searched for those responsible for the murder of captured SAS personnel by the Germans during World War II. The unit, set up by Brian Franks and headed by Major Eric Barkwoth, was responsible for the capture of several former Gestapo officers.
(SEE *Barkworth, Major Eric; Franks, Lieutenant-Colonel Brian*)

RHODESIAN SAS In the early 1950s,

Major Mike Calvert, founder of the Malayan Scouts, travelled to Rhodesia to recruit men for his unit. He selected 100 men for his Far East Volunteer Unit, who formed C Squadron, Malayan Scouts (SAS), and wore Rhodesian shoulder flashes. The squadron was organised and led by two officers: Peter Walls and Lieutenant Ron Campbell-Morrison. The Rhodesians stayed in Malaya for two years, losing only two men in action.

Once back in Rhodesia many men returned to civilian life, however Walls and a few others stayed in the army and conducted counter-insurgency training. In the early 1960s, the small team of men from the original unit was ordered to select and train recruits after they had spent some time with the British SAS. Six 'Sabre' Troops of 184 men in total were formed. Following Rhodesia's Unilateral Declaration of Independence from Britain in late 1965, the Rhodesian SAS began operations against black nationalist groups, although their initial role was one of reconnaissance. These missions included cross-border raids into Mozambique, Zambia and Botswana in pursuit of guerrillas.

By 1978 the unit totalled nearly 250 officers and men and was renamed 1 Special Air Service Regiment (Rhodesia). All members were trained in parachuting, small boat operations and long-range patrol techniques. Majority black rule in Rhodesia, however, led to the disbandment of the unit in 1980. Many former members went on to join the South African Defence Force.
(SEE *Calvert, Brigadier Mike; Malayan Scouts; Walls, General Peter*)

RIGID RAIDER Small, fast boat which is ideally suited for small-scale amphibious commando raids. Capable of carrying nine fully-equipped men or a payload of 900kg, it has a top speed of 40 knots.

Below: The Rigid Raider is a fast and highly manoeuvrable craft used by both SAS Boat Troops and the Royal Marines.

RILEY, PAT The first Regimental Sergeant-Major of the SAS and one of the originals of L Detachment.
(SEE *L Detachment*)

ROSE, LIEUTENANT-COLONEL MIKE Commander of 22 SAS during the Falklands War in 1982. It was Rose, together with Brigadier Peter de la Billière, who was responsible for the Regiment taking such an active part in the British operation to retake the islands. On hearing of the Argentinian invasion of the islands, he lobbied Brigadier Julian Thompson, commander of 3 Commando Brigade, Royal Marines, for inclusion of the Regiment in the Landing Force Task Group.

Towards the end of the campaign, Rose, with the assistance of a Royal Marines officer fluent in Spanish, conducted psychological warfare operations against the enemy headquarters at Port Stanley, highlighting the Argentinians' weak position and hopeless situation over the radio. This hastened the collapse of resistance, and on the afternoon of 14 June Rose flew into Port Stanley by helicopter to commence talks that eventually led to the formal surrender.
(SEE *de la Billière, General Sir Peter; Falkland Islands; South Georgia*)

'RTU'D' Returned to unit. Phrase generally applied to students who fail SAS Selection and Continuation Training, although it can also be used to describe members of the Regiment who have been returned to their original unit after a grave misdemeanour has resulted in their expulsion from the SAS.
(SEE *Continuation Training; Selection Training*)

RUBBER-COATED LADDERS Item of specialist kit used in hostage-rescue operations by a counter-terrorist unit. Because of their covering, the ladders can be placed noiselessly against an entry point. During GSG 9's successful operation at Mogadishu in 1977, for example, rubber-coated ladders were placed at the aircraft's emergency exits over the wings and at the front and rear of the Boeing 737. They are just one item in the armoury of the modern counter-terrorist unit.
(SEE *GSG 9; Counter Revolutionary Warfare Equipment; Mogadishu*)

RULES OF ENGAGEMENT The SAS, like other British Army units, is governed by specific rules concerning the use of force in its operations outside of wartime. These rules apply to SAS activities in Northern Ireland, where the Regiment is often accused of operating a shoot-to-kill policy against members of the Irish Republican Army (IRA) in Ulster. This may at first seem confusing, as it would appear reasonable for SAS soldiers to shoot terrorists who are, after all, trying to kill the soldiers. However, in Ulster the situation is far from simple, although the rules governing the behaviour of British troops appear unambiguous.

SAS teams are not allowed to use more force than is necessary and soldiers can open fire only if they have reasonable grounds for believing the suspect/suspects is committing, or about to commit, any action which could endanger their lives, any other lives, or if there is no way of preventing this. Firing without warning is allowed, but only if the giving of a warning or any delay in firing could lead to death or injury to the SAS or any other person, or the giving of a warning is impracticable. If the rules regarding firing without warning do not apply, then SAS soldiers must give a clear warning and indicate to the suspect/suspects that failure to obey will result in the opening of fire.

All the above appears fine, until one realises that the people the soldiers are giving the warnings to are dangerous armed terrorists who are often highly trained in the use of firearms. This being the case, British soldiers, especially the SAS, have as their first priority the safety of themselves and their comrades. In a contact with terrorists that is often over in seconds, the quick reactions of the terrorists render the issuing of a warning useless. The SAS in particular is aware that its own soldiers have died because they were too slow in an engagement. This being the case, it seems likely that there will always be controversy surrounding the attempted arrest of known terrorists. Incidents such as the SAS operation at Gibraltar illustrate that even the most highly trained soldiers in the world cannot strictly adhere to the rules of engagement laid down by the British government, which are, after all, drawn up by lawyers sitting in offices.
(SEE *Gibraltar; Irish Republican Army; Jones, Lance-Corporal David; Northern Ireland*)

'RUPERT' SAS term for an officer, often used disparagingly.

'RUPERT', OPERATION One of a number of World War II SAS missions which suffered from unfortunate delays. 'Rupert' was originally scheduled to begin just after D-Day, but objections from senior SOE figures forced a postponement until 23 July 1944. The object was to destroy as many railway lines as possible in the Verdun, Reims and Metz area of eastern France, and also establish contact with local *Maquis* forces.

The lead party, consisting of 58 men of 2 SAS, was to be parachuted into the area on 23 July. However, the aircraft crashed, killing all on board. The main group was dropped on 4 August, with further reinforcements under Major Rooney joining the base on the 24th. However, by this time General George Patton's US Third Army was in the area and the SAS party was too near the main front to carry out effective sabotage operations. 'Rupert' ended on 10 September, having achieved little.
(SEE Maquis; *Northwest Europe; SOE*)

S

S-61 Predominantly used as a search and rescue aircraft, the Sea King helicopter has been employed by the SAS for aggressive operations, notably during the Pebble Island raid in the 1982 Falklands War. The Sea King is an extremely rugged and versatile aircraft which can operate in all weathers.

Type: anti-submarine and search and rescue helicopter
Crew: four
Range: 480km
Payload: 9525kg
Maximum speed: 208km/hr
Armament: none
Passengers: 19
(SEE *Falkland Islands; Pebble Island*)

SA-80 The new individual weapon of the British Army which is a replacement for the SLR. Despite teething problems, the SA-80 has proved itself to be an accurate, well-balanced weapon which is easy to strip and clean in the field – all qualities which make it attractive for SAS teams on extended operations. The gun is self-loading and is capable of single-shot or full-automatic fire. In addition, a grenade launcher, designed to fit under the barrel and fire 40mm ammunition out to a range of 350m, is currently under development.

Type: assault rifle
Designation: L85A1

Left: The SA-80 rifle. Its bullpup design, whereby the firing mechanism is set back in the stock, means it is more compact than its predecessor, the SLR. Right: The SA 330 transport helicopter.

Calibre: 5.56mm
Weight: 4.98kg (with loaded magazine and optical sight)
Length: 785mm
Effective range: 400m
Rate of fire: 650-800 rounds per minute (cyclic)
Feed: 30-round box magazine
Muzzle velocity: 940 metres per second
(SEE *Grenades; SLR*)

SA 330 The Puma tactical transport helicopter is used extensively by the SAS, particularly in Northern Ireland. A reliable aircraft, it has a large cabin which can accommodate up to 20 lightly armed, or 16 fully equipped, troops. In addition, loads of up to 2500kg can be slung beneath its fuselage (making it ideal for transporting Light Strike Vehicles). The Puma can be used in all types of terrain. For example, special 'polyvalent' air intakes have been fitted to some models as protection for the engines, allowing the aircraft to be used in arctic conditions.

Type: tactical transport helicopter
Crew: two
Range: 550km
Payload: 7400kg
Maximum speed: 293km/hr
Armament: none
Passengers: up to 20
(SEE *Light Strike Vehicle*)

'SABRE' Name given to each of the four combat squadrons of the Special Air Service. The 'Sabre' Squadrons

Above: Two members of the Greek Sacred Squadron relax after participating in a Special Boat Squadron raid in the Aegean, 1943.

are A, B, D and G, with R Squadron being a reserve. Each has a paper strength of 64 men divided into four troops, all commanded by a major. (SEE *Special Air Service*)

SACRED SQUADRON A World War II Greek unit which was composed of men who had escaped from the German invaders of their country in April 1941. In the autumn of 1942, the unit was attached to the SAS (David Stirling had been lobbying for the Greeks to be part of his force because he believed their knowledge would be an asset to any SAS operations in the Balkans). The Sacred Squadron took part in the campaign in North Africa, numbering 121 men in January 1943. Later that year some of the Greeks were attached to the Special Boat Squadron and performed heroically in the Aegean. However, by this stage they had effectively left the SAS. The remainder were returned to the control of the Greek authorities in March 1943.

(SEE *North Africa; Special Air Service; Special Boat Squadron; Stirling, Lieutenant-Colonel David*)

SAID BIN TAIMUR, SULTAN Autocratic ruler of Oman whose despotism and refusal to make any effort to modernise his country led to rebellion breaking out in northern Oman (1957) and in the province of Dhofar (1962). As matters worsened, SAS detachments were sent to deal with each uprising. Under his rule there were few schools, hospitals or roads in Oman. The state of the country may be judged by the comments of the British economist John Townsend, who visited the country in 1969: 'No man could leave his village and seek work without the permission of the Sultan. No man could repair his house without the permission of the Sultan. This remote old man, who never left his palace in Salalah and ruled by radio-telephone through expatriates, had instilled such a fear in his people that very few of them dared defy him and undertake any initiative to improve their lot.'

This dire state of affairs was partly ended by the Sultan's son, Qaboos, who mounted a bloodless palace coup in 1970 (although his father did manage to shoot himself in the foot during the episode). Said bin Taimur was banished to London, where he lived out the last two years of his life in great luxury.
(SEE *Jebel Akhdar; Oman; Qaboos, Sultan*)

SALAHADIN, FIRQAT Name of the first *firqat* unit formed during the SAS's campaign in Oman (1970–76). In September 1970, Salim Mubarak, a leading figure within the Dhofar Liberation Front (DLF), together with 24 of his men, fought his way off the Jebel Dhofar and surrendered to Sultan Qaboos. He and his followers were disillusioned by the communist-based ideology of the powerful People's Front for the Liberation of the Occupied Arabian Gulf (which by

Right: Unlike this simple sangar, those encountered by the SAS in Aden (1964–67) were like small forts.

1970 dominted both the Jebel Dhofar and the DLF). In January 1971, Salim met Major Tony Jeapes, 22 SAS, and suggested the formation of a *firqat*, an irregular company, to fight on behalf of the Sultan. He would do this if Jeapes could organise training facilities and weapons. After consulting his superiors and the Sultan, Jeapes agreed and training began. The unit was named the *Firqat Salahadin* after the great Moslem leader who had fought the infidels in the early Middle Ages.

The *Firqat Salahadin* was blooded at Sudh in February 1971, where it achieved an easy victory and took the town. One of the unique features about the unit was that it was multi-tribal, a fact which, perhaps surprisingly, encouraged military discipline. Other *firqats* tended to be run like communes which was very democratic but infuriating for the SAS instructors. In March Salim died of a heart attack, but his ideas flourished. More tribal leaders stepped forward to form *firqat* units. By late April the *Firqat Salahadin* was 68-strong, although this was reduced to 28 when the other 40 decided to enlist under the leadership of Qartoob, an ex-DLF leader who had joined after the success at Sudh. Nevertheless, the *Firqat Salahadin* and the vision of Salim

Mubarak had established a viable concept that was to prove an invaluable asset to the SAS in Oman.
(SEE *Dhofar Liberation Front;* Firqat; *Jeapes, Brigadier Tony; Oman; People's Front for the Liberation of the Occupied Arabian Gulf; Qaboos, Sultan*)

'SAMSON', OPERATION Conducted by 24 men of 3 French Parachute Battalion (3 SAS) between 10 August and 27 September 1944. The party was parachuted into the area west of Limoges, southern France, to disrupt enemy road traffic and stiffen local *Maquis* forces. 'Samson' was moderately successful, with some German vehicles being destroyed and the SAS inflicting approximately 100 casualties.
(SEE Maquis*; Northwest Europe*)

'SAMWEST', OPERATION Between 6 and 9 June 1944, 116 men of 4 French Parachute Battalion, led by Captain Le Blond, were dropped into northern Brittany to establish a base near St. Brieuc. Their task, in common with the other SAS parties dropped immediately after D-Day, was to prevent the movement of German forces from western Brittany to Normandy.

After landing the party received a very warm reception from the local population, who believed that libera-

tion was at hand. However, though the local *Maquis* was armed, its rather poor security measures led to the SAS base being attacked by the Germans on 12 June. Despite a ferocious battle in which the enemy lost a substantial number of casualties, the SAS and *Maquis* were scattered. Most of the French SAS subsequently joined the 'Dingson' base.

(SEE *'Dingson', Operation;* Maquis*; Northwest Europe*)

SANGAR An improvised wall of rocks or other materials, for example sandbags, often arranged in a circle and usually built where the ground does not allow defensive positions to be dug in. Sangars are employed by armies throughout the world, and were widely used by the SAS during its operations in Aden and Oman.

(SEE *Aden; Oman*)

SARAWAK RANGERS Official title of the unit composed of Iban trackers who were employed by the British during the Malayan Emergency (1948-60). As the name suggests, the trackers came from the Sarawak region of Borneo. The SAS was involved in teaching the Rangers basic military skills while the latter, in turn, shared the secrets of their considerable tracking abilities. Later, during the campaign in Borneo (1963-66), the SAS recruited several ex-Sarawak Rangers in their fight against the Indonesians.

(SEE *Borneo; Iban Tribesmen; Malaya*)

SARBE Surface-to-air rescue beacon. A small radio used for communications between an aircraft and parties on the ground. Used extensively by the SAS, particularly during its campaign in Oman.

(SEE *Oman*)

SAS Special Air Service.

(SEE *Special Air Service*)

SAS REGIMENTAL PRAYER 'O Lord, who didst call on Thy disciples to

Above: Major Sandy Scratchley, who fought with 2 SAS in Sicily and Italy during World War II, caught in jovial mood.

venture all to win all men to Thee, grant that we, the chosen members of the Special Air Service Regiment, may by our works and our ways, dare all to win all, and in doing so render special service to Thee and our fellow men in all the world. Through the same Jesus Christ, Our Lord, Amen.'

SAS WAR CRIMES INVESTIGATION TEAM

(SEE *Barker, Major Eric*)

SAVESAKI, TROOPER Fijian member of the SAS team that fought at the Battle of Mirbat in Oman on 19 July 1972. A top-class rugby player, Savesaki made a heroic dash over

open ground under fire to reach a wounded comrade. He was badly wounded in the action but later recovered.

(SEE *Mirbat*)

'SAXIFRAGE', OPERATION Run in conjunction with Operation 'Candytuft', 'Saxifrage' was supposed to cut the railway line between Ancona and Pescara on the east Italian coast. The four parties from 2 SAS, led by Major Roy Farran and Lieutenant Grant Hibbert, were landed by torpedo boat on 27 October 1943 and remained behind enemy lines for six days. Despite the fact that it rained continuously, the parties managed to

cut the railway line in several places and mine the coast road. Only two men were captured, the rest being evacuated by torpedo boat.
(SEE 'Candytuft', Operation; Farran, Major Roy; Italy)

'SCRAN' SAS slang for food.

SCRATCHLEY, MAJOR SANDY
Joined the SAS as a lieutenant in early 1942 and subsequently took part in operations in North Africa. He was with 2 SAS in Sicily and Italy, taking part in Operation 'Sleepy Lad', and stayed on the Italian peninsula until the end of the war in 1945.
(SEE Italy; North Africa; Sicily; 'Sleepy Lad', Operation)

SEALs The US Navy's Sea, Air and Land (SEAL) units are predominantly concerned with unconventional warfare operations: beach and coastal reconnaissance, deception, counter-insurgency, and special operations in a hostile environment. However, SEAL Team 6, established in November 1980, specialises in counter-terrorism and is part of Delta Force. Team 6 has 100 top-grade volunteers taken from other SEAL Teams, who are all highly trained in the use of small arms and operate in four-man assault squads. Their specialities include preventing terrorist attacks on oil rigs in the Gulf of Mexico and on US ships in general. SEAL Team 6 has worked closely with the SAS in the area of counter-terrorist warfare and has carried out exchange training with its British counterpart.
(SEE Delta Force)

SECRET INTELLIGENCE SERVICE
(SEE MI6)

SEEKINGS, SERGEANT-MAJOR REG
One of the originals of L Detachment, Reg Seekings came from No 7 Commando. He was a member of the first SAS operation in November 1941, and went on to take part in the many raids against Axis airfields in North Africa. He was a member of the Special Raiding Squadron during the Sicilian and Italian campaigns, being awarded the Military Medal (he already had a Distinguished Conduct Medal). At Termoli in October 1943, he had a lucky escape while sitting in the cab of a truck. A German shell landed in the back, killing all the occupants. In June 1944, he was one of the advance party for Operation 'Bulbasket', being later shot through the neck, the bullet narrowly missing his spine. By this time he held the rank of sergeant-major. Seekings survived the war and later joined the Rhodesian Police.
(SEE 'Bulbasket', Operation; North Africa; Sicily; Special Raiding Squadron; Termoli)

SELECTION TRAINING
The first hurdle a soldier must overcome on his way to becoming a member of the Special Air Service. The Regiment's selection procedures are specifically designed to weed out the unsuitable and enlist only those with the right qualities: a man who is mentally and physically tough, self-reliant, and has the intelligence to think through a situation regardless of the conditions or circumstances.

It is impossible to enter the SAS directly, each volunteer must have had previous service with a regular unit. As a result, most men who volunteer are in their mid-20s. In addition, a further rule stipulates that they must have a minimum of three years and three months left to serve from the date that, if successful, they pass Selection Training. The course is run twice a year, once in the summer and once in the winter, and each volunteer must wait until there is a vacancy before he is called. If he is sensible he will begin getting his body into shape long before this time.

The course, which lasts for one month, is run by Training Wing, 22 SAS, and is based on the one designed by Major John Woodhouse when he returned from Malaya in 1953. There is a three-week build-up period for soldiers (two weeks for officers) before Test Week, the culmination of Selection. Each student will have been pronounced fit by his own Regimental Medical Officer before being accepted on Selection, but the SAS likes to give each man a chance of getting up to its physical requirements. Therefore, the volunteers begin with sets of road runs which increase in length during the first week. Each man must be capable of passing the standard Battle Fitness Test (BFT) in the time allotted for infantry/airborne soldiers, although this standard is the bare minimum.

As the course progresses there are a number of rigorous cross-country marches over the Black Mountains and Brecon Beacons of South Wales. Physical fitness is not the only requirement, however, as students must also be proficient in map-reading and navigation. At the start of Selection they are divided into pairs, but as the course progresses they undertake the marches alone. Each man is given a bergen, a map and a compass, and is then given the grid reference for the first rendezvous (RV). He sets off knowing that he must complete the course as quickly as possible, although only the directing staff know the time limit. On reaching the first RV he is informed of the next one and so on. This uncertainty induces stress which the student must conquer if he is going to pass. All the time he is continually being watched and assessed.

By Test Week the numbers on the course will have dropped. Some will have left of their own accord, others will have been 'binned'. In addition, the weight of the bergens will have been increased from 11kg to 25kg to add to the difficulties. The culmination of Test Week is 'Long Drag' or the 'Fan Dance', a 60km land-navigation exercise over the highest points in the Brecon Beacons which has to be completed in 20 hours regardless of the weather conditions (which can be appalling). Most students who get this far usually pass the 'Fan Dance'. However, the successful candidates are not yet in the SAS. Now they must endure Continuation Training. (SEE *Bergen; BFT; 'Bin'; Brecon Beacons; Continuation Training; 'Fan Dance'; Special Air Service; Woodhouse, Lieutenant-Colonel John*)

SELOUS SCOUTS An elite Rhodesian unit that had links with the Rhodesian SAS. The Selous Scouts specialised in counter-insurgency warfare, specifically the highly dangerous infiltration of guerrilla-dominated areas disguised as the enemy. An officer from the SAS, Mike Graham, was one of the founders of the Scouts, which consisted of personnel from both Rhodesia and overseas. However, its secrecy and 'special' status aroused resentment in the regular forces, and

the Scouts were also accused of gun-running and poaching. The Scouts' commander resigned in 1979 and the next year, following the implementation of black majority rule, the unit was disbanded. (SEE *Rhodesian SAS*)

SENNYBRIDGE TRAINING AREA British Army training area located in South Wales which is close to Stirling Lines, the Regiment's base at Hereford. It is used extensively by the SAS for live-firing exercises and range drills. (SEE *Stirling Lines*)

'SHAKE OUT' SAS slang for preparing for combat.

'SHAKESPEARE', OPERATION Conducted by a small detachment of the Belgian Independent Parachute

Company between 31 July and 15 August 1944. The party, 22 men led by Lieutenants Debefre and Limbosen, was tasked with harassing the retreating Germans west of Paris. The Belgians were dropped by parachute into the area northwest of Le Mans but, because they were on foot, they only encountered the tail of the retreating enemy forces. However, they did assist in the rescue of 150 downed Allied airmen. (SEE *Belgian Independent Parachute Company; Northwest Europe*)

'SHOOT AND SCOOT' An SAS standard operating procedure (SOP) designed by Lieutenant-Colonel John Woodhouse for four-man patrols fighting in the jungle. It basically advocates making a rapid withdrawal during a chance encounter with the enemy. This tactic was designed to prevent casualties when there was no point in holding ground. When the enemy opened fire, for example, the

Below: Weapons checked, every man briefed, adrenalin levels high – a patrol 'shakes out' in wooded terrain deep behind enemy lines.

Above: A 'Sim Cas' exercise being conducted in the Far East. Medical expertise is essential in units which, because of their role, will often be behind enemy lines.

patrol would instantly return a heavy barrage of fire and, while the enemy were working out their next move, the patrol would 'scoot' to the emergency rendezvous, with each man taking a different route to confuse the opposition. SAS casualties would have to make their own way to any pre-arranged extraction point.
(SEE *Woodhouse, Lieutenant-Colonel John; SOPs*)

SHOTGUNS The SAS first employed shotguns during the Malayan Emergency (1948-60), when patrol lead scouts were issued with FN-Browning autoloaders. At present the Regiment employs shotguns for counter-terrorist duties, specifically hostage-rescue work. They are favoured because of the heavy close-range firepower they can put down

and their ability to handle a wide variety of cartridge types: buckshot, baton rounds, birdshot, armour-piercing, rubber ball, CS rounds, Hatton rounds (designed to blow hinges off doors without injuring the occupants of the room), and so on. The model most favoured by the SAS is the Remington 870 semi-automatic pump-action, although other models used have included the Franchi SPAS 12 and SPAS 15 12-gauge weapons, together with the USAS-12 combat shotgun designed by the Gilbert Equipment Company of the USA.
(SEE *Remington 870; Franchi SPAS 12; Franchi SPAS 15*)

SICILY Both the Special Raiding Squadron (SRS), 1 SAS temporarily renamed, and 2 SAS were involved in the Allied capture of Sicily in July-

August 1943 under their respective commanders, Lieutenant-Colonel 'Paddy' Mayne and Lieutenant-Colonel William Stirling. The SRS assaulted Capo Murro di Porco on 10 July and Augusta two days later, both operations being successful. 1 SAS had rather mixed fortunes, conducting two operations, 'Narcissus' and 'Chestnut', the latter being unsuccessful. However, overall the SAS made a significant contribution to the Allied success on the island.
(SEE *'Chestnut', Operation; Italy; Mayne, Lieutenant-Colonel 'Paddy' Blair; 'Narcissus', Operation; Stirling, Lieutenant-Colonel William*)

SIDI BARRANI Axis airfield in North Africa. Target of an SAS raid in July 1942 which was part of David Stirling's efforts to support an Eighth Army offensive. The SAS party, led by Captains Warr and Schott, was supposed to hit the airfield on the

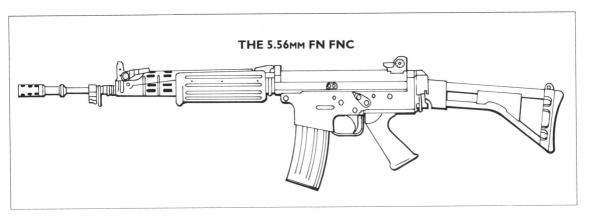

THE 5.56MM FN FNC

night of 12 July. However, owing to an error over maps the raiders were unable to carry out the mission. The only tangible result was the shooting-up of some enemy vehicles by the party's Long Range Desert Group guide, Lieutenant Timpson.
(SEE *Bagoush; El Daba; Fuka; Long Range Desert Group; North Africa; Stirling, Lieutenant-Colonel David*)

SIDI HANEISH Axis airfield in North Africa, located near Fuka. It was raided by the SAS on the night of 26 July 1942. David Stirling led 14 jeeps – two columns of seven commanded by George Jellicoe and 'Paddy' Mayne respectively – in a spectacular night-time operation. The jeeps, armed with Vickers 'K' machine guns, drove onto the airfield in formation and riddled the parked aircraft with gunfire as they passed. They destroyed 40 aircraft in the space of a few minutes before retreating into the night. SAS losses were small: one man killed and two jeeps destroyed.
(SEE *Fuka; Jeep; Jellicoe, Earl George; Mayne, Lieutenant-Colonel 'Paddy' Blair; North Africa; Stirling, Lieutenant-Colonel David; Vickers 'K'*)

SILENCED STERLING
(SEE *Sterling Submachine Gun*)

Left: The SLR. The SAS has used the rifle for over 30 years, being particularly attracted to the stopping power of its 7.62mm round.

'SIM CAS' SAS slang for simulated casualty.

SIRTE Axis airfield in North Africa, one of several which were raided by the Special Air Service during December 1941. On 8 December, David Stirling and 'Paddy' Mayne left Jalo with a Long Range Desert Group party to attack the airfields at Tamit and Sirte. Mayne was tasked with hitting Tamit while Stirling and three others headed for Sirte. However, they could not breach the airfield's security and so were restricted to placing their Lewes bombs on some vehicles parked by the side of the road. A second attempt by Stirling on Sirte on 25 December suffered the same fate.
(SEE *Agedabia; Agheila; Jalo; Lewes bomb; Long Range Desert Group; Mayne, Lieutenant-Colonel 'Paddy' Blair; North Africa; Stirling, Lieutenant-Colonel David; Tamit*)

'SIT REP' SAS slang for situation report.

SIWA OASIS Situated approximately 600km west of Cairo, Siwa was the main base of the Long Range Desert Group (LRDG) in North Africa. It was frequently used by SAS teams which were often transported to targets by the LRDG. In June 1942, Siwa was the base from where the SAS mounted a series of raids on enemy airfields to assist a convoy of

17 ships trying to reach Malta (only two would get through).
(SEE *Benghazi; Benina; Berka; Derna; Long Range Desert Group; North Africa*)

'SLEEPY LAD', OPERATION On 18 December 1943, several parties from 2 SAS were landed by the Royal Navy on the Italian east coast. Their task was to interdict German road and rail communications between Ancona and Pescara. Considerable damage was inflicted on road traffic and the railway line was cut in several places. Despite the fact that the Royal Navy failed to keep the rendezvous to extract the SAS, most of the men made it back to friendly lines by acquiring a local sailing boat.
(SEE *Italy*)

SLOANE, LIEUTENANT-COLONEL JOHN Nicknamed 'Tod' by the SAS, he commanded the Malayan Scouts from late 1951 until 1953, by which time it had become 22 SAS. Sloane, of the Argyll and Sutherland Highlanders, was a methodical man who was responsible for instilling discipline into the unit and reorganising it for deep-penetration jungle operations.
(SEE *Malaya; Malayan Scouts*)

SLR The self-loading rifle (SLR) was the standard British Army individual weapon from the mid-1950s to the late 1980s. Extremely reliable,

robust and easy to maintain and use, it was employed by the Regiment in every campaign from Oman to the Falklands. Although now replaced by the SA-80, because of the stopping power of its 7.62mm bullet it will no doubt still be carried by SAS soldiers on future missions (a 5.56mm version of the FN FAL is called the FN FNC).

Type: semi-automatic rifle
Designation: FN FAL
Calibre: 7.62mm
Weight: 5.07kg
Length: 1090mm
Effective range: 600m
Feed: 20-round steel or light box magazine
Muzzle velocity: 840 metres per second

(SEE *SA-80*)

'SNAPDRAGON', OPERATION Pointless exercise involving 2 SAS. On the night of 28 May 1943, a party was inserted onto the Italian island of Pantelleria in the Mediterranean. Its task was one of reconnaissance but the team achieved little and returned to the rendezvous submarine empty handed, though having suffered no casualties.

(SEE *Italy*)

'SNELGROVE', OPERATION Codename for an operation carried out by 28 men of 3 French Parachute Battalion (3 SAS) commanded by Lieutenant Hubler. The party was parachuted into the area around Creuse, east of Limoges, southern France, on 13 August 1944 with orders to disrupt enemy movements and support local *Maquis* forces. 'Snelgrove' lasted until 24 August, by which time the *Maquis* had been armed and the enemy had been attacked on a number of occasions.

(SEE Maquis; *Northwest Europe*)

Left: Modern sniper systems, be they of the infra-red or image-intesifying variety, allow standard infantry assault rifles to be used accurately in low light.

Above: As shown by this Royal Marine, standard operating procedures (SOPs) include keeping one's weapon within reach at all times.

SNIPER SIGHTS The SAS, like other special forces, employs a wide variety of specialist rifle sights for use in low light and dark conditions. These sights are particularly useful for counter-terrorist work, whether a stakeout in Northern Ireland or sniper cover during a hostage-rescue operation. There are a plethora of models available, most of them being thermal-imaging or image-intensifying sights. The former work by emitting beams in the infra-red wavelength to 'illuminate' the target; the latter by taking the light available and intensifying it thousands of times (modern systems can work in virtually no light at all).

Models available include the Orion 80 passive night sight built by the German firm Eltro Gmbh. This sight uses a three-stage image intensifier system and can be fitted to a number of submachine guns and rifles including the Heckler & Koch MP5.

Advisor Systems of the UK build the Model 1500 Night Sight, an image intensifier for use at short and medium ranges; and the Dutch firm Officine Galileo have the OGVN 7 miniaturised night sight, an image intensifier which is suitable for observation and aiming. There are also the conventional optical telescopic sights which are intended for daylight use. They usually give a magnification of between four and six, making them ideal for long-range observation.

(SEE *Heckler & Koch MP5 Submachine Gun*)

SOE Special Operations Executive. World War II British intelligence and espionage organisation established in 1940. Although it did contain military men, most of its members were in fact civilians. There were SOE schools in Britain, North Africa, Italy and the Far East, and by 1944 there

Above: A panoramic view of Leith, South Georgia. The SAS established a number of observation posts overlooking the whaling station during the Falklands War.

were 7500 SOE spies and saboteurs available for missions in northwest Europe. Operations behind enemy lines carried out by SOE and the SAS were supposed to be coordinated, though the former often regarded the latter as being under its control. SOE also tended to over-protect its missions and resented SAS forces dropping into an area where its agents were working, thinking its operatives would be compromised. SOE, for example, had some SAS operations prior to D-Day cancelled. However, when the actual drops took place SOE did cooperate; for example, by arranging reception parties for SAS groups. (SEE *Northwest Europe*)

SOPs Standard operating procedures. A set of rules and guidelines devised for use by SAS soldiers and patrols. Most SOPs have evolved as a consequence of the Regiment's experiences in the conflicts it has been involved in since 1941. Although there are too many to list in full, they include the following: 'shoot and scoot'; patrols must always use a different camp site each night; shooting is discouraged unless there is a visible target; personal weapons must always be kept within arm's reach; noise discipline to be maintained at all times; and extra vigilance at dusk and dawn, the times when soldiers are traditionally at their most vulnerable.

These SOPs form the cornerstone of the tactics used by SAS four-man patrols in the field and are designed to ensure their survival when working behind enemy lines for long periods of time. In essence, patrols using these skills should be able to carry out their missions of, say, reconnaissance, intelligence gathering or sabotage without coming into conflict with the enemy or, if they are compromised, should be able to deal with a threat without endangering either their lives or their operation. SOPs were created on the basis of much hard-earned experience and are drilled into team members during training.
(SEE *Four-man Patrol; Head-on Contact Drill; 'Shoot and Scoot'; Special Air Service; Woodhouse, Lieutenant-Colonel John*)

SOUTH ARABIA

(SEE *Aden; Oman*)

SOUTH ARMAGH

A region of County Armagh, Northern Ireland, on the border with Eire which has strong pro-Republican sympathies and, as a result, is an area where the Irish Republican Army (IRA) is particularly active. Though the SAS has been in the area since 1969, its presence in South Armagh was only made public by the British government at a later date as a way of intimidating the IRA. In January 1976, Downing Street announced: 'The government has decided to further reinforce the Army in Northern Ireland with elements of the SAS. These troops will be used in County Armagh for patrolling and surveillance, tasks to which the SAS are particularly well suited.' In fact the initial presence was small, only 11 extra men were deployed to Northern Ireland. However, this had increased to 60 by April.

Results were not slow in coming: on 12 March Sean Mckenna, an IRA member, was kidnapped in a cross-border raid; on 15 April Peter Cleary, another IRA figure, was arrested in South Armagh near the village of Belleeks. The SAS continue to operate in Armagh, mostly from the British Army barracks at Bessbrook. The area is largely agricultural and there are many secluded houses and roads with easy access to Eire. All this makes South Armagh, nicknamed 'bandit country', ideal for terrorist activity. Nevertheless, operating in the region gives the SAS an ideal opportunity to practise its observation and concealment skills.

(SEE *'Bandit Country'; Irish Republican Army; Northern Ireland*)

SOUTH GEORGIA

Island in the South Atlantic. A British dependency, South Georgia was taken by Argentinian forces in early April 1982. Part of the British Task Force was despatched to retake the island – codenamed Operation 'Paraquet' – before the main landings on the Falklands as a way of demonstrating to the Argentinians that Britain would use force to retake all of her occupied possessions. The British naval units detailed to regain South Georgia were the destroyer *Antrim*, the frigate *Plymouth*, the ice patrol ship *Endurance*, and the Royal Fleet Auxiliary *Tidespring*. In addition, HMS *Brilliant* later joined the fleet. The troops involved were M Company, 42 Commando, Royal Marines, No 2 Section, Special Boat Squadron (SBS), D Squadron, 22 SAS, and a team from 148 Battery, 29 Commando Regiment, Royal Artillery.

The SAS teams were involved from the outset of the operation: establishing observation posts (OPs) around Stromness and Husvik, around Leith, and carrying out reconnaissances for a possible beach landing area in Fortuna Bay and a helicopter landing site. To this end, the squadron's Mountain Troop was landed on Fortuna Glacier on 22 April. However, the party, inserted by helicopter, encountered severe weather conditions and was forced to abandon its mission. Undeterred, the SAS commander, Major Cedric Delves, despatched Boat Troop, commanded by Captain Tim Burls, from *Antrim* in Stromness Bay in five Gemini dinghies. The target was Grass Island, though two out of the five boats were lost, their occupants being picked up later (the SBS had encountered similar problems in its attempts to reach Grytviken). Nevertheless, by 23 April the SAS had established a number of OPs around Leith.

A submarine alert temporarily dispersed the British ships, though *Endurance* remained among the icebergs to look after the observation parties on the islands. On 25 April, however, the force re-assembled and a plan was agreed to mount a heliborne assault on Grytviken. The Argentinian submarine *Santa Fe* was stranded there, having been forced to return to harbour after being attacked by British helicopters. The only ship not present was *Tidespring* which contained the bulk of the ground forces. Nevertheless, it was decided to attack before the Argentinians had time to organise their defences.

Some 75 men divided between three troops were assembled to mount the operation: one of Royal Marines, one of SBS, and a third composed of SAS soldiers under Major Delves. On the afternoon of 25 April, six helicopters put the force ashore. The Argentinian defenders numbered around 100 including the crew of the disabled submarine. As *Antrim* and *Plymouth* laid down a barrage of fire from their 4.5in guns, the invasion force advanced from Hestesletten towards Grytviken. At 1700 hours, the Argentinian forces surrendered without firing a shot. A small detachment of enemy Marines at Leith gave themselves up the following day.

(SEE *Delves, Major Cedric; Falkland Islands; Fortuna Glacier; Gemini landing craft*)

SPECIAL AIR SERVICE

Today, several decades after its formation in 1941, the SAS has several wartime roles of a strategic nature: to operate in small, self-contained groups deep behind enemy lines; to conduct sabotage and intelligence gathering missions; to prosecute counter-insurgency warfare (including winning 'hearts and minds'); to undertake long-range reconnaissance patrolling; and clandestine insertion. In addition, the SAS has a significant counter-terrorist and hostage-rescue capability.

Organisation History

July 1941: the formation of L Detachment, SAS Brigade.
17 November 1941: the official 'birthday' of the SAS, celebrated in honour of its first raid in North Africa.
October 1942: L Detachment officially named 1 SAS.
January 1943: David Stirling, the founder of the SAS, has under his command a French Squadron (94

men); the Greek Sacred Squadron (114 men); the Special Boat Section (55 men); 1 SAS (390 men); and the Special Interrogation Group.

April 1943: French and Greek Squadrons return to their respective national armies. Major Jellicoe is given command of the waterborne element of the SAS which becomes the Special Boat Squadron. From this date it effectively ceases to be a part of the SAS. 1 SAS becomes the Special Raiding Squadron.

May 1943: 2 SAS comes into existence. The Special Raiding Squadron reverts to 1 SAS later in the year.

January 1944: the SAS Brigade is formed under the umbrella of I Airborne Corps. It consists of:

HQ French Demi-Brigade
20 Liaison HQ (the SAS link with the Free French)
1 SAS
2 SAS
3 SAS (3 French Parachute Battalion)
4 SAS (4 French Parachute Battalion)
5 SAS (Belgian Independent Parachute Company)
F Squadron, GHQ Liaison Regiment

September 1945: the Belgian company is handed back to its own government.

October 1945: the French detachments are handed back to their government. In Britain the SAS is officially disbanded.

November 1945: SAS Regimental Association is formed.

1947: the War Office decides to establish a Territorial Army (TA) raiding unit which is attached to the Rifle Brigade. However, the unit merges with the Artists Rifles – originally a volunteer battalion raised from London's artistic community in 1859 – and is known as 21 SAS (Artists).

1950: Malayan Scouts are formed by Mike Calvert. A detachment from 21 SAS (Artists) joins the Scouts.

1952: 22 SAS is created from the Malayan Scouts.

1959: 23 SAS (TA) is established.

1987: The UK Special Forces Group is set up. Headed by a brigadier, it controls the SAS and Special Boat Squadron. The Group's HQ is located in the Duke of York's Barracks, Chelsea, London.

Current Organisation

22 SAS: based at Stirling Lines, Hereford, commanded by a lieutenant-colonel.

Composed of:
Training Wing
Counter Revolutionary Warfare Wing
Operations Research Wing
Demolitions Wing
Operations Planning & Intelligence (the 'Kremlin')
264 SAS Signals Squadron (detached from the Royal Corps of Signals)
Four 'Sabre' (fighting) Squadrons: A, B, D and G. In addition, there is R Squadron, a reserve. C Squadron, which became the Rhodesian SAS, no longer exists, but it is still recognised by the SAS out of respect for its assistance during the campaign in Malaya.

Each 'Sabre' Squadron has four troops, each one having it own speciality: Mountain Troop (mountain and winter warfare); Boat Troop (amphibious warfare); Mobility Troop (vehicles and motorcycles); and Air Troop (freefall parachuting).

Each troop consists of four four-man patrols, with each patrol member having his own speciality: demolitions, medicine, languages or signals.

Additional support

Army Air Corps 'S' Flight (helicopters)
RAF Special Forces Flight, 47 Squadron, RAF Lyneham
Royal Corps of Transport Motor Pool

21 SAS (TA): Four squadrons – A, B, C and S – plus an HQ.

HQ, A and B are based at the Duke of York's Barracks, London.

C Squadron is based at Hitchin, Hertfordshire.

S Squadron and 63 SAS Signals Squadron (TA) are based at Portsmouth, Hampshire.

23 SAS (TA): Four squadrons – A, B, C and D – plus an HQ.

HQ and A Squadron are based at Birmingham, West Midlands.

B Squadron is based at Leeds, Yorkshire.

C Squadron is based at Doncaster, Yorkshire.

D Squadron is based in Scotland.

The guiding principles of the SAS (*as laid down by David Stirling*)

Engage in the never-ending pursuit of excellence.

Maintain the highest standards of self-discipline in all aspects of daily life.

Tolerate no sense of class, all ranks in the SAS belong to one company. All ranks to possess humility and humour.

(SEE *Air Troop; Artists Rifles; Belgian Independent Parachute Company; Boat Troop; Calvert, Brigadier Mike; Duke of York's Barracks, London; Free French SAS; Four-man Patrol; 'Hearts and Minds'; Jellicoe, Earl George; 'Kremlin'; L Detachment; Malaya; Malayan Scouts; Mobility Troop; Mountain Troop; North Africa; Northwest Europe; Patrol Skills; Phantom; Rhodesian SAS; 'Sabre'; Sacred Squadron; Special Boat Section; Special Boat Squadron; Special Interrogation Group; Special Raiding Squadron; Stirling, Lieutenant-Colonel David; Stirling Lines; Territorial Army; Troop Skills*)

SPECIAL BOAT SECTION World War II special forces canoeist raiding unit formed in the spring of 1941 on the Suez Canal. It was originally used by Layforce for beach and harbour reconnaissance, though No 1 SBS, because of heavy losses, was absorbed into the SAS in November 1942. Other Special Boat Section units continued to serve until 1945, most

Above: A member of the Special Boat Squadron undergoing aquatic training. Like the SAS, the SBS saw service in Oman, Borneo and the Falklands.

notably in the Adriatic, Aegean and eastern Mediterranean.
(SEE *Kabrit; Layforce; Special Air Service*)

SPECIAL BOAT SQUADRON This British unit was first established in the late summer of 1940 as a raiding unit called the Folbot (canoe) Section commanded by Major Roger Courtney. In February 1941, Courtney and 15 men were sent to the Middle East with Layforce, being designated 'Z' Section. By the end of 1941, 'Z' Section and the Special Boat Section had received substantial casualties and so were absorbed into the SAS, in addition to three groups of canoeists under Earl Jellicoe. The latter reorganised these groups into three Special Boat Sections in the autumn of 1942.

In the spring of 1943, these sections, called M, L and S respectively, were elevated to squadrons and effectively became separate from the SAS. In November 1943, Jellicoe's Special Boat Squadron came under the command of Brigadier D.J.T. Turnbull's Raiding Forces Middle East and was renamed the Special Boat Service. It came under the control of Land Forces Adriatic and, until the end of the war, operated in the Mediterranean, Adriatic and Aegean Seas.

In the years following World War II, the SBS went through a number of changes and reorganisations. In 1975, the Special Boat Company was renamed the Special Boat Squadron of Special Boat Sections.
(SEE *Jellicoe, Earl George; Layforce; Special Air Service; Special Boat Section*)

SPECIAL INTERROGATION GROUP
Small British unit which was formed in North Africa during World War II.

Established by a Captain Buck, it consisted of 12 Jewish immigrants to Palestine who were fluent in German. They were trained in the highly dangerous task of infiltrating enemy lines dressed as German soldiers and driving captured enemy vehicles. In March 1942, the SIG was moved to Kabrit to begin training with the SAS. The unit took part in a number of SAS actions, most notably at Derna, although by the end of 1942 SIG was all but defunct owing to the difficulties of finding suitable recruits.
(SEE *Derna; Kabrit; North Africa*)

SPECIAL PROJECTS TEAM All SAS 'Sabre' Squadrons are rotated through counter-terrorist training at Hereford and, at any one time, there is a squadron on 24-hour standby for anti-terrorist and hostage-rescue operations. The squadron on duty is always divided into four operational troops, called Special Projects Teams, which consist of one officer, usually a captain, and 15 other ranks. The Special

Projects Teams are further divided into four-man assault teams. There is always a team on permanent standby in the London area and at Hereford.
(SEE *Counter Revolutionary Warfare; Counter Revolutionary Warfare Equipment; Princes Gate; 'Sabre'; Special Air Service*)

SPECIAL RAIDING SQUADRON

During World War II, 1 SAS was temporarily renamed the Special Raiding Squadron, fighting under this name in Sicily and Italy in 1943.
(SEE *Special Air Service*)

SPECIAL SUPPORT UNIT

Armed intelligence gathering unit of the Royal Ulster Constabulary (RUC) which was set up at the beginning of the 1980s as part of an overall drive against terrorism in Northern Ireland. The SSU, which numbered 30 men, was trained in all aspects of undercover work by the SAS at Hereford, despite the grave misgivings the Regiment had at the time about the poor calibre of the recruits it was instructing.

In 1982, the SSU shot and killed seven men in extremely dubious circumstances. In 1984, John Stalker, Deputy Chief Constable of Greater Manchester, was called in to hold an independent enquiry into the shootings. Despite no prosecutions being brought, the SSU was subsequently disbanded.
(SEE *Northern Ireland*)

'SPEEDWELL', OPERATION A classic World War II SAS mission which was a superb example of how small parties could inflict substantial damage on the enemy and remain behind their lines for long periods. On 7 September 1943, two seven-man parties from 2 SAS, commanded by Captain Pinckney and Captain Dudgeon, were dropped into the Spezia/Genoa area of northeast Italy to cut the railway lines which were transporting enemy reinforcements to the front.

After landing, the two sticks split into smaller parties. Over the next few weeks the SAS derailed a number of trains and blew up railway lines, although many of the men suffered from illnesses brought on by a combination of poor diet and bad weather. There were losses too, most notably Dudgeon, who was captured by the Germans and shot. Some men got back to Allied lines after operating for 54 days, others after 73 days. However, one man, Sergeant 'Tanky' Challenor, returned after seven months behind enemy lines, a period which included a spell in an enemy hospital.
(SEE *Challenor, Sergeant 'Tanky'; Italy*)

'SPENSER', OPERATION Conducted between 29 August and 14 September 1944 by 317 men of 4 French Parachute Battalion (4 SAS) commanded by Commandant Bourgoin.

The party, mounted on 54 jeeps, was infiltrated through Allied lines into the area east of Bourges, central France. The intention was to inflict maximum damage on the retreating Germans as they pulled back over the River Loire. 'Spenser' was very successful: 120 enemy vehicles were destroyed and the SAS took 2500 prisoners. In addition, the SAS assisted in the surrender of over 20,000 German troops to nearby American forces.
(SEE *Jeep; Northwest Europe*)

'SPIDER' SAS slang for sleeping quarters. The central section of the barracks building has eight dormitory wings running off it, thus resembling a spider's legs.

S-PHONE Used by the SAS during World War II, particularly in northwest Europe, the S-Phone was a beacon which transmitted a signal that could be detected by an aircraft flying up to 10km away and at an altitude of 3000m. It was used as a direction-finding device for aircraft when dropping supplies to waiting SAS parties.

'SPORTS AND SOCIAL' SAS nickname for the barracks at Hereford. A play on the letters SAS.
(SEE *Stirling Lines*)

SSG 69. Sniper rifle manufactured by the Austrian company Steyr-Mannlicher GmbH. This weapon has

---

THE SSG 69 SNIPER RIFLE

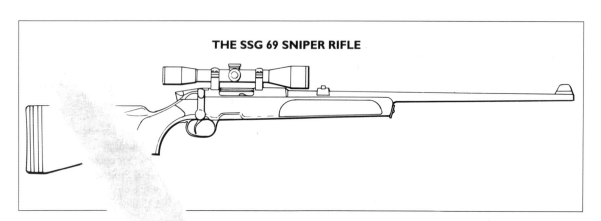

Above: The Sterling submachine gun (right). This is the standard model; the silenced version is used by the SAS in Northern Ireland.

been periodically used by the Regiment in preference to the L42 sniper rifle. Extremely well-made and accurate, it is also used by the Austrian Army, the German counter-terrorist unit GSG 9, and the British Royal Marines.

Type: bolt-action sniper rifle
Designation: Scharfschutzengewehr 69
Calibre: 7.62mm
Weight: 4.6kg (empty, with tele-scopic sight)
Length: 1140mm
Effective range: 800m
Feed: 5-round magazine
Muzzle velocity: 860 metres per second
(SEE *GSG 9; L42A1*)

STANLEY, LIEUTENANT-COMMANDER IAN

(SEE *Fortuna Glacier*)

'STARTREK' SAS slang for air strike.

STATIC-LINE PARACHUTING COURSE

The last and perhaps easiest of the training phases which a student has to pass before becoming a member of the Special Air Service, it follows Jungle Training which is held in the Far East (for those students from the Parachute Regiment attendance on the course is unnecessary as they are already para-qualified). The course lasts four weeks and is conducted at No 1 Parachute Training School at RAF Brize Norton, Oxfordshire. The students make a total of eight jumps including one from a balloon, one at night, and an operational descent (the latter being the most difficult). At the end of the course all SAS students are awarded their 'Sabre' wings. They then return to Hereford where they are 'badged' SAS.
(SEE *'Badged'; Continuation Training; Escape and Evasion; Jungle Training; 'Sabre'; Selection Training; Test Week; 'Wings'*)

STEN GUN British equivalent of the American Thompson submachine gun used by the SAS and Commandos in World War II. Millions of Stens were produced during the war. It was very cheap and lightweight, though it could be highly unreliable and unstable. Nevertheless, its simplicity and minimal lubrication requirements made it an attractive weapon to special forces and partisans.

Type: submachine gun
Designation: machine carbine, 9mm Sten
Calibre: 9mm
Weight: 2.95kg (unloaded)
Length: 762mm
Effective range: 160m
Rate of fire: 550 rounds per minute (cyclic)
Feed: 32-round box magazine
Muzzle velocity: 305 metres per second
(SEE *Thompson Submachine Gun*)

STERLING SUBMACHINE GUN Used by the Regiment alongside the Heckler & Koch MP5 for counter-

Muzzle velocity: 293–310 metres per second
(SEE *Heckler & Koch MP5 Submachine Gun; Northern Ireland*)

'STEP-UP' Drill evolved by the SAS during its campaign in Borneo (1963-66) when small-sized patrols were deployed along the jungle border to detect Indonesian and guerrilla incursions. Once a cross-border incident was detected, the SAS would radio for infantry reinforcements to be flown into the area and landed on cleared jungle landing sites by helicopter. The SAS would then guide the infantry to an ambush point to await the enemy. 'Step-up' was a simple but effective answer to the problem of three- and four-man SAS patrols being thinly spread along the 1500km-long Borneo frontier.
(SEE *Borneo; Four-man Patrol*)

STINGER US-made surface-to-air missile (SAM) system. First used operationally by the Regiment in the Falklands in 1982, Stinger employs an infra-red guidance system and fires a missile equipped with a high explosive warhead.

Type: man-portable surface-to-air missile (SAM) system
Calibre: 70mm
Weight: 13.4kg
Length: 1524mm
Maximum range: 8000m
Flight speed: Mach 2
(SEE *Falkland Islands*)

STIRLING, LIEUTENANT-COLONEL DAVID The founder of the Special Air Service who was born in 1915. In 1940, Stirling was a lieutenant in the Scots Guards when he volunteered for No 8 Commando which, under its commander, Captain Robert Laycock, was despatched to the Middle East as part of Layforce. He took part in a

Above: The Stinger surface-to-air missile (SAM) is an effective hand-held anti-aircraft weapon. It was used by the SAS during the Falklands War.

terrorist work, although not for hostage-rescue missions, the Sterling first entered British Army service in 1955. The silenced version is often employed in ambushes and covert operations in Northern Ireland. Reliable, easy to strip and clean in the field, the Sterling also performs well in adverse weather conditions. Despite its age, it seems set to remain in the Regiment's armoury well into the twenty-first century.

Standard version
Type: submachine gun
Designation: L2A3
Calibre: 9mm
Weight: 3.5kg
Length: 690mm (butt extended); 483mm (butt retracted)

Effective range: 200m
Rate of fire: 550 rounds per minute (cyclic)
Feed: 34-round box magazine; 10- and 15-round and twin stacked magazines also available
Muzzle velocity: 390 metres per second

Silenced version
Type: silenced submachine gun
Designation: L34A1
Calibre: 9mm
Weight: 4.3kg
Length: 864mm (butt extended); 660mm (butt retracted)
Effective range: 150m
Rate of fire: 515–565 rounds per minute (cyclic)
Feed: 34-round box magazine

Right: The vision and drive of David Stirling (centre) led to the creation of the world's most famous elite special forces unit.

number of ineffectual raids on the North African coast which convinced him of the idea that small-sized units would be much more effective for raiding than the large-scale operations in which he had taken part. Luckily for the SAS, Stirling was then involved in a parachuting accident which forced him into hospital. There he formulated his plans for establishing a raiding unit, believing that 200 men split into five-man units could achieve surprise and hit several targets on the same night, as opposed to using a large number of men and Royal Navy ships to hit one target.

By using bluff and sheer audacity, he managed to personally see the Deputy Chief of Staff, General Neil Ritchie, who handed Stirling's memorandum to the Commander-in-Chief Middle East, General Claude Auchinleck – L Detachment, Special Air Service Brigade, was born.

Over the next few weeks Stirling organised training and recruits for the new unit. However, its first operation on the night of 16/17 November 1941 was a complete disaster. Disappointed but not dispirited, Stirling, after talking with Captain David Lloyd-Owen of the Long Range Desert Group (LRDG), decided that it would be better for his raiding parties to be transported to the target in LRDG vehicles. It was this ability to adapt and improvise which was Stirling's great strength. He also impressed upon his superiors that the SAS was to be used strategically to attack targets which would aid the overall grand plan, and not as combat troops just beyond the front line. Stirling's imprint on the unit was so strong that it ensured its survival after he was captured in North Africa in January 1943. By this time the SAS was a regiment and Stirling himself a lieutenant-colonel.

One of Stirling's great attributes, which was essential to the success of the SAS, was his ability to spot and enlist men of talent into his unit. This resulted in the organisation containing

Above: Sultan Qaboos reviewing members of the Sultan's Armed Forces. Though well disciplined and led, it could not on its own quell the two rebellions in Oman.

personalities of vision and charisma, men who were ideally suited to lead and train soldiers for the kind of missions David Stirling had in mind. Such men were 'Paddy' Mayne, 'Jock' Lewes, Johnny Cooper and Reg Seekings. Of them all, Mayne probably came closest to the archetypal SAS warrior – courageous, a superb leader of men who inspired by example, and a man who, like Stirling, had little time for red tape.

Stirling's personal bravery – some would say recklessness – ensured that he took an active part in all of the operations against enemy targets

throughout 1941-42 (this contrasts with his brother William, who, while not wanting for bravery, was more of an administrator than his brother). If he had a weakness, it was that he kept the future plans he had for the SAS to himself. This was to result in some confusion over its role after he had been captured and the war in North Africa had ended. Stirling was taken to an Italian prison camp at Gavi, from where he escaped four times. He was then sent to the German high security prison at Colditz, where he remained until the end of the war. Knighted for his services in the New

Year Honours list of 1990, David Stirling died in the same year.

Johnny Cooper, one of the original members of L Detachment, provides a fitting epitaph to David Stirling's efforts: 'We were carrying out David Stirling's initial insistence that small patrols of no more than three men could inflict enormous damage on an enemy owing to their ability to penetrate silently behind the lines. We certainly proved that in those early days. This was coupled naturally to the ability to change our operational methods to reflect changing circumstances and enemy response. It was this flexibility which David Stirling insisted upon that kept us one step ahead of the *Afrika Korps*. Ever since, those same basic principles have kept the enemy guessing in operations in Europe, Malaya, Oman, Borneo, the Falklands, and today in the counter-terrorist role in Northern Ireland and elsewhere; and, most recently, in the Gulf.'
(SEE *Athlit; Bagoush; Benghazi; Benina; 'Blitz Buggy'; Bouerat; Cooper, Lieutenant-Colonel Johnny; 'Crusader', Operation; Gabes Gap; L Detachment; Lewes, Lieutenant John Steel 'Jock'; Long Range Desert Group; Mayne, Lieutenant-Colonel 'Paddy' Blair; North Africa; Qattara Depression; Seekings, Sergeant-Major Reg; Sidi Haneish; Sirte; Stirling, Lieutenant-Colonel William; Stirling Lines; Zem Zem*)

STIRLING, LIEUTENANT-COLONEL WILLIAM The brother of David Stirling and commander of 2 SAS. William, an officer in the Scots Guards, became a member of No 62 Commando, being promoted to its commander as a lieutenant-colonel in September 1942. However, the unit was disbanded at the end of the year after being sent to Algeria. Allied Forces HQ gave Stirling permission to raise a second SAS regiment, 2 SAS, which was established on exactly the same principles as 1 SAS. However, William was continually at

loggerheads with his superiors concerning the proper use of his men, believing that they should have been employed in attacking strategic targets and not merely in the support role. Missions such as Operation 'Speedwell' in Italy were proof of the validity of his ideas. Despite these successes, the high command still insisted on using the SAS just ahead of the front line.

William Stirling's anger finally erupted on the eve of Operation 'Overlord', the Allied invasion of Europe. Supreme Headquarters Allied Expeditionary Force (SHAEF) wanted to use the SAS just behind the beaches, between the enemy infantry and the German armoured reserves. Stirling resigned, seeing this task as near suicidal and a complete waste of his unit. His resignation seriously threatened the future of 2 SAS, though Lieutenant-Colonel Brian Franks became its commander and turned out to be an excellent choice. Stirling himself, aggrieved, retired home to Scotland.

William was certainly less charismatic than his brother, nevertheless he was an excellent administrator who clearly understood the SAS's true role in war. Though he has been somewhat overshadowed by David, he deserves to be remembered for his efforts to impress upon the higher echelons of the British Army that the SAS was, and still is, a deep-penetration unit which, given proper support, can achieve results out of all proportion to its size.
(SEE *Franks, Lieutenant-Colonel Brian; Germany; Italy; 'Narcissus', Operation; North Africa; Northwest Europe; Sicily; Special Air Service; 'Speedwell', Operation; Stirling, Lieutenant-Colonel David*)

STIRLING LINES Name of the SAS barracks and headquarters at Hereford. The old buildings were called Bradbury Lines but, after the new barracks block was completed in 1984, the site was renamed after the

Regiment's founder, Lieutenant-Colonel David Stirling.
(SEE *Bradbury Lines; Stirling, Lieutenant-Colonel David*)

'STORM', OPERATION Codename of the plan devised in 1970 for the forthcoming Special Air Service campaign in Oman. The basic elements of the SAS strategy were: no indiscriminate reprisals against civilians, a large medical effort for the civilian population, intelligence gathering, as well as a 'hearts and minds' campaign. 'Storm' was really a blueprint which was refined by the SAS and would form the basis of Lieutenant-Colonel Watts' 'Five Fronts' Campaign.
(SEE *'Five Fronts' Campaign; 'Hearts and Minds'; Oman; Watts, Lieutenant-Colonel Johnny*)

STUN GRENADE One of the most effective items in the SAS counter-terrorist armoury. Originally developed by the Regiment at Hereford, the stun grenade, called a 'flash-bang', is ideally suited to hostage-rescue operations.

It is a small non-lethal device which contains magnesium powder and fulminate of mercury. When the ring is pulled and the grenade thrown the mercury fulminate detonates. This results in a large bang which ignites the magnesium and produces a blinding flash (up to 50,000 candlepower). The two combined result in extreme disorientation among the unprotected for up to 45 seconds, allowing the hostage-rescue team to disable any terrorists. Stun grenades were used to great effect at Mogadishu and Princes Gate.

Three examples of models currently available on the international market are the Condor SA GL-307, Royal Ordnance G60 and Haley and Weller's E180.

Condor SA GL-307
Diameter: 52mm
Length: 98.5mm
Weight: 145g

Weight of charge: 56g
Delay time: 2-4 seconds

Royal Ordnance G60

Diameter: 62mm
Length: 100mm
Weight: 200g
Noise: over 160dB
Flash: over 300,000cd

Haley and Weller E180

Diameter: 51mm
Length: 134mm
Weight: 250g
Noise: 187dB
Flash: 22 million candela for 10 milliseconds

(SEE *Counter Revolutionary Warfare; Counter Revolutionary Warfare Equipment; Counter Revolutionary Warfare Wing; Mogadishu; Princes Gate*)

SUBSKIMMER Vessel which can operate as a high-speed surface craft or as a submersible. Subskimmers are designed so conversion to submarine mode is simple: the pilot seals off the engine and instrument compartment and then deflates the side tubes. Underwater the craft is powered by an electric motor. For an approach to an objective it is possible to adopt a so-called 'snorkel' mode: only the air inlet, exhaust pipes and divers' heads are showing above the surface. This mode offers an extremely low profile which is difficult to pick out by the naked eye or on radar.

These vessels are useful for clandestine missions including those conducted by the Boat Troops of the SAS and the Special Boat Squadron, as well as the US Navy's SEAL teams. An example of the models currently available is Defence Boats' Subskimmer 180. It is designed to carry up to 10 fully equipped men at speeds of up to 30 knots to a range of 160km.

Length: 7m
Beam: 2.3m
Weight: 1500kg
Propulsion: two 1140cc outboard engines (surface); two electric motors (underwater)
Speed underwater: 2-3 knots
Surface speed: 30 knots (max)
Payload: 900kg
Maximum operating depth: 50m

(SEE *Boat Troop; SEALs; Special Boat Squadron*)

SULTAN'S ARMED FORCES The land forces of the Sultanate of Muscat and Oman. Britain helped to reorganise the SAF in 1958 when Colonel David Smiley was appointed Chief of Staff to the Sultan. At this time the core of the army was the 450-strong Northern Frontier Regiment, with detachments of the Trucial Oman Scouts also being enlisted. In 1957, the SAF was totally unprepared for the uprising on the Jebel Akhdar and had to request British assistance. Similarly, the SAF was barely able to contain the rebellion in the province of Dhofar which broke out in 1962. Though around 1000 men were deployed in the province, aid to the guerrillas from nearby Yemen forced the SAF onto the defensive and the Sultan, Said bin Taimur, again asked for British military help.

The SAS entered the war in 1970, and for the next six years the SAF, SAS and *firqat* units combined to defeat the guerrillas. The war in Dhofar was virtually over by the end of 1975, after the SAF had won a significant victory at Sarfait in October and had taken the Dorra Ridge in December.

(SEE *Baluchis; Firqat; Jebel Akhdar; Oman; Said bin Taimur, Sultan; Trucial Oman Scouts*)

SULTAN OF OMAN'S AIR FORCE

Omani Air Force. During the SAS involvement in Oman in the 1970s, the SOAF provided much-needed air support for ground forces against the guerrillas of the Dhofar Liberation Front and the People's Front for the Liberation of the Occupied Arabian Gulf, a notable example being at Mirbat in 1972. The main aircraft used by the SOAF were Strikemasters, Skyvans and Huey helicopters.

The SOAF was not badly trained or equipped. However, before the SAS arrived in Oman in 1970, the Sultan's Air Force had a rather haphazard approach to the war. For example, there was little or no liaison between the Air Force and the Sultan's Armed Forces (SAF). Thus a patrol would encounter a group of guerrillas, for example, near a village in Dhofar. Only when the battle was over would the SOAF hear about the incident and then despatch a number of aircraft to bomb the immediate vicinity. As the guerrillas would have long gone, this usually meant the nearest village would be bombed. This resulted in alienating the civilian population even further.

After the SAS arrived, there was a much greater degree of cooperation between the SAS and SOAF, instigated by the soldiers from Britain. This would reap substantial rewards during actions undertaken by both the SAS and SAF later in the war.

(SEE *Dhofar Liberation Front; Mirbat; Oman; People's Front for the Liberation of the Occupied Arabian Gulf; Sultan's Armed Forces*)

'SWORD', OPERATION Codename for a sweep by the SAS deep in the Malayan jungle during the 'Emergency' (1948-60). The party was dropped in January 1954, but three men were killed as a result of 'tree-jumping'. One of the men, wounded when he hit the jungle canopy, was also killed when he cut himself free of his harness and fell 100m to the ground.

(SEE *Malaya; 'Tree-jumping'*)

SYCAMORE Light assault and reconnaissance helicopter used by the SAS in Malaya, Oman and Borneo in the 1950s and early 1960s. The Sycamore had five seats and had a top speed of 204km/hr.

(SEE *Borneo; Malaya; Oman*)

T–V

TA Territorial Army. A British force composed of part-time soldiers which, in times of a general mobilisation, would reinforce the regular British Army. There are two TA SAS regiments: 21 and 23 SAS. Though part-time, the soldiers of these units must pass through the same selection courses as the regulars. Indeed, the TA SAS soldiers are recognised throughout the British Army as being highly trained and extremely well motivated.
(SEE *Selection Training; Special Air Service*)

'TAB' In SAS parlance, a word used to describe a forced march carrying a heavy load. Similar to the Royal Marines' term 'yomp'.

'TAILEND CHARLIE' Name for the soldier situated at the rear of a four-man patrol's order of march. 'Tailend Charlies', who are often equipped with machine guns, are tasked with covering the rear of the patrol. This entails regularly swinging round and facing the opposite direction to that in which the patrol is moving to ensure all-round defence.

TAMIT Axis airfield in North Africa. Raided by the SAS on two occasions

Below: 'Tailend Charlie' ensures that a patrol on the move has constant all-round defence. He guards against the unit being ambushed from the rear.

Above: A detachment of 2 SAS photographed after the action at Termoli in October 1943. The officer at the front wearing the peaked cap is Major Sandy Scratchley.

in late 1941. On the night of 12 December, Captain 'Paddy' Mayne and eight men, after being dropped off by the Long Range Desert Group (LRDG), simply walked onto the airfield and planted their bombs on each parked aircraft. Very soon there were a number ablaze but Mayne, not content with this, disabled one aircraft by wrenching out the instrument panel in the cockpit with his hands. Later, he burst into the officer's mess

on the airfield and raked it with machine-gun fire. The SAS party then withdrew into the night, having suffered no casualties.

Twelve days later Mayne was back, this time with five men. This raid was as successful as the first, with 27 enemy aircraft being destroyed on the ground.

(SEE *Long Range Desert Group; Mayne, Lieutenant-Colonel 'Paddy' Blair; North Africa*)

TERMOLI Port on Italy's Adriatic coast. In October 1943, the Special Raiding Squadron (SRS) under Lieutenant-Colonel 'Paddy' Mayne, operating with the Special Service Brigade – composed of a number of Commandos – was tasked with capturing Termoli to assist the Eighth Army's attempt to breach the so-called Termoli line. The mission, codenamed 'Devon', got under way on 3 October when the 207-strong SRS, two Commandos and support units went ashore by landing craft. The force cleared the town relatively easily, and at midday forward elements of the Lancashire Fusiliers and a party of 2 SAS arrived.

The SRS was about to re-embark on the morning of the 5th when the Germans launched a massive counterattack on Termoli. The battle around the cemetery and astride the railway line was particularly fierce, and the situation was saved only by the arrival of a detachment of Royal Irish Rangers and some Canadian Sherman tanks. The action at Termoli was the last SRS operation in Italy.

(SEE *Italy; Mayne, Lieutenant-Colonel 'Paddy' Blair; Special Raiding Squadron*)

TEST WEEK The culmination of Selection Training.

(SEE *Selection Training*)

'THE PALUDRINE CLUB' Name of the SAS bar at Stirling Lines. It derives from the anti-Malaria drug Paludrine, which is administered to individual troopers when they go on overseas operations.

(SEE *Stirling Lines*)

THESIGER, MAJOR WILFRED
Explorer and adventurer who held a fascination for Arab culture. Served briefly with B Squadron, 1 SAS, in late 1942 and early 1943 during the later stages of the war in North Africa.

(SEE *North Africa*)

THOMPSON, MAJOR HARRY
Originally of the Royal Highland Fusiliers, Thompson commanded one of the last SAS guerrilla hunts in Malaya. In February 1958, leading 37 men of D Squadron, 22 SAS, he parachuted into the Telok Anson Swamp to hunt down the terrorist leader Ah Hoi, nicknamed 'Baby Killer'. After 20 days in the swamp, Thompson's men had surrounded the terrorists' camp and forced them to surrender. Thompson went on to fight with the Regiment in Borneo as Operations Officer, before being killed

in a helicopter accident in May 1963.
(SEE *Ah Hoi; Borneo; Malaya*)

THOMPSON SUBMACHINE GUN The famous 'Tommy gun' of World War II. The American Thompson was used by the SAS in its operations throughout the war.

Type: submachine gun
Designation: M1A1
Calibre: .45in
Weight: 5.63kg
Length: 852mm
Effective range: 200m
Rate of fire: 120 rounds per minute (cyclic)
Feed: 20- or 30-round box or 50-round drum magazine
Muzzle velocity: 282 metres per second

THOMPSON, TROOPER IAN A member of D Squadron, 22 SAS, who in February 1965 was wounded in a contact with Indonesian troops in Borneo. His subsequent actions provide an excellent example of the calibre of SAS soldiers. After his patrol was fired upon Thompson, wounded in the thigh, hopped to where Sergeant Lillico, also wounded, was firing. The latter, apparently seeing Thompson walking, ordered him to go back up the track they had come down and fetch the rest of the patrol.

Thompson then spent the rest of the day and part of the next dragging himself to where he expected to find the patrol, all the time suffering from a shattered thigh. He was not evacuated until nearly 48 hours after the contact. For his conduct he was Mentioned in Despatches.

(SEE *Borneo; Lillico, Sergeant Eddie*)

3 SAS

(SEE *Special Air Service*)

THUMIER SAS base in the Radfan area of Aden. First established by A Squadron, 22 SAS, in April 1964, it was located off the Dhala road near the Habilayn airstrip. Air support for SAS patrols was often flown from

Habilayn. Thumier was only 50km from the border with North Yemen and was thus well placed to interdict weapons and supplies destined for the guerrillas coming from the north. The SAS retained a presence at Thumier until its withdrawal from Aden in 1967.

(SEE *Aden; Radfan*)

TIKKA M55 Finnish-built sniper rifle used by the SAS during the 1980s and before the introduction of the Accuracy International PM.

Type: bolt-action sniper rifle
Designation: M55 Super Sporter
Calibre: various (.223, .243, 7mm)
Weight: 3.27kg
Length: 1010mm
Effective range: 550m
Feed: 4-shot magazine
Muzzle velocity: 900 metres per second

(SEE *Accuracy International PM*)

'TITANIC', OPERATION One of the least successful SAS operations of World War II. Very early on the morning of 6 June 1944, seven men of 1 SAS were dropped into the area south of Carentan, Normandy. A number of containers filled with sand, dummy parachutists, small bombs which fired Very cartridges on landing, and detonators designed to simulate small-arms fire were also dropped. All these devices were supposed to fool the Germans into thinking that a full-scale airborne landing was taking place. However, on landing both the men and containers were widely scattered.

Without the containers the men could do little but hide. They did this until 10 July, when three of them were wounded in a gun battle with the enemy. The party was then surrounded and forced to surrender.

(SEE *Northwest Europe*)

'TOMBOLA', OPERATION An extremely successful operation which was characterised by typical SAS daring and panache. On 4 March 1945,

Above: SAS soldiers 'tree-jumping' in Malaya. This highly dangerous tactic was devised as a way of reaching guerrilla bases situated deep in the jungle.

an advance party from 2 SAS was dropped into the area midway between Spezia and Bologna, northern Italy, with orders to establish a base, organise the local partisans and harass the enemy. Offensive operations were also to be launched when the US Fifth Army mounted its expected attack in the region. Major Roy Farran, technically a despatcher in the aircraft, also dropped with the party.

Once on the ground the SAS quickly established contact with the partisans, established a base and started to organise a force. By 23 March, 'Tombola' numbered 50 SAS men from 3 Squadron, local partisan units and 70 escaped Russians, all armed by air drops. This force was called the 'Battaglione Alleata'.

Its first action was at the end of March, when Farran attacked a German HQ at Albinea. The Russians guarded the perimeter while the SAS and Italians assaulted the two buildings. A furious battle ensued which forced Farran to retreat, though not before 30 Germans had been killed and the two buildings destroyed. In the first week of April, the Germans

launched an attack on Farran's base, though it was beaten off. 'Alleata' was then ordered to support the Fifth Army's offensive by attacking Highway 12, the main route of the retreating Germans. From 10 April the composite force conducted a series of ambushes and mortar attacks against enemy forces. The town of Sassuolo was shelled by Farran's 75mm howitzer, and the whole force advanced to Modena. 'Tombola'

effectively ended on 24 April, by which time the party had inflicted 600 enemy casualties and taken over 400 prisoners.
(SEE *Farran, Major Roy; Italy*)

'TOMMY GUN'
(SEE *Thompson Submachine Gun*)

'TRAIN HARD, FIGHT EASY' The motto of Training Wing, 22 SAS.

'TREE-JUMPING' A parachute technique pioneered by the SAS during its campaign in Malaya. The Communist Terrorists' (CTs) camps were often situated deep in the jungle and, while they could be spotted from the air (they had to clear patches of jungle to grow food), it took foot patrols a long time to reach them. The SAS also wanted a method of sealing areas off quickly. Captain Johnny Cooper and Alistair MacGregor, both of the Malayan Scouts, saw possibilities in dropping men by parachute onto the jungle canopy – their fall would be broken by the tall trees – and then descending to the ground by rope (all men would eventually be issued with rope which was knotted every 450mm).

The first operational jump was carried out by 54 men in February 1952. Their role was to act as a blocking party in an operation involving Gurkhas, Royal Marines, Malay Police and SAS foot patrols. There were very few casualties and so the technique was judged a great success. 'Tree-jumping' therefore became a standard tactic until the end of the Malayan campaign. Unfortunately, subsequent operations were not so free of casualties. Three SAS men died after smashing into the canopy during Operation 'Sword' in January 1954. Because of the high incidence of casualties and the introduction into service of more capable helicopters, 'tree-jumping' was never again employed by the SAS.
(SEE *Communist Terrorist; Cooper, Lieutenant-Colonel Johnny; Malaya;*

Malayan Races Liberation Army; Malayan Scouts; 'Sword', Operation)

TROOP SKILLS Each SAS 'Sabre' Squadron is composed of four troops, each having its own speciality: Boat Troop (all aspects of amphibious warfare); Mobility Troop (Land Rovers, fast attack vehicles and motorcycles); Air Troop (freefall parachuting); and Mountain Troop (mountaineering and winter warfare operations). All soldiers are rotated through different troops during their three-year service with the Regiment. This ensures that each man has at least two troop skills in addition to his patrol skills. This cross-training guarantees that each four-men patrol contains a broad cross-section of military expertise.
(SEE *Air Troop; Boat Troop; Mobility Troop; Mountain Troop; Patrol Skills*)

TRUCIAL OMAN SCOUTS A battalion led by British officers which was raised in 1951 in the Trucial Oman States (now the United Arab Emirates) for internal security duties and general frontier patrol work. Elements from the Trucial Scouts fought in Oman (1958-59) and in Dhofar after 1965. They were well-trained troops who established a good relationship with the SAS.
(SEE *Jebel Akhdar; Oman*)

'TRUEFORM', OPERATION A disappointing operation which suffered from beginning too late. On 17 August 1944, soldiers of 1 and 2 SAS and the Belgian Independent Parachute Company – 102 in all – were dropped in 25 parties onto 12 dropping zones northwest of Paris. They were ordered to harass the retreating Germans and inflict as much damage as possible. However, they had been dropped too late and, despite destroying a few vehicles and some petrol dumps, the 'Trueform' parties were reached by Allied forces nine days later.
(SEE *Belgian Independent Parachute Company; Northwest Europe*)

Above: A detachment of Trucial Oman Scouts on patrol in Oman. They established an excellent relationship with the SAS during the latter's campaign in the country.

TURNBULL, SERGEANT BOB The epitome of the archetypal SAS soldier. Turnbull fought in Malaya, where he became an expert linguist and tracker. Tough, patient and resilient, he was an expert with a semi-automatic shotgun. On one occasion, after tracking four terrorists to a jungle hut, he killed them all single-handedly.

21 SAS
(SEE *Special Air Service*)

22 SAS
(SEE *Special Air Service*)

23 SAS
(SEE *Special Air Service*)

2 SAS
(SEE *Special Air Service*)

U

ULSTER
(SEE *Northern Ireland*)

Ulu Malay word used by the SAS to describe jungle.

US NAVY SEALs
(SEE *SEALs*)

US SPECIAL FORCES The SAS has long-standing ties with the US Special Forces, the Green Berets. The latter have a great many similarities with their British counterpart: all recruits are highly proficient in a number of skills – signalling, medicine, engineering, intelligence gathering, weapons handling, combat survival, languages and demolitions – and undergo exchange training with other special forces units. Unlike the SAS, the Green Berets operate in 12-man units called 'A Teams'. However, they are trained to fight in much the same way. They fight in small teams deep inside enemy territory, relying for survival on their own skills and equipment to conduct clandestine warfare against the foe.

The close link between the two organisations is illustrated by the fact that in 1962 the head of the Green Berets, Major-General William Yarborough, was made an honorary member of the SAS. A Green Beret officer, Charles Beckwith, was responsible for the formation of Delta Force, the US anti-terrorist group modelled closely on the SAS.

(SEE *Beckwith, Colonel Charles; Delta Force*)

UZI PISTOL A shortened and lightened version of the Uzi submachine gun, it can fire in the semi-automatic mode only. Though large in comparison with other handguns, the Uzi's bulk means that it is easy to control during the one-handed firing of a rapid succession of shots.

Type: semi-automatic pistol
Calibre: 9mm
Weight: 1.65kg (empty); 2.005kg (loaded)
Length: 240mm
Effective range: 60m
Feed: 20-round magazine
Muzzle velocity: 350 metres per second
(SEE *Uzi Submachine Gun*)

UZI SUBMACHINE GUN In existence since 1949, the well-known Uzi, specifically the Mini and Micro versions, is widely used by counterterrorist units around the world. Though not normally carried by SAS hostage-rescue teams, the wide-scale use of the Uzi by anti-terrorist organisations around the world and the close liaison between those units and the SAS, means that all Special Air Service personnel are familiar with the weapon.

Mini-Uzi
Type: submachine gun
Calibre: 9mm
Weight: 2.70kg (empty)
Length: 600mm (butt extended); 360mm (butt retracted)
Effective range: 150m
Rate of fire: 950 rounds per minute (cyclic)
Feed: 20-, 25- or 32-round box magazines
Muzzle velocity: 352 metres per second

Right: A US Special Forces soldier conducting weapons training. Like the SAS, the Green Berets are tasked with operating deep behind enemy lines.

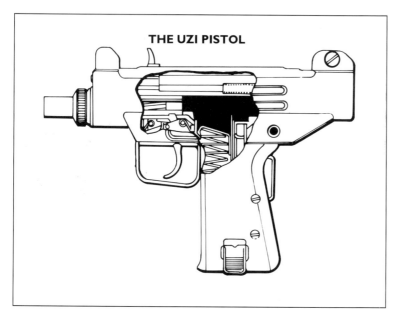

THE UZI PISTOL

Micro-Uzi
Type: submachine gun
Calibre: 9mm
Weight: 1.95kg (empty)
Length: 460mm (butt extended);
250mm (butt folded)
Effective range: 150m
Rate of fire: 1250 rounds per minute
(cyclic)
Feed: 20-round box magazine

Muzzle velocity: 350 metres per
second

V

VALETTA An extremely capable and
durable aircraft which was employed
on SAS operations in Malaya. The
twin-engined Vickers Valetta was produced between 1947 and 1952,
although there were still many in service in the 1960s. It had a four-man
crew and could transport 34 troops or
20 paratroopers. The Valetta had a
maximum speed of 473km/hr, a
cruising speed of 277km/hr and a
maximum range of 2250km, although
this dropped to 853km with the
troops on board.

VICKERS 'K' Machine gun which was
fitted to World War II SAS jeeps,
usually in pairs mounted front and
rear. It was known as the Vickers Gas
Operated (VGO). Originally used by
the RAF as an aircraft gun, the SAS
found that the Vickers withstood the
desert conditions of North Africa
extremely well and its high rate of fire
was ideal for hit-and-run raids.
Type: machine gun
Calibre: .303in
Weight: 8.86kg (unloaded)
Length: 1016mm
Effective range: 1800m
Rate of fire: 950 rounds per minute
(cyclic)
Feed: 100-round flat drum magazine
Muzzle velocity: 745 metres per
second
(SEE *Jeep; North Africa*)

Below: The Vickers Valetta was used by the SAS for parachute drops in Malaya.

W–Z

WADDY, COLONEL JOHN The commander of 22 SAS in the late 1960s and early 1970s. He wrote an important paper concerning the future role of the Regiment with particular regard to counter-terrorism. While the SAS was still training for its traditional roles of intelligence gathering and sabotage behind enemy lines, Waddy believed that it could also be used in clandestine operations such as those it had recently carried in Northern Ireland. He envisaged the SAS in the covert intelligence gathering role and working closely with the intelligence services: MI5, MI6 and Special Branch. Events were to prove him right, and today the Regiment undertakes a wide variety of undercover tasks in the Province.
(SEE *E4A; MI5; MI6; Northern Ireland*)

'WADS' SAS slang for sandwiches.

WALKER, MAJOR-GENERAL WALTER The Director of Operations in Borneo. A tough ex-jungle veteran of Burma and Malaya, Walker was tasked with containing Indonesian and communist incursions into Borneo. He recognised the worth of the SAS in this task, ordering the top secret 'Claret' operations and recommending the expansion of the Regiment, a request which led to the reformation of B Squadron. His famous statement concerning the SAS is worth repeating: 'I regard 70 troopers of the SAS as being as valuable to me as 700 infantry in the role of "hearts and minds", border surveillance, early warning, stay behind, and eyes and ears with a sting.' Walker was eventually replaced as Director of Operations Borneo by the SAS veteran, Major-General George Lea.
(SEE *Borneo; 'Claret' Operations; 'Hearts and Minds'; Lea, Major-General George; Malaya*)

WALKER, CAPTAIN RODERIC 'RORY' An officer with D Squadron, 22 SAS, Walker served in Malaya and Oman, where he took part in the assault on the Jebel Akhdar in 1959. His most famous exploit, however, was in the Indonesian capital, Jakarta. After Sarawak and North Borneo had opted to join the Malaysian Federation, a mob attacked the British Embassy in the city. As stone-throwers rioted outside the compound, Walker marched up and down in front of the building playing a set of bagpipes!
(SEE *Jebel Akhdar; Malaya; Oman*)

'WALLACE', OPERATION Conducted by 60 men of 2 SAS, 'Wallace' included a great jeep drive in true SAS tradition. The 23 vehicles, commanded by Major Roy Farran, landed at Rennes on 19 August 1944. The party was tasked with strengthening existing SAS bases and increasing offensive operations against the Germans. Farran immediately drove to the north bank of the River Loire, avoiding German forces on the way as he wanted to delay any action until he reached the 'Hardy' base.

On 22 August, the squadron was split into three groups: five jeeps under Captain Lee, eight under Farran and the rest under Lieutenant Leigh. However, the next few days witnessed several brief encounters with the enemy, one of which resulted in the death of Leigh. Eventually the party linked up with the rest of 2 SAS under Major Grant Hibbert at the 'Hardy' base in the Chatillon forest. On 27 August, aggressive jeep patrolling began.

The most famous exploit of 'Wallace' ('Hardy' by this time must be considered part of 'Wallace') was the attack on the German HQ in the town of Chatillon itself on 30 August. A prior meeting with the local *Maquis* commander resulted in the latter ostensibly agreeing to help the SAS in the attack. However, on the morning of the assault the French failed to turn up. Farran's force became engaged in a fierce battle with the garrison and a German column which was approaching the town. He had no choice but to call off the action, but not before the enemy had lost 100 killed and nine lorries, four cars and a motorcycle destroyed. That night the SAS received several jeeps by parachute, bringing the total to 18.

Farran then split the vehicles into two columns of nine, one under Hibbert and one commanded by himself, and headed for the Belfort Gap, an area between the Vosges mountains and the Swiss border. German forces were retreating to the area to try to prevent the Allies from reaching the Rhine. The two columns set off on 2

Above: The Wessex helicopter has been in service since the early 1960s. Though being gradually phased out, it is still used by the SAS in Northern Ireland.

September, heading for the gap between two US armies: the Third to the north and the Seventh in the south. Several targets were shot up as the SAS entered enemy territory, though the large numbers of Germans in the area made operations difficult. On 19 August, 'Wallace' came to an end when the SAS linked up with US forces. It had been a great success: for the loss of seven killed, seven wounded, two captured and 16 jeeps destroyed, the SAS had killed or wounded 500 enemy personnel, destroyed 59 vehicles and derailed one train.

(SEE *Farran, Major Roy; 'Hardy', Operation; Jeep; Maquis; Northwest Europe*)

WALLS, GENERAL PETER The commander of C Squadron, Malayan Scouts, during the Malayan Emergency, Walls later became the head of Rhodesia's armed forces following the country's Unilateral Declaration of Independence in 1965. (SEE *Malaya; Malayan Scouts; Rhodesian SAS*)

WARBURTON, TROOPER J.N. A member of the ill-fated Edwards patrol which took part in the Radfan campaign at the end of April 1964. Warburton, an ex-sapper who was the patrol's signaller, and Edwards, the

patrol leader, were both killed by guerrillas and decapitated. Their heads were later put on public display in North Yemen. The families of the two men were initially told that they had been killed during a training exercise on Salisbury Plain.
(SEE *Edwards, Captain Robin; Radfan*)

WARR, CAPTAIN PETER One of the first parachute instructors of the SAS. He joined L Detachment at Kabrit, North Africa, from the British Parachute School at Manchester after

David Stirling had requested help. He subsequently went on to take part in some of the early raids in the desert.
(SEE *Kabrit; L Detachment; North Africa; Stirling, Lieutenant-Colonel David*)

'WASH', OPERATION Part of Operation 'Samwest'.
(SEE *Northwest Europe; 'Samwest', Operation*)

'WASHUP' SAS slang for a debriefing.

WATTS, LIEUTENANT-COLONEL JOHNNY An SAS squadron commander who eventually went on to command the Regiment, the SAS Group and the Sultan of Oman's Armed Forces. In November 1958, Major Watts was in Malaya commanding D Squadron when he and his men were ordered to Oman to take part in the successful Jebel Akhdar campaign (1958-59). During this conflict Watts, in typical SAS style, undertook several lone reconnaissance patrols to search for a way onto the inhospitable plateau.

He was given command of the re-formed B Squadron in 1964, and by October the unit was ready for its first tour in Borneo which lasted from November to February 1965. During this time Watts led his men in the area south of Pensiangan and in western Sarawak, conducting several cross-border operations. In mid-1970, now commanding the Regiment, Watts was sent to Oman to report on the state of the country. This was to result in his 'Five Fronts' campaign which would enable Sultan Qaboos to win the war in Dhofar. He commanded 22 SAS in Oman and launched several operations against the enemy. One of these was 'Jaguar' in October 1971, when the SAS, *firqat* units and elements of the Sultan's Armed Forces launched an attack onto the Jebel Dhofar. Led personally by Watts, the operation threatened to grind to a halt when the *firqat* decided to stop fighting and

observe Ramadan. At this Watts erupted and threatened to withdraw all SAS support for the *firqats*. The latter, knowing their existence depended on the British soldiers, opted to go back on the offensive. Watts relinquished command of the Regiment at the end of 1971. Tony Jeapes, who served under him in Oman, provides a fitting epitaph to the efforts of his commander: 'More than anyone else it was the strategy he had devised and the groundwork he had completed that was to lead to the ultimate defeat of the enemy.'
(SEE *Dhofar; Firqat; 'Five Fronts' Campaign; 'Jaguar', Operation; Jeapes, Brigadier Tony; Jebel Akhdar; Malaya; Oman; Qaboos, Sultan; Sultan's Armed Forces*)

WEGENER, ULRICH
(SEE *GSG 9*)

WESSEX This British general purpose helicopter first entered service in 1963. Although now largely relegated to the search and rescue role, it is still used as a tactical transport, especially in Northern Ireland. The aircraft is used to transport SAS soldiers in the Province, though the most famous exploit involving the Wessex and the Regiment was during the Falklands War, when one flown by a Royal Navy officer (Lieutenant-Commander Ian Stanley) evacuated an SAS troop from Fortuna Glacier, South Georgia.
   Type: general purpose transport helicopter
   Crew: three
   Range: 770km
   Payload: 6150kg
   Maximum speed: 212km/hr
   Weapons: generally none, although can be armed with machine guns, cannon and AS-12 air-to-surface missiles
   Passengers: up to 16
(SEE *Fortuna Glacier; Northern Ireland; South Georgia*)

WESTMACOTT, CAPTAIN RICHARD
One of the first SAS fatalities in

Northern Ireland. On 2 May 1980, he was in command of an eight-man SAS unit operating in two unmarked cars in Belfast. The soldiers were in plain clothes but were armed with handguns and automatic weapons. Westmacott received instructions over the radio to go to a house in Antrim Road, where suspicious activity had been reported. Shortly after 1400 hours, one SAS car pulled up at the rear of the house while Westmacott's drew up at the front. Inside the house were four armed escaped Irish Republican Army terrorists, who opened fire as soon as the men got out the car at the front. Westmacott was killed instantly. The SAS believed they were being fired at from number 369, and this they stormed and cleared room by room. However, the terrorists were in fact next door in No 371. As soon as the shooting started Army and Royal Ulster Constabulary units sealed off the area and the gunmen were persuaded to surrender. The incident does illustrate how, even at the beginning of the 1980s, the SAS was still refining its tactics in the Province. It would now be inconceivable for a unit to be ordered to intervene so readily in such a situation; rather, the house would be placed under surveillance before any SAS action.
(SEE *Counter Revolutionary Warfare; Irish Republican Army; Jones, Lance-Corporal David; Northern Ireland; Rules of Engagement*)

'WET-JUMP' SAS term for a parachute drop into water.
(SEE *Parachutes*)

'WET REP' SAS slang for weather report.

WHIRLWIND A medium-lift helicopter, the Sikorsky S-55 Whirlwind

Left: The M60 machine gun which killed Captain Westmacott in May 1980. The incident highlighted initial shortcomings in SAS tactics in Ulster.

Above: The Whirlwind was one of the first helicopters to enter service with the RAF. It was used to insert SAS teams into the jungle in Malaya.

was used by the Special Air Service in Malaya.
(SEE *Malaya*)

'WHITE-OUT' Often experienced by troops operating in arctic conditions, a white-out occurs when visibility is suddenly reduced to zero by blizzards or cloud. This happened to an SAS party being evacuated from Fortuna Glacier, South Georgia, with disastrous results.
(SEE *Fortuna Glacier; South Georgia*)

'WHO DARES WINS' The motto of the Special Air Service, reportedly coined by David Stirling.
(SEE *Special Air Service; Stirling, Lieutenant-Colonel David; Winged Dagger*)

WILLYS JEEP
(SEE *Jeep*)

WINGATE-GRAY, LIEUTENANT-COLONEL MIKE The second-in-command of 22 SAS when John Woodhouse was its CO. The latter had insisted that before becoming second-in-command, Wingate-Gray must pass SAS Selection (Woodhouse was determined that whoever held the post would eventually succeed him as commander). Despite being 42 years old at the time, Wingate-Gray passed and, in January 1965, he replaced Woodhouse as commander of 22 SAS. He allowed the Regiment's cross-border patrols in Borneo to take on a more aggressive aspect, and during the next few months A, B and D

Above: The SAS winged dagger badge. Originally, the design was supposed to represent King Arthur's sword Excalibur, the symbol of truth and justice.

Squadrons were involved in offensive cross-border patrols.
(SEE *Borneo; 'Claret' Operations; Selection Training; Woodhouse, Lieutenant-Colonel John*)

WINGED DAGGER The badge of the SAS. Reportedly the creation of Sergeant Bob Tait, who won a competition for the choice of a badge for the new unit in North Africa at the end of 1941. Another story maintains that the weapon was not originally a dagger, but was supposed to represent King Arthur's sword, Excalibur. However, the tailor produced a design more like a dagger and this was retained. The colours of the wings are Oxford and Cambridge blue, selected because in the original L Detachment 'Jock' Lewes had rowed for Oxford and Lieutenant Langton for Cambridge.

The badge was originally worn on a white beret. However, this colour headgear was derided by other units, especially the New Zealanders and Australians, and it was subsequently withdrawn. It was replaced with a khaki forage cap and then the famous beige beret, and the latter has remained to this day.
(SEE *Lewes, Lieutenant John Steel 'Jock'; North Africa; Special Air Service*)

'WINGED STAGGER' The drinking club of the Rhodesian Special Air Service.
(SEE *Rhodesian SAS*)

'WINGS' The parachute wings badge of the SAS was originally designed by 'Jock' Lewes in late 1941. He reportedly got the idea after seeing a fresco of an ibis, a large wading bird with a long curved bill, in an Egyptian hotel. Those members of the SAS who had made three parachute drops behind enemy lines were permitted to wear the wings over the left breast pocket instead of on the sleeve, which was common British military custom at the time. This practice was also adopted by the Special Boat Squadron.
(SEE *Lewes, Lieutenant John Steel 'Jock'; North Africa; Special Air Service; Special Boat Squadron; Winged Dagger*)

WOODHOUSE, LIEUTENANT-COLONEL JOHN Regarded as the father of the modern SAS and, alongside Daivd Stirling, 'Paddy' Mayne and Mike Calvert, one of the outstanding personalities to have served with the Regiment. He joined the British Army in 1941 as a private, having just left public school. He was one of the original members of the Malayan Scouts, being drafted in by Mike Calvert to work in its intelligence cell in 1950 (at this time Woodhouse was a major). However, together with Major Dare Newell he set about reorganising the Scouts to fight in the jungle and mount deep-penetration patrols. He insisted on the highest levels of professionalism, physical fitness and discipline. In February of that year, for example, he led an operation in the Belum Valley in northern Malaya.

In the summer of 1952, Woodhouse returned to England to organise SAS recruitment procedures. The course he devised was to form the basis of the current SAS Selection and Continuation Training which is undertaken by the Regiment at Hereford. He spent nearly two years in England before returning to Malaya as a squadron commander at the end of 1954. By 1962 he was commanding 22 SAS in Borneo, a choice that was extremely popular within the Regiment. He continued to use the SAS with flair and imagination, advocating the use of four-man patrols for cross-border reconnaissance work in early 1964. Later that year authorisation was granted for such patrols and the 'Claret' operations were born. In October of that year Woodhouse went on his last operational patrol, before leaving the Army in January 1965. (SEE *Borneo; Calvert, Brigadier Mike; 'Claret' Operations; Continuation Training; Cross-training; Four-man Patrol; Jungle Training; Malaya; Malayan Scouts; Mayne, Lieutenant-Colonel 'Paddy' Blair; Newell, Major Dare; Patrol Skills; Selection Training; Special Air Service; Stirling, Lieutenant-Colonel David; Stirling Lines; Troop Skills*)

'WOLSEY', OPERATION A very successful small-scale joint SAS/Phantom mission conducted in the area around Compiègne and Soissons, northeast France, between 26 August and 3 September 1944. The five-man party, led by Lieutenant McDevitt, was parachuted in to collect intelligence concerning enemy dispositions and movements in the area. The party gathered some good information, most notably on an enemy convoy which was subsequently destroyed by 44 RAF Mosquito aircraft. (SEE *Northwest Europe; Phantom*)

Z

ZEM ZEM Located southeast of Tripoli, North Africa. In November 1942, David Stirling with B Squadron was operating in the area around Zem Zem in an attempt to harass enemy forces as the Eighth Army advanced west after the Battle of El Alamein. The SAS depot at this time was at Benghazi, though B Squadron's forward base was at El Fascia. By 13 December the squadron was in place and ready for action, having a total of 24 jeeps. At the same time, A Squadron under Major 'Paddy' Mayne was operating along the road between Agheila and Bouerat. However, Stirling's men found that the area was swarming with enemy soldiers and unfriendly locals, and within a few days most of the patrols had been captured or killed.

The SAS operations in Tunisia were, on the whole, disappointing when compared to the earlier successes of 1942. This was not realy surprising; German and Italian forces were being squeezed into an ever-smaller pocket by US and British forces. As a consequence, the SAS was forced to operate in a relatively small area. This is why so many jeep-mounted patrols, including David Stirling's at Gabes, ran into difficulties. The countryside was filled with columns of retreating Axis forces. (SEE *Benghazi; El Fascia; Gabes Gap; Mayne, Lieutenant-Colonel 'Paddy' Blair; North Africa; Stirling, Lieutenant-Colonel David*)

ZIRNHELD, LIEUTENANT ANDRE
Popular young Free French officer who served with the SAS during its early operations in North Africa. He led one of the raids against enemy airfields in mid-June 1942, destroying 11 aircraft at Berka Main. In early July he was raiding again, this time against El Daba airfield. However, due to a lack of targets he was forced to lay ambushes on the nearby road. His last action was on the night of 26 July 1942, when he took part in the spectacular action at Sidi Haneish airfield. However, on the way back his three Free French SAS jeeps were strafed by Stuka aircraft and he was killed. (SEE *Berka; Free French SAS; North Africa; Sidi Haneish*)

Below: Two SAS soldiers take a break during a mission in Tunisia, late 1942. SAS operations during the final stages of the war in North Africa were disappointing.

ACKNOWLEDGEMENTS

RECOMMENDED READING

Adams, James, *Secret Armies*, Hutchinson, 1987

Adams, James, Morgan, Robin and Bambridge, Anthony, *Ambush: The War between the SAS and the IRA*, Pan Books Limited, 1988

Bradford, Roy and Dillon, Martin, *Rogue Warrior of the SAS*, Arrow Books Limited, 1989

Chappell, Mike, *The British Army in the 1980s*, Osprey Publishing Limited, 1987

Cooper, Johnny, *One of the Originals*, Pan Books Limited, 1991

Dickens, Peter, *SAS: The Jungle Frontier*, Book Club Associates, 1983

Ferguson, Gregor, *The Paras: British Airborne Forces 1940-1984*, Osprey Publishing Limited, 1987

Geraghty, Tony, *Who Dares Wins*, Fontana/Collins, 1981

Jeapes, Colonel Tony, *SAS: Operation Oman*, William Kimber & Co. Limited, 1983

Kemp, Anthony, *The SAS at War*, John Murray Limited, 1991

Kennedy, Michael Paul, *Soldier 'I' SAS*, Bloomsbury Publishing Limited, 1990

Ladd, James, *Commandos and Rangers of World War II*, David & Charles, 1989

Ladd, James, *SAS Operations*, Robert Hale Limited, 1989

Ladd, James, *SBS: The Invisible Raiders*, David & Charles, 1989

Laffin, John, *Brassey's Battles*, Brassey's Defence Publishers Limited, 1986

Large, Lofty, *One Man's SAS*, William Kimber & Co. Limited, 1987

Markham, George, *Guns of the Elite*, Book Club Associates, 1989

Middlebrook, Martin, *Task Force: The Falklands War 1982*, Penguin Books, 1987

Murray, Raymond, *The SAS in Ireland*, The Mercier Press, 1990

Scurr, John, *The Malayan Campaign 1948-60*, Osprey Publishing Limited, 1984

Seymour William, *British Special Forces*, Sidgwick & Jackson, 1985

Shortt, James G., *British Special Forces 1945 to the Present*, Arms & Armour Press, 1986

Smith, Gordon, *Battles of the Falklands War*, Ian Allan Limited, 1989

Strawson, John, *A History of the SAS Regiment*, Secker & Warburg Limited, 1984

Thompson, Leroy, *The Rescuers: The World's Top Anti-Terrorist Units*, David & Charles, 1986

Warner, Philip, *The SAS*, Sphere Books Limited, 1988

Weeks, John, *The Airborne Soldier*, Blandford Press, 1986